RESOURCE AND DEVELOPMENT IN INDIA

Books by the Same Author

1. Education in North East India: Experience and Challenge (Jointly Edited with Biloris Lyndem
2. Look East Policy and North East India : Achievements and Constraints
3. Health and Health Care in Indian Sub-Continent: Special Focus North East India (With Premananda Bharati)

About the Editor

Utpal Kumar De is currently Professor of Economics at the North Eastern Hill University, Shillong, India. Prof. De has been engaged in teaching at post-graduate level since 1994. His research interests include agricultural economics and rural development, issues on environment and natural resources, climate change adaptation, and empowerment of women. Prof. De has visited several countries of Europe and Asia in connection with research and delivered keynote lectures at a number of conferences. Besides presenting over 60 research papers in various international and national conferences he has published nine volumes, completed half a dozen research projects and published over 85 research articles in reputed national and international journals. The Marquis Who's Who Publications Board certifies that Utpal Kumar De is a subject of biographical record in Who's Who in the World 2013 Pearl Anniversary Edition, inclusion in which is limited to those individuals who have demonstrated outstanding achievement in their own fields of endeavour and who have, thereby, contributed significantly to the betterment of contemporary society. He has successfully guided 10 research scholars for their Ph.D. degree.

Resource and Development in India

Special Focus on Tourism, Entrepreneurship and Natural Resources of North East

Edited by

Utpal Kumar De

CONCEPT PUBLISHING COMPANY PVT. LTD.
NEW DELHI-110059

ISBN-13: 978-93-86682-75-8

First Published 2019

Published and Printed by:

Concept Since 1974

Concept Publishing Company Pvt. Ltd.
A/15-16, Commercial Block, Mohan Garden,
New Delhi-110059 (INDIA)
T : +91 11 25351460, +91 11 25351794
E : publishing@conceptpub.com, *W* : www.conceptpub.com

Cataloging in Publication Data--Courtesy: D.K. Agencies (P) Ltd. <docinfo@dkagencies.com>

Resource and development in India : special focus on tourism, entrepreneurship and natural resources of North East / edited by Utpal Kumar De.
pages cm
Includes bibliographical references and index.
ISBN 9789386682758

1. Sustainable development—India, Northeastern. 2. Tourism—India, Northeastern. 3. Rural development—India, Northeastern. 4. Entrepreneurship—India, Northeastern. 5. Conservation of natural resources—India, Northeastern. I. De, Utpal Kumar, 1968- editor.

LCC HC440.E5R47 2019 | DDC 338.92709541 23

Preface

Resource and development are intricately linked with each other. As availability of productive resources is important for the development of any region; planning for proper use of such resources is equally important for maintaining sustainable progress. Again, development activities in many cases have serious adverse impacts on various resources in several ways that seriously affect availability of such resources with required productivity in future. Land, water, forest, mineral and other natural resources are highly important from the employment and earning perspectives, especially in a region where industrial progress is very limited and confined to natural resource base. The natural scenario, landscape, parks, waterfalls, caves and other natural resources also contribute significantly towards development through tourism and hospitality in different ways, whose multiple impacts on the society cannot be ignored. Thus, maintenance of such resources is crucial for any society and studies may help in generating knowledge base on the direct and indirect utility of those resources and to provide mechanism on sustainable use of such resources. Micro-entrepreneurship encompassing such natural resource base is also a crucial way to overcome various obstacles including access to capital, managing the activities jointly and achieve inclusive development.

This book is a humble attempt that addresses various aspects of tourism and hospitality sector, entrepreneurship, agricultural as well as environmental perspectives of development in India in general and North East India in particular. Sixteen chapters divided into three sections have attempted to provide scientific investigations on issues related to resource and development dynamics with a special focus on North East India. The studies included in this book, therefore, tried to answer several questions related to intricate issues for removing development bottlenecks in the region. It will, thus, be helpful to researchers and academicians to undertake further studies on issues that remained untouched here and students for enriching their knowledge and policy-makers for making plans towards sustainable development.

Utpal Kumar De

Contents

List of Contributors

A.N. Tripathi, Division of Crop Protection, ICAR-Central Research Institute for Jute and Allied Fibre, Barrackpore, Kolkata-700120. **E-mail:** *antripathi_patho@rediffmail.com*

Abdul Basith Laskar, Research Scholar, Department of Economics, Assam University, Silchar-788011, Assam. **E-mail:** *abdulbasith510@gmail.com*

Anil K. Srivastava, ICAR Consultant-Central, Agriculture University, Jhansi; Integrated Farming Systems Ex-Director, ICAR, VPKAS, Almora, Uttarakhand. **E-mail:** *aksrivastva4@yahoo.com, aksrivastva2@gmail.com*

B.K. Tiwari, Professor, Department of Environmental Studies, North Eastern Hill University, Shillong-793022, Meghalaya. **E-mail:** *bktiwarinehu@gmail.com*

Bhaskar Jyoti Neog, Research Scholar, Department of Humanities and Social Sciences, IIT Kharagpur, Kharagpur-721302, West Bengal. **E-mail:** *bneog8@gmail.com*

Bimal Kishore Sahoo (Dr.), Assistant Professor, Department of Humanities and Social Sciences, IIT Kharagpur, Kharagpur-721302, West Bengal. **E-mail:** *bimalkishore.sahoo@gmail.com*

Dipanjan Chakraborty (Dr.), Associate Professor, Department of Commerce, Darrang College, Sonitpur-784001, Assam. **E-mail:** *dipjan_2005@rediffmail.com*

Etiban Lapasam, Department of Environmental Studies, North Eastern Hill University, Shillong-793022.

Jagdish Jadhav (Dr.), Associate Professor, Department of Social Work, Central University of Rajasthan, Ajmer-305801, Rajasthan. **E-mail:** *jagdishjadhav_sw@curaj.ac.in*

Juban Nongbri, Department of Economics, North Eastern Hill University, Shillong-793022, Meghalaya. **E-mail:** *jubans2@gmail.com*

Malabika Das Gupta (Prof.), Professor of Economics (Retd.), Tripura University, Visiting Professor of Economics, Institute of Development Studies, Kolkata and Honorary Associate, Centre for Urban Economic

Studies, Department of Economics, Calcutta University, 1, Reformatory Street, Kolkata-700027.
E-mail: *dasgupta.dg@rediffmail.com*

Niranjan Das, North East Centre for Social Science Research, Murhateteli, Tezpur-784001, Assam.
E-mail: *das_niranjan2002@Yahoo.com; niranjannameri@gmail.com*

P.K. Ryngnga (Dr.), Assistant Professor, Department of Geography, North Eastern Hill University, Shillong-793022, Meghalaya.
E-mail: *kryngnga@yahoo.com*

Parthsarathi Dehury, M.Phil. Scholar, Tata Institute of Social Sciences, V.N. Purav Marg, Eden Gardens, Deonar, Mumbai-400088, Maharashtra.
E-mail: *parthsarathidehury@gmail.com*

Rajib Kumar De, Division of Crop Protection, ICAR-Central Research Institute for Jute and Allied Fibre, Barrackpore-700120, Kolkata.

Raju Mandal (Dr.), Assistant Professor, Department of Economics, Assam University, Silchar-788011, Assam. **E-mail:** *rajum06@gmail.com*

Ruma Kundu (Dr.), Assistant Professor, Department of Economics, Sikkim University, Gangtok-737102, Sikkim.
E-mail: *rumakundu76@gmail.com,* Ph: 09733123434.

Sandip Rudra Paul, Department of Economics, Assam University, Silchar-788011, Assam.
E-mail: *sandips_rhythm@yahoo.com*

Sazzad Parwez, Senior Research Fellow, Centre for Studies in Economics and Planning, School of Social Sciences, Central University of Gujarat, Gandhinagar, Sector 29, Gandhinagar-382030, Gujarat.
E-mail: *sazzad.parwez@gmail.com*

Subrata Barman (Dr.), Assistant Professor, Department of Economics, Nalbari College, Nalbari-781335, Assam.

Sujata Deori (Dr.), Assistant Professor, Department of Geography, North Gauhati College, Guwahati-784031, Kamrup, Assam.
E-mail: *sujatadeori@yahoo.com*

Sushmita Sharma, Research Scholar, Department of Commerce, Assam University, Diphu Campus, Karbi Anglong, Diphu-782462, Assam.
E-mail: *sushmita.bharadwaj123@gmail.com*

Tumbenthung Humtsoe, Ph.D. Student (JRF), School of Economics, University of Hyderabad, Hyderabad-500046, Telangana.
E-mail: *benthunghmt@gmail.com*

Utpal Kumar De (Dr.), Professor, Department of Economics, North Eastern Hill University, Shillong-793022, Meghalaya.
E-mail: *utpalkde@gmail.com,* Ph: +91-9436102066.

Introduction

Environmental sustainability was one of the important Millennium Development Goals (MDGs) that were targeted to be achieved by the end of 2015. Sustainable resource management is very crucial from the achievement of continuity in the development process. After thorough deliberations and looking at the success and failure in the past decades, United Nations substituted the eight MDGs by seventeen Sustainable Development Goals (SDGs) with specific targets to be achieved over the next 15 years, i.e. by 2030.

In this volume, we concentrate on the three aspects of development, namely Tourism and Hospitality, Environment and Natural Resource and Sustainable Development. Special thrust is given on institutional and entrepreneurial aspects of development along with environmental and tourism perspectives.

Here, research papers are included specific to tourism, entrepreneurship, agricultural and environmental resources and development. Articles have been shortlisted on the basis of their quality and relevance to the present day situation. On the basis of the comments of honourable referees in the respective fields and after due modifications we selected the final papers as included in this book.

Eradication of extreme poverty and reduction in inequality were in the forefront of MDGs declaration. So far as amelioration of poverty is concerned, a significant reduction in the percentage of population living under poverty has already been achieved in India. Incidence of poverty in India was brought down from almost 51 per cent in 1990-91 to 37 per cent in 2004-05 and further to an overall figure of 22 per cent in 2011-12. The head count ratios of poverty in rural and urban India came down to about 26 per cent and 14 per cent respectively. Though, a remarkable progress has been achieved so far, there are more than 250 million people still living under poor conditions of which over 200 million are in rural areas only. Still, now almost 1 in every 5 persons in India is well below the national poverty line.

Across the countries in the world, socio-economic progress has been commendable. According to the most recent estimates, in 2011, about 17 per cent of people in the developing world live below $1.25 income a day. That is significantly lower than 43 per cent figure of 1990. This means that, in 2011, just over one billion people lived on less than $1.25 a day, as compared with 1.91 billion in 1990.

Apart from the significant improvement in the form of poverty reduction in both rural and urban areas, there is significant rural-urban variation in achievement across the states. The rural urban gap in poverty ratio varied from 1 per cent in Uttar Pradesh to 29 per cent in Mizoram during 2011-12. Also, there is a significant variation in male female poverty ratio. We have to search for ways and means to tackle the issues of inequality to improve the welfare across all sections of the society.

Social relations and entrepreneurship are important from the point of view of addressing development, food security and employment generation. A proper institutional mechanism can help in fostering social welfare of the citizens of a region. Whatever institutional attempts have been undertaken in India so far, the benefits did not reach to all sections of the society.

Quality of environment is also directly and indirectly linked with the growth process. Thus, achieving sustainable progress is another target that remains elusive. In terms of reduction in pollution, carbon dioxide emission, deforestation etc. India is far behind the expectations. Nature based tourism can contribute a lot to generate employment and income along with maintenance of sustainable environment.

Tourism is one of the fastest growing industries and enterprises based on tourism and hospitality has been playing significant role in the generation of employment, earning and removal of poverty. Nature based tourism may occupy a special position in North East India that provides ample scope of sustainable development with appropriate use of available natural resources. These aspects are the prime focus of this book.

From the above discussion it is clear that we could not achieve the MDGs in all targets and there are also significant spatial variations. Thus, it is high time we review our achievements and lapses incurred in comparison with the targets of the MDGs.

We hope that the readers of this book will be highly benefited and be encouraged to do further studies to meet up the gaps which still remain. The research outputs presented here will also help the planners, politicians and the social workers.

This book is divided in three Parts—1. *Tourism, Hospitality and Development*, 2. *Entrepreneurship and Socio-Economic Development*, 3. *Agricultural and Environmental Perspectives of Development*. There are 6, 5 and 5 numbers of papers (total 16 papers) included in respective categories.

In Chapter 1 of Part 1, *Niranjan Das, Utpal Kumar De* and *Sujata Deori* examine the tourists' behaviour and evaluate their expectations and demands in order to make strategies for promotion of tourism in the area. It aims at dealing with the profile and perceptions of the tourists visiting Nameri National Park of Assam. The chapter reveals a wide gap between the expected and actual number of tourists visiting the park and other tourist spots in the states. It also suggests for the improvement of transport and hotel infrastructure along with massive campaign for the improvement of tourism in the area.

In the next Chapter, *Subrata Barman* and *Raju Mandal* estimate the recreation benefit of Kaziranga National Park, Assam by using individual travel cost method. The chapter reveals substantial amount of consumer's surplus enjoyed by the visitors to this unique tourist site of the region.

Malabika Das Gupta in Chapter 3 tries to examine the status and potential of tourism in an archaeological site, Devtamura in North Tripura. It also highlights how the sustainable tourism management in Devtamura can provide a fillip to the local economy without causing environmental damage.

In Chapter 4, *Ruma Kundu* tries to examine the relationship between tourism and economic development in Sikkim. She has used growth rate of NSDP as a proxy for economic development in the analysis. This chapter reveals that there exists a long run relationship between NSDP and income from industry but not between income from tourism activities and NSDP, which may be due to the non-reporting of several informal tourism activities and thereby earning.

Utpal Kumar De and *Jaban Nongbri,* in Chapter 5 try to explore how far the state of Meghalaya meets those requirements for the appropriate growth of tourism in the state. It is done through the examination of the opinion of the visiting tourists obtained by a primary survey. Especially, those who are the repeated visitors, their opinions are taken as they can better explain the changes in those factors over the years and also the variation in environmental conditions, especially, the climate for which many visitors prefer to visit Shillong and its surrounding areas during the summer time.

P.K. Ryngnga in Chapter 6, however, assesses the role that tourism plays in livelihood strategies of two indigenous communities in Meghalaya from an indigenous perspective using the sustainable livelihood framework as an organizing framework. It is one of the first studies of tourism to employ the concept of sustainable livelihoods, to emphasise that tourism should be understood in the broader economic and cultural context in which it takes place, and it illustrates the kinds of information that can be generated by adopting such an approach.

Chapter 7 in Part 2 by *Sazzad Parwez* describes the socio-economic implication of the policy of special economic zone for the rural indigenous population in India on a theoretical model.

Chapter 8 by *Sushmita Sharma* and *Dipanjan Chakraborty,* however attempts to analyse the impact of microenterprises on the development of rural areas in Assam. The study was conducted in Sonitpur district of Assam. It was done by analyzing the primary data obtained through a personal interview of rural entrepreneurs registered in District Industries and Commerce Centre, Sonitpur selected by simple random sampling method. The result shows that microenterprises have a positive impact on development of rural areas.

Spatio-temporal variation in private tuition and its effect on the educational scenario across the States of North East India is examined by *Abdul Basith Laskar* in Chapter 9. Large variations in private tuition across the major states of India are observed by the author. It is the highest in West Bengal followed by Tripura, while it is lowest in Chhattisgarh followed by Mizoram. However, the highest intensity of private tuition in eastern region is followed by North-Eastern region and it is the lowest in the central region.

Using a panel data set and applying fixed effect model, *Bimal Kishore Sahoo* and *Bhaskar Jyoti* in Chapter 10 shows trend and patterns of informal and formal employment in organised and unorganised non-agriculture sector with special reference to North East India. The investigation of the determinants of informality at the individual level has given us crucial inputs on its nature at the micro-level. However, in order to comprehend better on its determinants at the macro-level it becomes necessary investigate further the variation in the incidence of informality across States. Looking at the prevalence of informality across States, the chapter finds that informality is significantly lower in the North Eastern States, Union Territories as well as in the northern States of Jammu & Kashmir, Himachal Pradesh. Finally, regarding the determinants of informality at the macro-level the chapter finds that among the multiple factors it is tax-SDP ratio, expenditure-SDP ratio are important factors that forces people to undertake activities in informal sectors.

The last Chapter 11 of Part 2 by *Sandip Rudra Paul* provides a brief investigation of expenditure on tobacco products in North East India. The chapter reveals considerably high, but differentiated use of tobacco in North East Indian states.

Etiban Lapasam and *B.K. Tiwari* in Chapter 12 of Part 3 investigate the effect of plant density on cash income of the farmers cultivating broom grass. The experiments are laid in Mynska village of Jaintia Hills in Meghalaya. The production of panicles in the plantations with lower plant density is found significantly higher than those grown in higher plant density. The study concludes that plantation rose at a density of 3500 plants/ha (1.5 × 2.0 m spacing) gave highest net present value of Rs. 126199.8 ha^{-1} $year^{-1}$ up to three harvests. Hence, the recommendation follows.

The economic viability of resource conservation farming system in rural India has been described by *Anil K. Srivastava* in Chapter 13. The study at farm holding levels involved evaluating the promising farming system the terrace level.

Adaptive coping mechanism for agricultural sustainability against rising climate uncertainty in two Agro-Climatic Zones of Rajasthan has been explained *Parthsarathi Dehury* and *Jagdish Jadhav* in Chapter 14. Mixed method is used with semi-structured interview schedule; observation methods and focus group discussion are conducted for collecting information.

The next Chapter 15 by *A.N. Tripathi* and *Rajib Kumar De* is on the Characterization of isolates of *Ralstonia Solanacearum*

(E.F. Smith) Yabuuchi *et al.* Causing Bacterial (Hooghly) Wilt of Jute (*Corchorus* spp.) in West Bengal.

On the other hand, growth of urban areas, transportation issues in Kohima has been highlighted by *Tumbenthung Humtsoe* in Chapter 16.

The book, therefore, addresses a wide range of issues including tourism and hospitality aspects of development, entrepreneurship and socio-economic development interface, which are crucial for understanding overall progress of a region. Also, it provides the guidelines for the future actions by the policy-makers and further studies to unearth other related socio-economic issues concerning welfare. The book, therefore, will surely attract the researchers, academicians and policy-makers and benefit all sections of readers.

Utpal Kumar De

PART 1
Tourism, Hospitality and Development

1
Characteristics of Tourists in Nameri National Park, Assam
An Assessment

Niranjan Das, Utpal Kumar De and *Sujata Deori*

Introduction

Ecotourism is a field of human activity where conservation and development can wisely effectively be balanced to achieve a mutual goal to the benefit of the people in the community. The term 'Ecotourism' was first coined by *Hector Ceballos Lascurain* in 1983, and was initially used to describe nature-based travel to relatively undisturbed area with an emphasis on Education. This new approach of tourism is becoming an increasingly popular expression to conservation and sustainable development of the biodiversity (Yadav, 2002). It involves education and interpretation of natural environment and to manage it in an ecologically sustainable way. Here 'natural environment' includes cultural components and the term 'ecologically sustainable' involves appropriate returnees to the local community and long term conservation of resources (Grant, 1995). In this way a person eventually acquires a consciousness and knowledge of the natural environment, together with cultural aspects, that will convert people keenly involved in conservation issues (Cebaballos, 1998).

Study Area

The study region covers Nameri National Park of Assam located in 26°50′48″ N to 27°03′43″ N Latitudes and 92°39′ E to 92°59′ E

Longitudes covering an area of 200 km^2 on the northern bank of river Brahmaputra in Sonitpur district. The area is criss-cross by the river Jia-Bhoreli and its tributaries, namely Diji, Dinai, Doigurung, Nameri, Dikorai, Khari etc. Nameri is covered by Tropical evergreen, semi-evergreen, moist deciduous forest with cane and bamboo brakes and narrow stripes of open grassland along rivers. Grassland comprises less than 10 per cent of the total area of the park while the semi-evergreen and moist deciduous species dominate the area. The area is influenced by the tropical monsoon regime. The predominance of the south-west monsoon in this region causes precipitation to be highly seasonal (Barthakur, 1986) (*see* Map 1.1).

Objectives

The study is carried out within the Nameri National Park and the objectives are—

(i) to highlight how the physiographic base can be an attraction for tourists;
(ii) to examine the tourist-flow pattern and their preferred destinations and needs; and
(iii) to evaluate the status of existing tourist resources and facilities in the park.

Methodology

The present chapter entitled "Characteristics of Tourists in Nameri National Park Assam," is based on research study; data and information were obtained on the spot observation of the ecotourism resources by the researcher supported by secondary information sources like books, papers, reports, maps and information of local people. For this study, data related with tourist flow from Government Tourist Department, Department of Forest, field survey for primary information and data from different tourism promotion organisation are used.

The survey was designed to explore the nature of arrivals and the pattern of tourist demands. Attempts have also been made to study the tourists according to their origin, age, sex, occupation as well as economic level. By the study of their behavioural

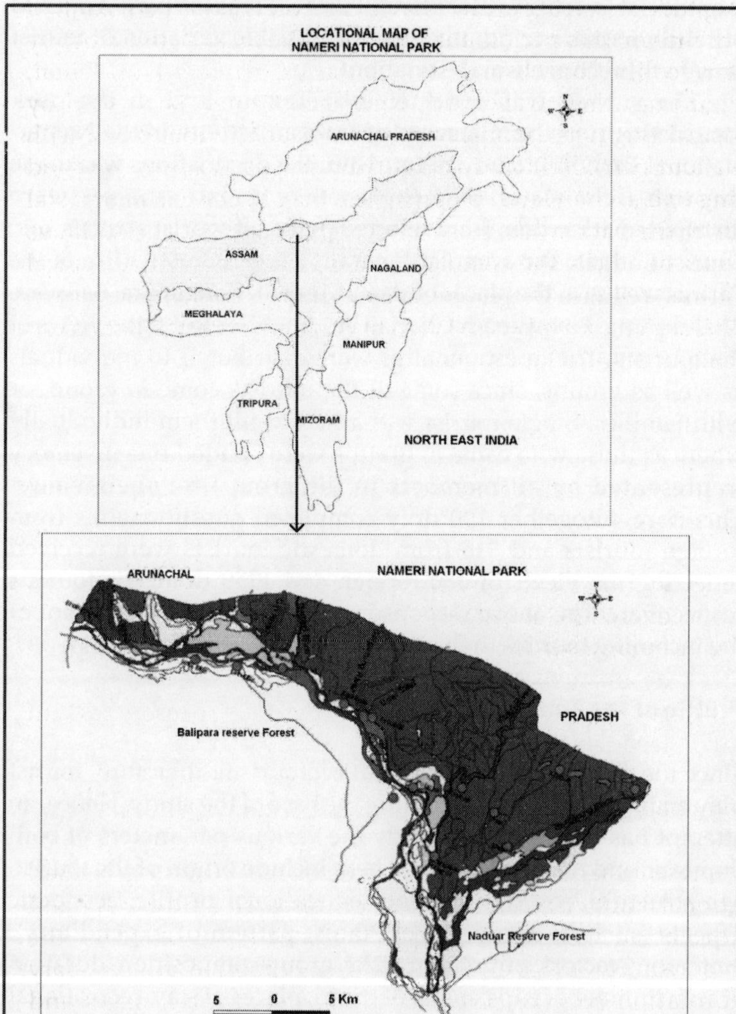

Map 1.1: Map of Nameri National Park

characteristics, attempt have also been made to cover their nature of travel, source of travel motivation, area of interest, mode of mobility as well as their perception towards infrastructural facilities. The survey was conducted for one tourist season, i.e. six months (1st October to 31st March, 2010-2011) as the park is opened officially in this period, to judge the possible variation of tourist flow to this ecotourism destination.

The survey was conducted at Tezpur and in the park considering it as the 'Gateway' of tourism activity in the Nameri National Park. The study of tourist in the destinations was made through field visits. Self-explanatory questionnaires were distributed at random from selected points of tourist arrivals, viz. Tourist Lodges, Eco-camp at Potasali, Range Forest Office of the Park as well as in the places of stay in Tezpur, Rangapara, Balipara, Bhalukpung, Bishwanath Chariali etc., in order to get the views of the tourists. The questionnaires were distributed to individuals as well as groups, since some of the tourists come in group, or with families. Single tourist was asked to fill them individually where as those who came in groups were handed one inventory (represented by all members in the group) for their views. Therefore, altogether 100 duly completed questionnaires from foreign tourists and 315 from domestic tourists were received reflecting the views of 380 foreign and 1250 domestic tourists respectively. The above response represents about 40 per cent of the incoming tourists to the Park, during the year 2010-2011.

Profile of the Tourists

Since the present work deals with ecotourism, therefore, tourist play an important role in forming the base of the study. Hence, an attempt has been made to study the various parameters of both domestic and foreign tourists. These include origin of the tourist, age structure, sex composition, educational profile, economic aspects (such as occupational status, pattern of expenditure), motivating factors, purpose of visits, group composition, duration of stay, number of trips, mode of travel, places of stay, recreational activities, perception on entry formalities, perception on tourism infrastructure and services, perception on climate, future travel prospect etc. Through these parameters an analysis has been made to examine the tourist's opinion towards ecotourism resources of the Park.

Origin of Domestic and Foreign Tourists

Domestic tourists visiting Nameri National Park are mostly from

West Bengal. The share of visitors from this state constitutes 38.09 per cent followed by Delhi 20 per cent (Table 1.1) to get relief from stress and strain of urban environment. Though, the home state Assam gets third position in tourist flow, its share of tourists is only 7.61 per cent, due to low economic level, slow pace of urbanisation and lack of travel component.

Table 1.1: Origin of the Domestic Tourists Visiting in Nameri National Park

Sl. No.	*States*	*No. of Tourists*	*Per cent*	*Sl. No.*	*States*	*No. of Tourists*	*Per cent*
1.	West Bengal	120	38.09	9.	Odhisha	9	2.85
2.	Delhi	63	20	10.	Tamil Nadu	8	2.53
3.	Assam	24	7.61	11.	Bihar	6	1.9
4.	Maharashtra	20	6.34	12.	Punjab	4	1.26
5.	Uttar Pradesh	17	5.39	13.	Tripura	4	1.26
6.	Meghalaya	13	4.12	14.	Haryana	1	0.31
7.	Karnataka	13	4.12	15.	Gujarat	1	0.31
8.	Rajasthan	11	3.49	16.	Andhra Pradesh	1	0.31
			Total			**315**	**100**

Source: Primary Survey.

A study on the origin of the tourists visiting in the Park reveals that foreign tourists came from the countries of Europe, North America, Africa, Asia and Australia. However, lion share of the tourist traffic is 52 per cent goes to tourists of European origin (Table 1.2). A country-wise breakup of the foreign tourists to

Table 1.2: Origin of the Foreign Tourists Visiting Nameri National Park

Sl. No.	*Countries*	*No. of Tourists*	*Percentage of Tourists*	*Sl. No.*	*Countries*	*No. of Tourists*	*Per of*
1.	USA	16	16	9.	France	5	
2.	Germany	13	13	10.	China	4	
3.	UK	11	11	11.	Denmark	4	
4.	Australia	9	9	12.	Philippine	3	
5.	Switzerland	9	9	13.	Nepal	2	
6.	Holland	8	8	14.	Belgium	2	
7.	Zimbabwe	7	7	15.	Bhutan	1	
8.	Japan	5	5	16.	Bangladesh	1	
			Total			**100**	

Source: Primary Survey.

Nameri National Park shows that USA and Germany each account for 16 per cent and 13 per cent of the share of foreign tourists, followed by UK, Australia and Switzerland with 11 per cent, 9 per cent and 9 per cent of share respectively.

Age Structure of Domestic/Foreign Tourists

Age structure is one of the most important characteristics of population composition. Age statistics form a vital component of population analysis, as most of the analysis is based on age-sex structure of the population. It is an important variable in measuring potential tourist flow of a particular tourist destination.

Observation on the age structure of domestic tourists reveals that majority of them 50.47 per cent belong to the age group of 20-40 years, followed by 35.87 per cent belonging to the age group of 40-60 years. Tourists of the age group of more than 60 years and less than 20 years represent 5.07 per cent and 8.57 per cent respectively (Table 1.3). Scenic beauty and fragility of the destination continues to be one of the motivating factors for young group of tourists coming to the State.

Table 1.3: Composition of Sample Tourists as per Different Age Groups

Age Groups	*Domestic*		*Foreign*
	No. of Tourists	*Percentage*	*Number and Percentage of Tourists*
Less than 20 years	27	8.57	7
20 to 40 years	159	50.47	48
40 to 60 years	113	35.87	33
Above 60 years	16	5.07	12
Total	**315**	**100**	**100**

Source: Primary Survey.

So far as the age structure of the foreign tourists is concerned, Nameri hosts a large youthful population (belonging to 20-40 years of age), which constitute 48 per cent of the total foreign tourists (Table 1.3). Another 33 per cent belong to the age group of 40-60 years. Presence of sizeable proportion (12%) of elderly tourists (above 60 years of age) may be due to the present low priced tourism amenities that attract some of the retired foreign tourists to the Park and its surrounding.

Sex Composition of Domestic/Foreign Tourists

Sex composition is an important aspect which determines the male/female ratio in an area and hence useful for incoming tourists analysis. The sex composition of the domestic tourists shows that male tourists dominate the overall tourist scene accounting for 89.52 per cent (Table 1.4). The share of the female tourists is low, i.e. 10.47 per cent due to lack of information feedback and negative publicity in the national media regarding the deteriorating law and order situation and relatively less safe tourism environment at the destination.

Table 1.4: Sex Composition of Sample Tourists

Sex	*Domestic*		*Foreign*
	Number	*Percentage*	*Number and Percentage*
Male	282	89.52	63
Female	33	10.47	37
Total	**315**	**100**	**100**

Source: Primary Survey.

The study of the sex composition of foreign tourists reveals that the share of female foreign tourists, i.e. 37 per cent is higher than that of the female segment of domestic tourists. However, the male tourists dominate the foreign segment like that of domestic tourists.

Educational Profile of Domestic and Foreign Tourists

Educational background of the tourists is one of the important aspects of tourist evaluation as it determines their economic level and urge of mobility. The observation reveals that only 14.92 per cent of domestic tourists belong to below graduate segment (Table 1.5). As a whole, an overwhelming number of domestic tourists 85.07 per cent have graduate, post-graduate and professional qualification.

The study reveals that only 9 per cent of foreign tourists belong to below graduate segment. As professional education is more

Table 1.5: Educational Qualification of Sample Tourists

Level of Education	Domestic Tourist		Foreign Tourist	
	Number	Percentage	Number	Percentage
Below Graduate	47	14.92	9	9
Graduate	119	37.77	31	31
Post-Graduate	86	27.30	19	19
Professional	63	20	41	41
Total	**315**	**100**	**100**	**100**

Source: Primary Survey.

emphasized in the Western world, the share of foreign tourists is comparatively more, i.e. 41 per cent in this segment than that of domestic tourist. As a whole, an overwhelming number of foreign tourists, i.e. 91 per cent have graduate, post-graduate and professional qualification (Table 1.5).

Economic Status of Sample Tourists

Occupation and income of tourists determine their affordable limit to avail tourist facilities and services. There exists a threshold level of income above which expenditure on recreational activities begins to increase rapidly (Cosgrove and Jackson, 1972). Low-income group generally have lowest activity rates in recreational pursuit than the higher income group.

Occupational Status of Domestic and Foreign Tourists

An analysis of the occupational status of domestic tourists visiting the Park reveals that most of the domestic tourists occupationally belong to the secondary and tertiary sectors. Of the domestic tourists 83.48 per cent occupationally belongs to these sectors (Table 1.6). It is also observed that the Park did attract 9.84 per cent of domestic tourist belonging to student's community. The share of tourists who are basically in household occupation has been found to be around 3 per cent in the case of domestic tourists. The elderly and retired person constitutes 3.80 per cent of the domestic tourists.

Information gathered from the foreign tourists visiting the Park also revealed that most of them occupationally belong to secondary

Table 1.6: Occupational Structure of the Sample Tourists

Occupational Category	Domestic		Foreign	
	No. of Tourists	Percentage	No. of Tourists	Percentage
Primary	–	–	–	–
Secondary	44	13.96	33	33
Tertiary	219	69.52	55	55
Student	31	9.84	3	3
Retired	12	3.80	6	6
Housewife	9	2.85	3	3
Total	**315**	**100**	**100**	**100**

Source: Primary Survey.

and tertiary sectors (88%) (Table 1.6). The share of tourists who are basically in household occupation has been found to be around 3 per cent in the case of domestic and foreign tourists. The elderly and retired persons constitute 6 per cent of the foreign tourists.

Domestic Tourists/Foreign Tourists and Their Level of Income

Income of tourists determines their mobility and level of consumption of goods and services provided by tourism industry (Bagri, 1995). An evaluation of economic status of the domestic tourist reveals that 10.47 per cent of them belong to the group having income range from 3,000; 25.07 per cent belong to the group having income range from Rs. 3,000 to Rs. 5000; 40.63 per cent to the group having an income range of Rs. 5,000 to Rs. 10,000 and 23.80 per cent to the group with a monthly income of more than Rs. 10,000 (Table 1.7).

Table 1.7: Distribuion of Domestic Tourists According to Income Level

Monthly Income of Tourists (in Rs.)	No. of Tourists	Percentage
<3000	33	10.47
3000–5000	79	25.07
5000–10,000	128	40.63
>10,000	75	23.80
Total	**315**	**100**

Source: Primary Survey.

In contrast to the domestic tourists, the foreign visitors were generally of higher economic background. Only 2 per cent of them have monthly income of less than Rs. 10,000, 5 per cent earn between Rs. 10,000 and 20,000, 3 per cent earn from Rs. 20,000 to Rs. 30,000, 4 per cent from Rs. 30,000 to 50,000 and 42 per cent from Rs. 50,000 to Rs. 1,00,000 (Table 1.8). The remaining 44 per cent of the foreign tourists belong to the group having a monthly income of Rs. 1,00,000 and above.

Table 1.8: Monthly Income Distribution of Foreign Tourists

Monthly Income (Rs)	*No. of Tourists*
<10,000	2
10,000–20,000	5
20,000–30,000	3
30,000–50,000	4
50,000–1,00,000	42
>1,00,000	44
Total	**100**

Note: Amount converted from equivalent $ and £ value at the exchange rate of 2010.

Source: Primary Survey.

Though compared to the Indian tourists the foreign tourists are rich enough with more purchasing power of goods and services of tourism industry in the context of their economy, most of the foreign tourists belong to the middle or lower income group, i.e. 44 per cent of them belong to the group having monthly earning of more than Rs. 1,00,000 and remaining 56 per cent earn monthly income from Rs. 10,000 to Rs. 1,00,000.

Pattern of Expenditure of Domestic/Foreign Tourists

As the economic condition of the domestic tourists is not sound enough, the bulk of them (about 61.26%) have daily expenditure ranging Rs. 200 to Rs. 500, while 24.76 per cent could spend even less than Rs. 200 per day, 10.79 per cent could afford Rs. 500 to Rs. 1000 per day per head during the tour period (Table 1.9). In contrast, a sizeable number of foreign tourists (29%) spent from Rs. 500 to 1000 per day (Table 1.10). Similarly, 59 per cent of the foreign tourists spent over Rs. 1000. Only, 12 per cent of them spent less than Rs. 500 per head in their tour period in the state.

Table 1.9: Daily Expenditure of Domestic Tourists

Expenditure (Rs.)	*No. of Tourist*	*Percentage*
<200	78	24.76
200–500	193	61.26
500–1000	34	10.79
1000–1500	10	3.17
Total	**315**	**100**

Source: Primary Survey.

Table 1.10: Daily Expenditure of Foreign Tourists

Expenditure (Rs.)	*No. and Percentage of Tourist*
<500	12
500–1000	29
1000–1500	38
>1500	21
Total	**100**

Source: Primary Survey.

Paying capacity of foreign tourists is much higher (Rs. 1055 per head per day) than that of the domestic tourists (Rs. 356 per capita per day). Thus, they generally expect quality and comfortable tourists' services.

Motivating Factors of Domestic and Foreign Tourists

Human motivations are the driving force for actions and decisions made by individuals. However, motivations vary and individual attributes including age, gender, cultural orientation, occupation etc. do influence what motivates their desire and the resulting choices (Singh *et al.*, 1996).

Here, we tried is to find out how tourists are motivated to undertake a travel trip to Nameri National Park. In case of domestic tourists, 35.23 per cent got motivated by the tourists' information bureaus of the Central and State Governments, while only 2.22 per cent were motivated by the travel agencies, and who are generally interested in handling foreign tourists for more profit. They make limited effort to motivate domestic tourists (Table 1.11).

Table 1.11: Sources of Motivation of Tourists Visiting the Park

Motivating Factors	*Domestic Tourists*		*Foreign Tourists*	
	No. of Tourists	*Percentage*	*No. of Tourists*	*Percentage*
Tourist Information Bureau	111	35.23	21	21
Travel Agencies	7	2.22	12	12
Friends and Relatives	127	40.31	32	32
Own Experience	62	19.68	27	27
Any other	8	2.53	8	8
Total	**315**	**100**	**100**	**100**

Source: Primary Survey.

A sizeable proportion about 40.31 per cent of the domestic tourists is motivated by their friends and relatives, and 19.68 per cent of them visited the State on the basis of their previous experiences in the State. Only 2.53 per cent of the domestic tourists were motivated by other motivating factors, such as travel literatures and such other publications in the state.

Among the foreign tourists, 21 per cent were motivated to visit the state by Tourist Information Bureau and 12 per cent by travel agencies (Table 1.11). However, friends and relatives had an important role in motivating 32 per cent of the foreign tourists to visit the State. As many as 27 per cent of the foreign tourists continue to get motivated by their own experience in the State and 8 per cent of them were motivated by other sources, viz. travel literature, and other related publications. It was also found that the bulk of the foreign tourists were motivated by the guidebook '*Lonely Planet*'[1], published by a UK based publication agency, which generally emphasise on least known tourist destinations of the world.

Visit Group Structure and Purpose of Domestic/Foreign Tourists

The purpose of visitors to the Park varies from person to person. Study of the purpose of visit of the tourists is essential to identify their expectations and to reorient the nature of tourist amenities and services per demand. An observation in this regard indicates that majority of the domestic tourists 80.31 per cent belong to the pleasure-seeking category. Hence, tourism promotional activities in the Park should be oriented towards creating more facilities to generate fun and pleasure excursion (Table 1.12).

Apart from pleasure excursionist, it is found that only around 3.49 per cent of the domestic tourists visited for business purposes. Around 6.03 per cent of the domestic tourists came for official work. Approximately 7.30 per cent of the domestic tourists came for academic purposes (i.e. to study wildlife, environmental status, native culture etc.). Besides, 2.85 per cent of the domestic tourist came for special purposes such as assigned photographic projects, visiting friends and relatives, attending seminars etc.

It is indicated that majority of the foreign tourists (68%) belong to the pleasure-seeking category. Apart from pleasure excursionist, it is found that only 9 per cent of the foreign tourists visited for business purposes. About 7 per cent of foreign tourists came for official work (Table 1.12). Approximately, 12 per cent of foreign tourists came for academic purposes (i.e. to study wildlife, environmental status, native culture etc.) and 4 per cent of the foreign tourists came for special purposes, such as assigned photographic projects, visiting friends and relatives, attending seminars etc. After the lifting of RAP[2], a class of foreign business tourists have started coming to the State in relation to travel industry, i.e. as tour organisers, translators and tour leaders.

Table 1.12: Distribution of Tourists as per the Purpose of Visit to Nameri National Park

Purpose	*Domestic*		*Foreign*	
	No.	*Per cent*	*No.*	*Per cent*
Pleasure excursion	253	80.31	68	68
Business	11	3.49	9	9
Official work	29	9.20	7	7
Academic interest	23	7.30	12	12
Any other	9	2.85	4	4
Total	**315**	**100**	**100**	**100**

Source: Primary Survey.

Duration of Stay of Domestic and Foreign Tourists

The duration of stay of the tourists is also one of the important aspects of tourist evaluation, because, it determines the economic return from the guest population (Kaul, 1994). 67.61 per cent of domestic tourists stay from 3 to 5 days and 10.15 per cent stay for one or more days (Table 1.13). This group represents a part of the tourists of the home state as well as those from other states (especially from West Bengal) who spend part of their total tour duration at Tawang, Bomdila (Arunachal Pradesh), Kaziranga National Park (Assam), Shillong (Meghalaya), due to fascination towards these destinations.

Table 1.13: Length of Stay of the Tourists in Nameri National Park

No. of Days	*Domestic Tourists*		*Foreign Tourists*	
	No.	*Per cent*	*No.*	*Per cent*
0–1	32	10.15	14	14
2–3	72	22.85	19	19
4–5	141	44.76	21	21
6–7	23	7.30	13	13
8–9	13	4.12	9	9
10–11	8	2.53	8	8
12–13	6	1.90	7	7
14–15	13	4.12	4	4
>16	7	2.22	5	5
Total	**315**	**100**	**100**	**100**

Source: Primary Survey.

As 33.7 per cent of the domestic tourists stay for a short time, the package tours for a longer duration may not gain popularity among this segment of domestic tourists. About 40 per cent of the foreign tourists visiting the park and their length of stay vary from 3 to 5 days. Merely 14 per cent of them stay for one or more days.

This segment of tourists uses Tezpur as a transit point for overnight halt, before going to Nameri National Park. About 5 per cent of the foreign tourists are found to stay in the Park or in Tezpur for a comparatively longer duration (more than 16 days). However, such development has been noticed only after the lifting of RAP rule.

Number of Trips Made by Domestic and Foreign Individual Tourists

A study of the number of trips made by individual tourists to the park reveals that majority of the domestic tourists, i.e. 85.71 per cent visited the park for the first time (Table 1.14). Thus, there is

Table 1.14: Domestic Tourist According to Number of Visit

No. of Trips	*Domestic Tourists*		*Foreign Tourists*	
	No.	*Per cent*	*No.*	*Per cent*
First Visit	270	85.71	80	80
Twice	33	10.47	7	7
Three times or more	12	3.80	13	13
Total	**315**	**100**	**100**	**100**

Source: Primary Survey.

an urgent need to improve information feedback as well as tourist amenities, which can inspire tourists for future visit. In the domestic sector 3.80 per cent visitors came to the Park for more than three times, 10.47 per cent for the second time.

On the other hand, 80 per cent of foreign tourists visited the Park for the first time. Among the 20 per cent of the foreign visitors who came, 13 per cent did so for more than three times, 7 per cent for the second time. In both the cases, repetition of visits reflects the strength (attraction) of various tourist destinations of the Park.

Mode of Travel of Domestic and Foreign Tourists

Mode of travel is one of the important components of tourist inflow into a particular destination. It is also considered as an attribute of tourism resources in an area where host community provides tourism facilities and services. Of the three modes, railway constitute a major mode of domestic tourist arrivals (65.07%), followed by air and bus or car services representing 24.76 per cent and 10.15 per cent of tourists respectively (Table 1.15).

Table 1.15: Mode of Travel of the Domestic and Foreign Tourists

Travel Mode	*Domestic tourists*		*Foreign tourists*	
	No. of Tourists	*Per cent*	*No. of Tourists*	*Per cent*
Air	78	24.76	89	89
Train	205	65.07	2	2
Bus and Car	32	10.15	9	9
Total	**315**	**100**	**100**	**100**

Source: Primary Survey.

It is revealed that, among the foreign tourists, air service is the popular mode of travel, which is valid by 89 per cent of them. Only small portion of the foreign tourists avail train (2%) and bus or car services (9%) while coming to the Park.

Tourists always prefer to travel the fragile destination either on foot or by elephant riding and boating. This helps them to get acquainted with nature, landscape and the cultural identity of the area. Among 56.82 per cent domestic and 49 per cent of the foreign tourists visiting the Park take the advantage of walking or long trail through nature.

Table 1.16: Travel Mode of Tourists within the Nameri National Park

Travel Mode	*Domestic Tourists*		*Foreign Tourists*	
	No. of Tourists	*Per cent*	*No. of Tourists*	*Per cent*
Elephant	113	35.87	36	36
Walking/Hiking	179	56.82	49	49
Boating	23	7.30	15	15
Total	**315**	**100**	**100**	**100**

Note: Some of the tourists use more than one mode of travel.
Source: Primary Survey.

Though Elephant riding is a part of ecotourism venture, it is popular among female and young tourist enthusiast that consists of 35.87 per cent of domestic and 36 per cent of foreign tourists (Table 1.16). Travel through boating is not so familiar among the tourists; hence a small segment, i.e. 7.30 per cent of domestic and 15 per cent of foreign tourists are interested in such type of venture.

Domestic/Foreign Tourist and their Places of Stay

A better understanding of stay places of tourists is necessary for development of future strategies for accommodation of tourists (Zurick, 1992). From the query regarding places of stay of the tourists, it was found that Eco-camp is the main resort for the domestic (26.98 %) tourists. Government owned tourist lodges did attract 39.04 per cent of the domestic tourists. Rest of the government accommodations, viz. Dak bungalows and inspection bungalows of different government departments have recorded only about 1.90 per cent of the domestic tourists (Table 1.17). Only

2.85 per cent of domestic tourists stay with their friends and relatives during their tour period. Apart from that, paying guest system could accommodate only 6.03 per cent of the domestic tourists.

Table 1.17: Domestic Tourists and their Places of Stay

Travel Mode	*Domestic Tourists*		*Foreign Tourists*	
	No. of Tourists	*Per cent*	*No. of Tourists*	*Per cent*
Tourist Bungalow	123	39.04	19	19
Dak Bungalow	6	1.90	4	4
Circuit House	13	4.12	7	7
Hotel	52	16.50	27	27
With friend and relatives	9	2.85	4	4
As paying guest	19	6.03	5	5
Eco-camp	85	26.98	31	31
Any other government accommodation	8	2.53	3	3
Total	**315**	**100**	**100**	**100**

Note: Most of the tourists use more than one type of accommodation.
Source: Primary Survey.

On the other hand, it was found that eco-camp is the main resort for foreign tourists (31%) too. Government owned tourist lodges did attract 19 per cent of the foreign tourists from abroad. Rest of the government accommodations, viz. Dak bungalows and inspection bungalows of different government departments have recorded only about 1.90 per cent of the domestic tourists.

As foreign tourists are regarded as foreign guest, hence service of the 'Circuit Houses' located in Tezpur are generally extended to them. Four per cent of foreign tourists are found to stay with their friends and relatives during their tour period. Apart from it, paying guest system could accommodate only 5 per cent foreign tourists, because the local people do not yet offer such a provision of accommodation. However, there is every possibility to meet the seasonal demand of tourists by extending paying-guest facilities to them.

Demand of Domestic and Foreign Tourists for Recreational Activities

For a better planning and development of tourism, an evaluation of the attraction (both man-made and natural) is an urgent need (Bhattacharya, 1998). To identify the existing resource base and their significance, a recreational resource inventory for Nameri National Park was prepared and incorporated in the questionnaire.

The resulting preference pattern of domestic tourists indicates that there is a strong demand for three main attractions, namely rafting, observation of wildlife, scenery and natural landscapes (Table 1.18). These items of attraction, which belongs to tourist resource base of the Park, are preferred by 10.47 per cent, 9.84 per cent, and 8.57 per cent of tourists respectively. A second thrust of interest include items such as angling, adventure sports, observation of flora and fauna preferred by 8.57 per cent, 8.25 per cent and 7.93 per cent of tourists respectively. The third and moderately significant cluster of tourist attractions includes local dance and festival preferred by 7.30 per cent, native life and customs 6.66 per cent, art and handicraft 6.03 per cent, water sports 5.07 per cent, trekking 4.76 per cent and night life entertainment 4.76 per cent in the park and surrounding areas.

Table 1.18: Recreation Demand of Tourists on the Basis of Preference Pattern

Domestic Tourists			*Foreign Tourists*		
Attraction category	*No. of Tourists*	*Per cent*	*Attraction Category*	*No. of Tourists*	*Per cent*
Rafting	33	10.47	Wildlife	13	13
Wildlife	31	9.84	Scenery and natural landscape	10	10
Scenery and natural landscape	27	8.57	Water sports	9	9
Angling	27	8.57	Rafting	9	9
Adventure sports	26	8.25	Native life and customs	8	8
Flora and Fauna	25	7.93	Art and handicraft	7	7
Local dance and festivals	23	7.30	Angling	7	7
Native life and customs	21	6.66	Adventure sports	7	7
Art and handicraft	19	6.03	Flora and Fauna	6	6
Water sports	16	5.07	Local Dance and festivals	5	5
Trekking	15	4.76	Spa activities	4	4
Nightlife entertainment	15	4.76	Nightlife entertainment	4	4
Open air activities	13	4.12	Open air activities	4	4
Spa activities	13	4.12	Trekking	4	4
Research	11	3.49	Research	3	3

Note: Adventure sports include land and air based activities, i.e. trekking, hiking, rock climbing, cycling, parasailing, hang gliding, ballooning etc.

Source: Primary Survey.

A comparatively less significant group of attractions include open air activities (4.12%), Spa (Mineral bath) activities (4.12%), and research activities (3.49%) preferred by domestic tourists.

Unlike the domestic tourists, the priority areas of the foreign tourists are ecotourism in the Park. The items most sought for by the foreign tourists include wildlife (13%); scenery and natural landscape (10%), water sports (9%) and rafting (9%). The second group of item includes native life and customs (8%), art and handicraft (7%), angling (7%) and adventure sports (7%) and flora and fauna (6%). The third and moderately significant attractions of the inventory include Spa activities (4%), nightlife entertainment (4%), open air activities (4%) and trekking (4%). A comparatively less significant group of attractions of foreign tourist includes research (3%). Though the park has immense potentialities for conducting productive research, but it is in initial stage due to improper infrastructure and negative publicity in national and international level.

Tourists' Perception on Entry Formalities

Evaluation of tourist's perception towards the existing infrastructure is a vital need to identify potentials and limitations in this area and to reorient the development strategies (Brandon, 1992). In this context some questions regarding the entry formalities to the Park were asked in order to understand the reaction of the foreign tourists. Their opinion in this regard showed that 68 per cent of them were quite dissatisfied with the entry formalities prevailing then. Among them, 40 per cent commented for complete withdrawal and 30 per cent for modification of such formalities. Only 12 per cent of them opined that such formalities should be retained and 9 per cent of them did not respond to the query. Since majority of the tourists, i.e. 68 per cent, showed their dissatisfaction towards entry formalities, the rule was a major hurdle for tourists interested in visiting Nameri National Park.

Perception of Domestic and Foreign Tourist on Tourism Infrastructure and Services

The evaluation shows that, in domestic sphere, only 7.07 per cent tourists termed the room service in their places of stay as excellent, 40.30 per cent as good, 43.38 per cent as satisfactory and 5.84 per cent entirely unsatisfactory (Table 1.19). The remaining 3.38 per cent of tourists did not reply to the query. Regarding the quality of food and beverage of the destinations, only 4.92 per cent of the domestic tourists found it excellent, 31.69 per cent found it good 46.76 per cent found it satisfactory while 10.15 per cent found it unsatisfactory. The remaining 6.46 per cent domestic tourist did not reply to the query.

Behaviour of the staff is important because cordial and efficient hospitality in the places of stay can motivate tourists for future visits. The behaviour of the service staff at places of their stay reveals that among the domestic tourists, 12.9 per cent rated the behaviour of the staff as excellent, 46.46 per cent as good, 33.53 per cent as satisfactory, while 4.30 per cent rated it as unsatisfactory.

The query regarding quality of transport service available in the area revealed that 8.30 per cent of the domestic tourists termed it as excellent, 44.92 per cent as good, 36.61 per cent as satisfactory, while 10.15 per cent termed as unsatisfactory.

Table 1.19: Perception of Domestic Tourist on Tourism Infrastructure and Services

Opinion	Room Service		Food and Beverage		Staff Behaviour		Transport Service	
	Domestic		Domestic		Domestic		Domestic	
	No.	Per cent	No.	Per cent	No.	Per cent	No.	Per cent
Excellent	23	7.07	16	4.92	42	12.92	27	8.30
Good	131	40.30	103	31.69	151	46.46	146	44.92
Satisfactory	141	43.38	152	46.76	109	33.53	119	36.61
Unsatisfactory	19	5.84	33	10.15	14	4.30	33	10.15
No response	11	3.38	21	6.46	9	2.76	0	0
Total	**325**	**100**	**325**	**100**	**325**	**100**	**325**	**100**

Source: Primary Survey.

However, in the case of foreign tourists a comparatively improved picture of room service qualities was found to exist, because bulk of the foreign tourists stay in hotels and eco-camp in Nameri National Park, which offered better services to the tourist. Hence, 19 per cent of them expressed the quality of room service of their places of stay as excellent, 41 per cent as good, 33 per cent as satisfactory; while 5 per cent found them unsatisfactory. The remaining 2 per cent did not reply to this query. In the case of foreign tourist, their opinion reflects a comparatively improved picture with 65 per cent positive response, 31 per cent neutral and 4 per cent negative response (Table 1.20).

Table 1.20: Perception of Foreign Tourist on Tourism Infrastructure and Services

Opinion	Room Service		Food and Beverage		Staff Behaviour		Transport Service	
	Foreign		Foreign		Foreign		Foreign	
	No.	Per cent	No.	Per cent	No.	Per cent	No.	Per cent
Excellent	19	19	27	27	42	42	21	21
Good	41	41	38	38	46	46	31	31
Satisfactory	33	33	31	31	12	12	37	37
Unsatisfactory	5	5	4	4	0	0	11	11
No response	2	2	0	0	0	0	0	0
Total	**100**	**100**	**100**	**100**	**100**	**100**	**100**	**100**

Source: Primary Survey.

As far as foreign tourists are concerned, 42 per cent of them termed it as excellent, 46 per cent as good and 12 per cent as satisfactory. In general, it may be said that the tourist were by and large contended with the service provided by service staff. The evaluation further indicates that, regarding the behaviour of service staff, level of satisfaction is comparatively high among foreign tourists with 88 per cent giving positive response and 12 per cent giving neutral response. Service of transport plays a pivotal role in tourism industry. However, among the foreign tourists a large fraction of 21 per cent opined the existing transport service as excellent, while 31 per cent found it to be good, 37 per cent rated as satisfactory. The remaining 11 per cent opined it as unsatisfactory.

Perception on Climate of the Area

Climate is one of the important environmental factors that determine tourism activity in an area (West, 1991). As the whole range of tourist resources in the Park is meant for out-door recreation, hence climatic elements have direct control on exploitation of it.

Table 1.21: Perception of Climate by Tourists

Climatic perception	*Domestic tourist*		*Foreign tourist*		*Visiting Months*
	No.	*Per cent*	*No.*	*Per cent*	
Hot and humid	131	40.30	39	39	Mar., Apr.,
Cool and humid	194	59.69	61	61	Dec, Jan.,
Total	**325**	**100**	**100**	**100**	Feb.

Source: Primary Survey.

The evaluation in this regard reveals that 40.30 per cent of domestic and 39 per cent of the foreign tourist (who visited the Park in the month of March and April) perceived the climatic condition of the Park and the adjacent area as hot and humid, 59.69 per cent of domestic and 61 per cent of foreign tourists found it as cool and humid (who visited the Park in the months of September to February). As most of the foreign tourists belong to European and North American countries, they can expect their familiar summer conditions in the winter months of tropical destinations. Hence majority of them (61%) come in the month of December, January and February (Table 1.21).

Future Travel Prospect to Nameri National Park

An attempt has also been made to assess the minds of the tourists regarding their future plan to undertake visit to the Park. Queries in this regard reveal that majority of the tourists (77.84% domestic and 81% foreign) responded positively by stating that they had the desire to visit the Park in the near future, while 9.53 per cent of domestic and 17 per cent foreign tourists stated that they had no future plans to revisit the Park (Table 1.22). The remaining 12.61 per cent of domestic and 2 per cent of foreign tourists did not reply the query.

Conclusion

The above discussion reveals that the Assam tourism industry is yet to be developed, especially in respect to flow of foreign tourists. So far Assam is concerned, though the Department of Tourism

Table 1.22: Preference for Visiting Nameri National Park in Near Future

Response	*Domestic Tourists*		*Foreign Tourists*	
	No.	*Per cent*	*No.*	*Per cent*
Positive	253	77.84	81	81
Negative	31	9.53	17	17
No response	41	12.61	2	2
Total	**325**	**100**	**100**	**100**

Source: Primary Survey.

was started about half century ago, it has not been able to make required arrangement to attract both domestic and foreign tourists, in spite of the fact that the State has immense potentialities for both conventional and ecotourism development.

Ecotourism in Nameri National Park has remained far behind in comparison to some of the other destinations of India in terms of facilities and services. But, in context of travel pattern, Nameri National Park enjoys one of the better favourable position than the rest of the other destinations within the State. The above discussion reveals that travel demand of both domestic and foreign tourists visiting the Park is higher as compared to some of the ecotourism destinations in Assam. There is also a wide gap between the expected and actual number of tourists visiting the Park and other tourist spots in the States. Except Kaziranga National Park, Manas National Park, Pobitora Wildlife Sanctuaries, Majuli and Nameri National Parks, there is high potential for tourist in other ecotourism destinations of the state, which are unexplored. The existing insignificant tourism scenario is the result of lack of proper publicity and the coordination among the concerned authorities regarding entry formalities for the foreign and domestic tourists visiting the States. Besides their distant location from the mainland, the absence of improved transport service also slows down the growth of tourism. Hence, an integrated approach for tourism development is an urgent need to use the tourist potential of the Nameri National Park.

Notes

1. **Lonely Planet** is the largest travel guidebook and digital media

publisher in the world. Originally called Lonely Planet Publications, the company changed its name to Lonely Planet in July 2009 to reflect its broad travel industry offering and the emphasis on digital products. As of 2009, it published about 500 titles in 8 languages, as well as TV programmes, a magazine, mobile phone applications and websites.

2. The **Foreigners (Protected Areas) Order 1958** states that a **Restricted Area Permit (PAP)** is required for non-Indian citizens to visit certain areas in India (mainly in the North East). The previous RAP requirements have been lifted for Assam, Meghalaya, Tripura and Darjeeling area of West Bengal.

References

Bagri, S.C. (1995). "Tourism education; use and relevance for employment opportunities", *University News*, December 4, New Delhi, pp. 45-49.

Bhattacharya, P. (1998). "Some perspective on tourism and environment in assam", *Proceedings of National Association of Geographers* (Eastern Regions), Vol. 1, Cotton College, Guwahati, pp. 199-207.

Brandon, K.E. and Wells, M. (1992). "Planning for people and parks: Design dilemmas", *World Development Report*, 20(4): 557-570.

Cosgrove, I. and Jackson, R. (1972). *The Geography of Recreation and Leisure*, London: Hutchinson University Library, pp. 30-47.

Kaul, V. (1994). *Tourism and the Economy*, New Delhi: Har-Anand Publications, p. 67.

Singh, M.B., Singh, V.K. and Roy, B. (1996). "Behavarial analysis of foreign tourist in varanasi", *National Geographical Journals of India*, 42(1 and 2): 28-34.

West, P.C., and Brechin, S.R. (eds.) (1991). *Resident Peoples and National Parks*. Tucson: University of Arizona Press, pp. 67-81.

Zurick, D.N. (1992). "Adventure travel and sustainable tourism in the peripheral economy of Nepal". *Annals of the Association of American Geographers*. 82: 608-628.

2
Estimation of Recreational and Other Use Values of Kaziranga National Park
An Application of Individual Travel Cost Method

Subrata Barman and *Raju Mandal*

Introduction

The environment provides various goods and services, which are critical for human existence and well-being. With the passage of time rapid growth of population and growing demand for various goods have exerted excessive pressure on the environment which has led to environmental degradation of various forms like pollution of different kinds, deforestation, global warming etc. Thus, at one point of time the goods and services like clean air, water etc., which were considered to be free gifts of nature have now been increasingly getting scarce. It is because of growing awareness about implications of changes in environmental quality that valuation of environment has become an important issue in theoretical discourse and policy debate. Environmental valuation is of utmost importance from the point of view of formulating appropriate policies to combat environmental degradation, proper management and improving quality of the environment, and thereby increasing human well-being.

The environment provides amenities, among others[1], which are a great source of well-being of people. Environmental amenities like Kaziranga National Park (KNP) have both use and non-use values. As for the non-use values amenity is non-rival and non-excludable in nature, and hence is of the nature of public good. Conservation effort from this standpoint should be supported by general tax revenue of the State. However, the Park also generates recreational and other use values for which the amenity is excludable and to a large extent still non-rival. For this component of value generated by the amenity pricing is possible and there is, in fact, a system of price in the form of entry fee. However, the price being administratively determined it is not economically optimal. Moreover, valuation of such amenities poses difficulties because of non-existence of markets for them. This chapter aims at estimating recreational and other use values of environmental amenities of Kaziranga National Park (KNP) using non-market valuation technique of individual travel cost method.

The chapter is organised in five sections. Section II deals with data and methodology used. Specification of model is covered in Section III. Section IV focuses on the estimated results and their discussion. Section V concludes with policy recommendations.

Materials and Analytical Methodology

Study Area, Data Source and the Sample

Kaziranga National Park (KNP) is a world heritage site that covers an area of 430 sq. kms. along the river Brahmaputra on the north and Karbi Anglong Hills on the south. It is the oldest park in Assam which completed 100 years of its existence in 2005. It is famous for Great Indian one-horned rhinoceros. It is the home of world's largest population of one-horned rhinoceros (2048 nos. in 2009), apart from many mammals including tigers, elephants, panthers and bears, and thousands of birds. It has the highest ecological density of tigers (106 nos. in 2010) and largest population of Asiatic wild buffalo (1937 nos. in 2008).

The KNP is divided into four ranges, namely Central Range (Kohora), Eastern Range (Agoratali), Western Range (Bagori) and Burapahar. The Park is open for the visitors from November to April for six months every year. There are almost fifty lodges, resorts and hotels located in the surrounding area of the Park from Jakhalabandha to Bokakhat. There are also some resorts nearer to the core area of the Park. A few of them are managed and maintained by the Tourism Department of Assam, Assam Tourism Development Corporation, leased by the Assam Tourism Development Corporation and a large number of lodges and resorts belong to the private owners.

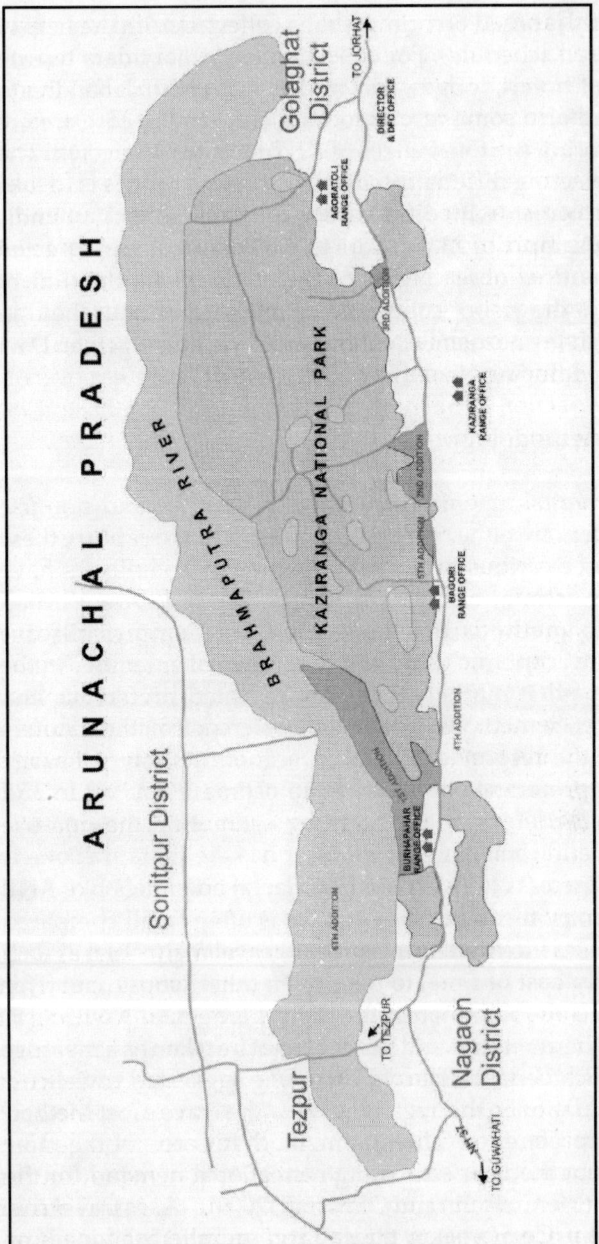

Map 2.1: Arunachal Pradesh

This study is based on primary data collected with the help of well-structured schedules. For collection of primary data twenty four different hotels, lodges, and resorts from Jakhalabandha to Bokakhat and also some resorts located close to the core area of the Park covering the four ranges of KNP have been selected. The reason for selecting different resorts from varied ranges is to take into account tourists with different socio-economic backgrounds. Thereafter, a sample of 233 visitors to the Park had been selected at random as final observations of the study. Here, the unit of observation is the visitor concerned or the head of household in case of more than one member of household visiting together. Data were collected during November 2008 to April 2009.

Analytical Methodology

An environmental amenity may have several use and non-use values. Markets are either absent or too imperfect to capture these values. Hence, various non-market valuation techniques have emerged for estimation of such values. There are two broad categories of methods that have been used empirically for estimating the economic value of environmental amenities in the absence of explicit markets. They are revealed preference and stated preference methods. The stated preference method suffers from bias of the respondents. Hence, economists rely primarily on revealed preference approaches to estimate use value and reserve stated preference methods for estimating the non-use values of the environment.

Although access to many environmental amenities like KNP requires an entry fee to be paid, that fee is often small compared to total expenses incurred by a visitor on travelling (actual as well as opportunity cost of time) to the site. In other words, entry fee does not reflect the amount that the visitors are actually willing to pay to enjoy the amenities and hence cannot be taken as a measure of value of such benefits. Harold Hotelling suggested travel cost method of valuation in this regard in 1949. The Travel Cost Method is a revealed preference valuation method. It is one of the most widely used methods of estimating recreational demand for the environment (Mendelsohn and Olmstead, 2009). It uses travel cost as an implicit price of visit to the site and seeks to examine how variations in travel cost affect the frequency of visits to the site.

Exploiting this empirical relationship between travel costs and visitation rates is an important step of estimation of demand function for recreation (Knetsch, 1963). The variants of travel cost method include zonal travel cost method, individual travel cost method, random utility model and hedonic travel cost method. They have been used in different contexts, each with its own merits and limitations.

To estimate the recreational and other use values of environmental amenities of KNP individual travel cost method has been used. The first step towards valuation/optimal pricing is estimation of the demand function for such amenities. The theory of demand suggests that quantity demanded of a commodity falls with increase in its price and *vice versa, ceteris paribus*. Likewise if cost of travelling to a recreational site is more, people tend to visit it less. Thus, amount paid by visitors to travel to a particular recreational site[2] is used as a proxy for the market price for recreational benefits of that site. The number of visits or visitation rate is used to illustrate the amount of recreation purchased at those prices. Relationship between these two variables, viz. price in the form of travel costs and the visitation rate has then been used to estimate a demand curve for the recreational activity.[3] A multiple regression model has been used for estimation of the demand curve. From the demand curve thus obtained, consumer surplus and total use value of recreation have been calculated.

Specification of the Model

In the application of travel cost method different functional forms and specifications of the model have been used by the researchers. In the present study two alternative specifications of the model have been used with the motive to check sensitivity of the results.

Variables

The travel cost method treats rate of visitation as the quantity demanded of the demand function. Thus, visitation rate, i.e. number of visits to KNP by a visitor per unit of time (to be discussed later) is taken as the dependent variable. In the travel cost method total expenditure incurred to make visits to the site concerned is taken as a proxy for the price of the recreational benefits paid by the visitors. Hence, the principal independent variable of concern is the travel cost (TC) incurred by the visitors. The travel cost has been computed as the sum the round trip travel expenses to and from KNP; opportunity cost of travel time; the expenses on food and beverages and lodging, and entry fee of the park. In case of visit of multiple sites particularly in case package tour a scale of priority to visit KNP have been used to rank their visit to KNP from 0 to 10. Depending upon the rank given by the visitors out of the total cost of the package tour the cost of visit to KNP is calculated. Finally, if the travel cost stated by the visitors relates to more than one person then the per head travel cost is calculated. Number of visits to the site and travel cost are expected to be inversely related.

Control Variables

The demand for any good or service depends not only on its price but also on some other factors. Likewise, apart from travel cost the number of visits by individuals to a recreational site also depends on some other factors such as their economic status; age, sex and educational attainment of the visitors; size of their households; location of the visitors, and quality of environmental amenity of the site concerned. Hence, these factors are used as control variables which may affect the visitation rate to the Park.

Economic Status of the Visitor

Economic status of the consumers is a crucial determinant of demand for any good or service. The most widely recommended measure of economic status of an individual is his income. However, it is very difficult to obtain the true income figures of individuals. Therefore, as a proxy for economic status of visitors an index of consumption standard has been constructed on the basis of the consumer durables possessed by them. The value of the index ranges from 0 to 1. Generally, higher the per capita income of a household better is its access to such assets and higher is the index value. It is expected that economic status of the visitors (ES) and number cf visit to the park are positively related.

Age: Age is an important factor that may affect the rate of visitation by individuals to a recreation site. Hence, age of the visitors in years (AG) is also taken into account as an explanatory variable. Age of the visitors may affect the visitation rate both positively and negatively, depending on the nature of the site concerned. In case of pilgrimage sites age may have a positive impact on the visitation rate whereas the reverse may be true for other types of sites like the KNP. It is expected that there is a negative relationship between the age of the visitors and the number of visits to the Park.

Sex: Gender of the visitors is taken as another explanatory variable, which may influence the demand for visits to KNP. To capture the possible impact of visitors' gender on visitation rate a dummy variable SX has been used, where SX = 1 for male and 0 otherwise. It is expected that because of their greater mobility in general males visit more to KNP than females.

Level of Education: Education makes an individual aware of the existence of environmental amenities and their importance as a source of recreation and other uses. Hence, to find out the impact of education on the demand for environmental amenities of KNP level of educational attainment (in years) of the visitors has been taken as another explanatory variable. It is expected that education (ED) has a positive impact on visitation rate.

Household Size: The number of members in the household of the visitors may also affect the visitation rate to KNP. Therefore, household size (HS) is taken as an explanatory variable.

Park Quality: The quality of the park as perceived by visitors may also affect visitation rate. It is assumed that the visitors have some knowledge about the quality of the park. They were asked to report about their perception about the quality of KNP. This perception about the quality of the park is taken as another explanatory variable and is captured by a dummy variable PQ, where PQ = 1, if perception of the visitor is good about quality of the park and 0 otherwise. It is expected that the sign of this variable is positive, that is, if the visitors know that the quality of the park is good than they will visit more to the park than others who have an opposite perception about quality of the park.

Location of the Visitors: The place of residence or locality of the visitors is another factor that may affect visitation rate, and hence considered as another independent variable. In this regard a dummy variable L is used where L = 1 for visitors from urban areas and 0 otherwise. It is expected that the sign of this explanatory variable is positive, that is the urban dwellers tend to visit more to the park than their rural counterparts.

The Model

Dependence of visitation rate on the factors mentioned above can be written as

$$VR_i = f(TC_i, ES_i, AG_i, SX_i, ED_i, HS_i, PQ_i, L_i) \qquad \dots (1)$$

where, VR_i represents visitation rate for the ith individual. Definitions of the explanatory variables are mentioned in Table 2.1. As mentioned earlier, to estimate the demand for environmental amenities of KNP two alternative specifications of the demand function and methods of estimation have been attempted in the present study.

In the first specification the dependent variable, visitation rate (VR) has been defined as the number of visits by a respondent in the last five years. Here the point to be noted is that the dependent variable visitation rate (VR) takes finite non-negative discrete values, i.e. it is a count variable. Because of the dependent variable is being a count variable a normal linear regression model will not be suitable. In such a situation count data regressions like poisson regression and negative binomial regression are commonly used. Poisson regression model is suitable when mean and variance of the dependent variable is identical. Since, the present case is one of under-dispersion the negative binomial formulation has been accepted and parameters are estimated by maximum likelihood method after affecting White's heterescadasticity correction procedure.

In an alternative formulation of the model the problem of count data can be avoided by redefining the dependent variable as the average number of visits by a sample visitor in a specified period. Thus in the present study while redefining visitation rate as the average annual visits by a sample visitor in the last five years, the dependent variable will not necessarily take discrete values but can take fractional values too. However, as the dependent variable can take only positive values a linear functional form may not be mathematically most suitable. Hence, the model can be specified as—

Table 2.1: Definition of the Explanatory Variables and Their Likely Impact on Visitation Rate to KNP

Variables	*Definition*	*Expected Sign of Co-efficients*
Travel Cost (TC)	Round trip travel expenses + opportunity cost of time + other expenses on food, lodging etc.+ entry fee	(–)
Economic Status (ES)	Index of Consumption Standard	(+)
Age (AG)	Age of the respondents in years	(–)
Sex (SX)	= 1 for male respondents, 0 otherwise	(+)
Education (ED)	Level of educational attainments of the respondents in years	(+)
Household Size (HS)	No. of members in the household of the respondents	(–)
Park Quality (PQ)	= 1 if perception about quality of the park is good and 0 otherwise	(+)
Location (L)	= 1 if the respondent is from urban area and 0 otherwise	(+)

Table 2.2: Descriptive Statistics of the Variables

Variables	*Unit*	*Mean*	*Standard Deviation*	*Minimum*	*Maximum*
Visitation Rate (VR)	Number	1.48	0.79	1	6
Travel Cost (TC)	INR	3417.79	5304.79	148	37750
Economic Status (ES)	Index	0.46	0.26	0.05	1
Age (AG)	Years	40.64	11.82	17	75
Sex (SX)	Categorical	0.88	0.33	0	1
Education (ED)	Years	14.68	2.78	2	19
Household Size (HS)	Number	4.09	1.25	1	8
Park Quality (PQ)	Categorical	0.93	0.26	0	1
Location (L)	Categorical	0.84	0.37	0	1

$$V_i = e^{\beta_0 + \beta_1 TC_i + \beta_2 ES_i + \beta_3 AG_i + \beta_4 SX_i + \beta_5 ED_i + \beta_6 HS_i + \beta_7 PQ_i + \beta_8 L_i + u_i} \quad \text{... (2)}$$

The advantage of this formulation is that its logarithmic transformation will be linear in coefficients and hence estimable by OLS or its variants. Thus, the estimable equation becomes—

$$\ln V_i = \beta_0 + \beta_1 TC_i + \beta_2 ES_i + \beta_3 AG_i + \beta_4 SX_i + \beta_5 ED_i + \beta_6 HS_i + \beta_7 PQ_i + \beta_8 L_i + u_i \ldots (3)$$

The demand function specified in equation (3) has been estimated by OLS method after affecting White's heterescadasticity correction procedure. After estimating the demand function consumer's surplus has been calculated as a measure of recreational and other use values of the KNP.

Results and Discussion

The regression results of recreational demand for the environmental amenities of KNP are shown in Table 2.3. The variable of prime concern for estimation of the demand function is TC, which is used as proxy for price of environmental amenity of KNP. As seen from Table 2.3 the co-efficient of TC turned out to be significant and negative. It implies that higher the amount of travel cost less is the visitation rate or demand for environmental amenity of KNP. This conforms to the usual theory of consumers' behaviour as far as the demand for any goods or service is concerned.

Other explanatory variables were also found to be significant with expected signs of their coefficients. The estimated coefficients of ED, SX, L, ES and PQ were found to be significant and positive whereas the coefficients of AG and HS turned out to be significant and negative. Higher the level of educational attainment greater is the desire to enjoy amenity of KNP and hence higher will be visitation rate. Males tend to visit more to the Park than females. Similarly, people from urban areas tend to visit more than their rural counterparts. The estimated results also suggest that the economic status and good perception about quality of KNP have positive impacts on demand for its environmental amenity. On the other hand, old aged people tend to visit less to KNP. Likewise, HS has a negative impact on the visitation rate. This is because large sized households have to support more with a given income and hence, have less capacity to visit KNP.

Taking average of the control variables a relationship between rate of visitation to the KNP and travel cost can be established. The intercept of the demand curve which represents the level of

Table 2.3: Regression Results of Demand for Environmental Amenities of Kaziranga National Park

Variables/ Particulars	*Coefficient (Negative Binomial Specification)*	*Coefficient (Semi-log Linear Specification)*
Travel Cost (TC)	–0.00003*** (6.42e-06)	–0.000025*** (4.78e-06)
Economic Status (ES)	0.466*** (0.161)	0.346*** (0.135)
Age (AG)	–0.0060** (0.003)	–0.0044** (0.002)
Sex (SX)	0.219*** (0.076)	0.136** (0.063)
Education (ED)	0.029** (0.011)	0.023** (0.009)
Household Size (HS)	–0.042* (0.023)	–0.042** (0.019)
Park Quality (PQ)	0.454*** (0.065)	0.34*** (0.05)
Location (L)	0.297*** (0.062)	0.229*** (0.05)
Constant	–0.61** (0.237)	–2.01*** (0.19)
	Wald χ^2 (8) = 109.58***	R^2 = 0.26
	Log pseudo likelihood = –291.413	F (8,224) = 11.09***

Notes: (i) Figures in the parentheses represent robust standard errors
(ii) *, ** and *** represent significant at 10 per cent, 5 per cent and 1 per cent respectively.

Source: Primary Survey.

travel cost at which the visitation rate to KNP becomes zero, which is also known as 'choke price', is determined. Having obtained the Marshallian type demand curve the consumer surplus per person is obtained by integrating area under the demand curve between the average travel cost of the visitors and the 'choke price' taking other explanatory variables at their average values. The estimates of average annual consumer's surplus are shown in Table 2.4. From the table it is clear that average annual consumer's surplus is as much as more than Rs. 9,000.

Table 2.4: Estimates of Consumer's Surplus

Model Specification	*Average Annual Consumer's Surplus (Rs.)*
Negative Binomial	9,704.19
Semi-log Linear	10,658.82

Source: Primary Survey.

Conclusion

The present chapter focuses on estimation of recreational and other use values of Kaziranga National Park. Estimation of such values may provide useful insights about the importance of such environmental amenities for human welfare, thereby inducing their conservation or promotional efforts. In view of the substantial average consumers' surplus there is obviously a scope for levying higher user charges from visitors of KNP keeping in view abysmally low existing charges. Higher user charges can be recovered in a number of possible ways such as by enhancing entry fee, charging higher rates for amateur and professional cameras and levy of cess on luxury resorts around the Park. While the first component is likely to be uniform, it will not be equitable to enhance this by a very high rate. On the other hand, the last component can be adjusted on the basis of standard of the resorts and can, hence, have a progressive structure.

Appendix

Measuring Economic Status of the Households

Economic status of the consumers is a crucial determinant of demand for any goods or service. The most common measure of the economic status of an individual is his income. But in many cases most of the people are either ignorant or refuse to disclose their actual income and hence, it is difficult to obtain their true income figures. In this study an index of consumption standard (CS) has been constructed and used as a proxy for the economic status of the households on the basis of the consumer durables possessed by them. First of all six items of consumer durables have been selected and assigned a score from 1 to 6 depending on less expensive to most expensive ones. The respective scores of the consumer durables possessed by an individual visitor are added and divided it by the grand total of the respective scores of each consumer durables assigned to it. If a visitor possesses all the six consumer durables then his index of CS will be equal to 1 and if he possesses nothing then his index of CS will be equal to 0. Thus, the value of the consumption standard index ranges from 0 to 1. It is reasonable to assume that the index has strong positive correlation with the household economic status or more specifically household per capita income.

Notes

1. Other benefits from the environment include materials and energy, global life support services and that environment acts as a waste sink.
2. Although Travel Cost Method was initially developed and used for valuation of environmental amenities of recreational sites its use has now been extended for valuation of heritage sites as well.
3. According to Mendelsohn and Olmstead (2009), "Exploiting the empirical relationship between travel cost and visitation rates permits the estimation of a demand function for recreation" (p. 330).

References

Knetsch, J.L. (1963). "Outdoor recreation demands and recreations." *Land Economics*, 39(4): 387-396.

Mendelsohn, R. and Olmstead, S. (2009). "The economic valuation of environmental amenities and disamenities: Methods and applications". *Annual Review of Environment and Resources*, 34: 325-347.

3
Policies for Encouraging Sustainable Tourism in Tripura
A Case Study of Devtamura: A Note

Malabika Das Gupta

Introduction

Devtamura or Chabimura, situated on the banks of the Gomati river in the Amarpur Subdivision of South Tripura District at a distance of 34 km from Udaipur town and 5 km from Amarpur town, is a site of historical and archaeological importance in Tripura. It is famous for its rock-cut panels in bas relief carved on the face of the steep rocky hills through which the Gomati river flows. There are around 37 mammoth bas relief panels on the sheer, nearly vertical rock faces of the hills through which the Gomati makes its way at Devtamura. Beautiful images of Shiva, Vishnu, Kartik, Mahishasurmardini Durga and other gods and goddesses dating back to the fifteenth and sixteenth centuries A.D. are carved on the rocky face of the gorge cut by the Gomati river as it flows through the Baramura-Devtamura range. The hills through which the Gomati flows in this stretch are picturesque and are thickly wooded and the area around Devtamura is the home of poor Jamatia tribals who eke out a living from fishing, collecting firewood and other forest produce and shifting agriculture (Bhattacharya, 2012).

Though Devtamura has a lot to offer to tourists by way of heritage tourism, unspoilt scenic beauty of the river, hills and virgin forests and gives tourists a chance to observe tribal life at close quarters, for various reasons it has remained a seldom-visited tourist spot of Tripura, unlike Matabari, Unokoti and Jampui Hills which are popular tourist destinations of the State. The reasons why Devtamura seldom experiences the footfall of tourists are not at all difficult to seek. Informal discussions that the author had with a few tourists who had visited Devtamura or were intending to visit the tourist spot whom she met at the Tourism Department's Office at Agartala in February 2012 indicated that the most important reason for the low turnout of tourists in this heritage tourism site is its inaccessibility. At one time, the Tourist Department of the Government of Tripura used to organise trips on demand for tourists to this spot of great tourist interest, but these trips have been discontinued. Tourists have to make their own arrangements to visit Devtamura at present and the journey to the tourist spot is arduous enough to dissuade anybody, but the extremely committed tourist. The author met a group of young and intrepid tourists from West Bengal at the Tourist Office in Agartala who had travelled from the State capital, spent the night in Udaipur at the Gomati Yatri Niwas and had taken a local bus to Rampur *via* Amarpur town. From there, they had hired a rickety and leaky country boat to get to Devtamura. Earlier, they had made an attempt to go to Devtamura from Amarpur by boat, but they were dissuaded from taking this route to visit the site as the boat trip from Amarpur to Devtamura would have involved travelling through an area covered with dense forests, which are supposed to be frequented by extremists and no boatman was willing to undertake the risky journey. Another reason for the lack of popularity of Devtamura as a tourist spot despite its attractions is the poor maintenance of the site. Although, it is a protected site of the Archaeological Survey of India, it is in a bad state of preservation. A number of its rock-cut bas relief panels like that of the dancing Shiva are partially covered with wild creepers. The entire bas relief panel of *Mahishasurmardini Durga* has fallen off the rocky slope on which it was carved and is lying in the river and is slowly sinking in the river bed. No attempt is being made to rescue it from its watery grave and restore it in its original site. Some of the other panels are in a sad state of disrepair and they, may break off from the hill side, topple into the river and disappear any day if restoration work is not undertaken immediately. Lack of suitable accommodation near the tourist site poses yet another problem for would-be tourists to Devtamura. There are no place where tourists can put up near Devtamura. The nearest place, where tourists can get government accommodation to visit this tourist spot is at Gomati Yatri Niwas at Udaipur town, which is 34 km away from Devtamura or at Gunawati Yatri Niwas at Matabari, which is close to Udaipur town. The other option is for tourists to stay in Amarpur town, which is 5 km away from Devtamura, but the town lacks suitable accommodation for tourists. All these factors combine to make Devtamura a not so sought after tourist destination of Tripura.

The Tourism Potential of Devtamura

Tourism has a lot of potential in Devtamura though it is untapped at present. Given the right infrastructure, Devtamura should be capable of drawing a large number of tourists who can enjoy the archaeological site, the natural beauty of the hills and forests of the area and their exposure to the life and culture of the local tribals. Encouraging tourism in Devtamura can enrich the coffers of the State and the local tribal economy can be given a big boost through the development of tourism in the area. But, care has to be taken to ensure that the local natural and human environment is not disturbed through the advent of a large number of tourists from outside in this unspoilt area so that Devtamura can remain a tourist destination in the years to come. Ecotourism with a strong emphasis on sustainable tourism has to be encouraged in and around Devtamura to tap the tourist potential of the area fully without endangering the environment while adding to the well-being of the resident population, so that tourism can maintain its viability in the area for an indefinite period of time.

At this stage, before the exact policy measures for making Devtamura a new tourist destination by promoting ecotourism with an emphasis on sustainable tourism are spelt out the two terms, 'ecotourism' and 'sustainable tourism' that have become buzzwords of tourist trade today have to be defined and their meanings clearly spelt out. Ecotourism is tourism that consists of travelling to relatively undisturbed or uncontaminated natural areas with the specific objective of studying, admiring and enjoying the scenery and its flora and fauna as well as any existing cultural manifestations, both past and present, found in these areas. Any form of tourism that does not reduce the availability of resources and does not inhibit future travellers from the same experience is called sustainable tourism. Sustainable tourism is thought of as tourism in a form which can maintain its viability in an area for an indefinite period of time.[1] Therefore, sustainable tourism is tourism which attempts to make a low impact on the environment and local culture while conserving the local ecosystems and helping to generate income and employment. Ecotourism has acquired a new meaning by incorporating within it the idea of sustainable tourism. It is increasingly being advocated as an environmentally benign means of preserving natural areas in peripheral locations and at the same time stimulating the well-being of the resident communities and imparting environmental education to tourists. It should involve responsible travel to natural areas which conserves and improves the environment and enhances the welfare of the local people. So, though the goals of ecotourism and sustainable tourism have become similar, the latter is still a broader concept and is concerned not only with ecotourism but with many other categories of tourism as well.[2]

Policies for creating benign forms of tourism like ecotourism that is sustainable should be based on cooperation among various agencies. They should be planned, implemented and monitored by regional, local and national authorities with a consultative mechanism and proactive participation of the local community. Local Non-Governmental Organisations can also spearhead sustainable tourism practices. Though the government, both state and local, have to play an important role in promoting sustainable tourism in remote areas, the management of tourist locations by the community is the hallmark of sustainable tourism and tourism activities and businesses have to be developed with their consent and support and operated by local community members who are directly or indirectly dependent on the location for their livelihood. Only community based tourism has a chance to survive—other forms of tourism cannot remain sustainable and ultimately decline.

Policies for Promoting Ecotourism with an Emphasis on Sustainable Tourism in Devtamura

If tourism is to be sustainable over time in Devtamura and achieve the goals of the maintenance of the environment and improve the well-being of the local people of the area, the Archaeological Survey of India, the Tourism Department of the Government of Tripura, the local panchayat, local NGOs and the tribal people of Devtamura will all have to collaborate to design and execute policies for encouraging ecotourism with a bias in favour of sustainable tourism in this tourist spot.

The Archaeological Survey of India, which has declared Devtamura as a protected site for its historical and archaeological importance, need to play a more proactive role in the upkeep of this heritage site. Many of the sculptured panels are half hidden by greenery at present and are in a bad state of repair. A number of those are ready to tumble down into the river from their steep perch on the hillside. The *Mahishasurmardini Durga* panel has slid off the rock face and is slowly getting submerged in the watery grave of the Gomati. The policy of neglect of this important and valuable tourist site followed so far by the Archaeological Survey of India will have to be replaced by a more vigorous policy of protecting and restoring the rock cut panels from further decay and ultimate oblivion.

The Government of Tripura and the local panchayat will have to adopt more imaginative policies for drawing more tourists to Devtamura while taking care to ensure that tourism in the region is sustainable, the local environment is preserved and the level of well-being of the resident community of the tribals of the area is improved. They will have to involve the local people in planning and executing these programmes and take their wishes into consideration while designing the programmes for promoting tourism in Devtamura. These agencies will have to provide the infrastructural support for tourism development in the area. This can take the form of repairing and maintaining the road from Amarpur to Rampur. Constructing a landing stage at Rampur, making nature trails in the hills and forests in the area where tourists can go trekking, setting up a tourist information centre and, a food court with stalls serving items made from local ingredients and specialities of the local cuisine, a picnic ground, a tourist lodge, a souvenir shop selling locally produced gift items following the local architectural design and using as far as possible, indigenous materials and providing drinking water and toilet facilities for the tourists will have to be on their agenda for attracting tourists to Devtamura. An ideal location for these central facilities could be at the scenic confluence of Gomati and Changanga rivers or at Rampur where tourists start their river trip to see the rock cut panels.

The tourist information centre can welcome the tourists and introduce them to the scenic and historical attractions of the Devtamura area, its flora and fauna and the tribal life of the area through photographs, audio-visual aids like film or slide shows and introductory talks. Tourists can be inducted into the underlying philosophy of ecotourism and sustainable tourism at this centre and told about the norms to be followed by them at the tourist site to enjoy nature, the archaeological site and glimpses of tribal life without harming the local ecology so that tourism can be sustained in the area over time. The importance of not using plastic in the area, not littering it, not defacing the hill sides with graffiti, not destroying the local flora and fauna, not playing loud music and not leaving carbon footprints in the area should be impressed upon the tourists at the tourist information centre. The tourist department should acquire small, solar battery operated buses to transport tourists in small groups from Amarpur to Rampur, which will not harm the environment. Solar power should be used to generate electricity to be used in the facilities, LPG cylinders for cooking should be provided in the tourist lodge and supplied to families which offer home stay facilities to tourists to save trees from being cut down for fuel and waste should be recycled in the tourist facilities so that the environment can be protected.

Once these facilities are set up by the state or local self-government bodies, they may be operated by local NGOs involving local people who require training to run the facilities by these agencies. For the purpose the locals may require advance for refurbishing their country boats and rafts for taking the tourists down the Gomati river to admire the rock-cut sculptures in bas relief at Chabimura, for setting up their homestay facilities and so on. The state level and local self-government bodies should evolve a profit-sharing formula with the local people through mutual discussions with them so that the profits and costs from tourism in the area can be shared equitably. They should obtain feedbacks from the tourists and locals on a regular basis for further improvement of tourist facilities offered in Devtamura.

With proper training and skill development, the local people of Devtamura can be important agents for promoting ecotourism and sustainable tourism at this tourist site. Tourism can improve their livelihood by providing them with supplementary sources of income. Their labour can be used in the infrastructure development activities of the state and local self-government agencies for the development of tourism in the Devtamura area. They can help in the construction work of the road, landing stage, nature trails, tourist information centre etc. They can get employment in the tourist centre, in the gift shop and as guides on trekking and sightseeing trips, as boatmen and in the running of the food court and the tourist lodge. They can earn extra income by opening up their homes for home stay by tourists, by producing local artefacts and handicrafts and selling local products like honey etc. They can act as guides for tourists following nature trails and walking through the forests, educating them on the local flora and fauna and their life cycle. They can also organise trips for tourists to nearby tribal villages giving them a chance to get a firsthand experience of rural life in remote tribal villages. They can form local cultural troupes for regaling the tourists with the local songs, dances and musical soirees at the tourist centre. The local people should be encouraged by the NGOs and the government to form cooperatives to manage and run the tourist facilities with support from the government.

All this will be possible with generous grants for the promotion of tourism from the Central Government and with an eradication of the blight of extremism in the area. Tourism development and the economic development of the people through tourism can act as a panacea to extremism. However, when tourism is developed in Devtamura, care has to be taken to see that tourism is sustainable and the social, cultural and natural environment of the area do not deteriorate with the opening up of the area to more tourist traffic.

If this model of tourism is successful at Devtamura, it can be replicated at the other tourist spots of Tripura for promoting ecotourism in the state in a sustainable manner.

Notes

1. Sustainable development is development that meets the needs of the present without compromising the ability of the future generations to meet their own needs. Thus, it encompasses a long-term perspective and notions of equity among individuals,

between the present and the future and between humans and other organisms. The tourism industry has endorsed the concept of sustainable development but from a narrow perspective.

2. For example, like ecotourism, adventure tourism and heritage tourism can also be guided by the philosophy of sustainable tourism.

References

Bhattacharya, Dipika (2012), "Gomati Pathe Debatamura", *Rong Route,* 2(4), February-March, 22-24 (in Bengali).

Government of Tripura, Directorate of Information, Cultural Affairs and Tourism, (Undated), *Tempting Tripura,* (pamphlet).

Jafari, J. (2000), *Encyclopaedia of Tourism,* London and New York: Routledge Keagan and Paul Pvt. Ltd.

Tripura Tourism Development Corporation Ltd. (Undated), *Tripura: Destination for Archaeological and Heritage Tourism,* (pamphlet).

Wahab, S. and Pigram, J.J. (1997), *Tourism Development and Growth: The Challenge of Sustainability,* London: Routledge Keagan and Paul Pvt. Ltd.

Websites

http://en.wikipedia.org/wiki/sustainable_tourism (visited on 9.4.2012)

http://www.preservearticle.com/2011p1072777/develop_sustainable_tourism_in_india (visited on 9.4.2012)

http://www.intamedpath.com/Ecotourism/what_is_ecotourism.html (visited on 10.4.2012)

http://www.ecoindia.com/sustainable_tourism/ (visited on 3.4.2012)

4

A Study of the Relationship between Tourism-based Activities and Economic Development in Sikkim

Ruma Kundu

Introduction

It would not be an exaggeration to say that tourism is the mainstay of the economy of Sikkim. About 3.5 lakh tourists visit the state every year from different parts of the world.[1] A majority of these are domestic in nature with an estimated 5.5 per cent coming from foreign nations. While the natural beauty offered by different locations of the state is undoubtedly a major attraction for the tourists, the state also provides ample resources of the taste of various kinds of visitors. Thus, different tourist activities are not only undertaken here, but also encouraged by the State Government. These include in addition to conventional tourism, niche categories like cultural, village and backpack tourism as well as ecotourism. The State Government has also been taking steps not only for developing these valuable resources, but also for leveraging it for the welfare of the local population. In fact, a significant proportion of the Sikkimese people depend directly or indirectly on tourism-based activities for their livelihood. In fact over a period of about a decade, tourism has emerged as lucrative employment option for the people of the state. Its economic importance can be judged from the fact that it helps to diversify the economy by introducing tertiary activities and new infrastructure in predominantly rural areas, creates additional demand in the village economy for agricultural produce and developing local markets, promotes local industries like food and beverage processing, souvenir and handicrafts etc. and provides a promising option for the youth in both rural and urban areas in terms of investment as well as employment.[2] If variables relating to transport and communication, trade, hotels and restaurants, and banking and insurance are taken as a proxy for tourism growth, then it will be found that these three sectors together have contributed 11.4 per cent of the GSDP of Sikkim (for the period from 1980-81 to 2006-07). Individually, the share of trade, hotels and restaurants is the largest with 6 per cent; that for transport and communication is 2.9 per cent, while the share of banking and insurance is 2.3 per cent.[3]

A natural question that would arise here is how far these tourism-based activities are contributing to the economic development of the state. This chapter thus tried to examine the contribution of tourism to the development of the economy of Sikkim and its people. The remaining part of the chapter is organised as follows. The next Section provides a brief outline of the available literatures and the justification of the present study. Thereafter, database and methodology of the study is described, which is followed by the results and discussions. The concluding remarks are given towards the end.

Review of Literature

Several studies have been conducted for the investigation of the effects of tourism and allied activities on the economic development of various countries or regions. It would be relevant to consider a few of them here.

Ghali (1973) carried out an empirical study relating tourism and economic growth in Hawaii. The methodology chosen involved developing an econometric model that replicated the characteristics of the economy under consideration as closely as possible. This model was then utilised for simulating the behaviour of the economy on the basis of the counter factual assumption of lack of growth in exports. The results revealed that the average rate of growth of income in the absence of tourism growth is 14 per cent lower than that obtained with growth in tourism. The total contribution of tourism growth to personal income over the 18-year period was measured by the discounted sum of the differences between the two time paths, deflating these differences by the Honolulu consumer price index and discounting back to 1953. It was found that the present value of the income generated by tourism growth was $1489 million, or about 1.5 times personal income during that year if the discount rate was 5 per cent. On the other hand, a discount rate of 10 per cent provided a present value contribution (in 1953) of $ 898 billion, which was approximately equal to personal income that year. With regard to stability of the growth it was found that although the standard deviation of the rate of growth in the absence of tourism growth was slightly lower than it would have otherwise been, the coefficient of variation was slightly larger. The results suggested that while growth in tourism had a role in economic growth, it also made this growth unstable.

Walton *et al.* (1993) attempted to document the recent trends in the development of the tourism industry among the nations of the ASEAN. At the same time, the paper tries to highlight some of the areas of concern in this regard like the inflationary effects of tourist expenditure on local prices and displacement of labour in other industries. The consensus is that the benefits in the form of foreign exchange earnings, income generation and employment creation outweigh any perceived problems. Tooman (1997) developed a case study focusing on tourism development in the Smoky Mountain gateway communities of Gatlinburg, Pigeon Forge, Tennessee, and Cherokee, North Carolina, USA. The study period was taken from 1970 so as to evaluate the second and third order economic impacts of the industry. According to the author, the impacts appeared to be beneficial on an overall basis, though they were more questionable from the viewpoint of the local population. On the one hand, total growth and income demonstrated an upward trajectory, while other social welfare indicators were not so positive. The author was of the view that tourism should be better managed, if it is to serve as an effective tool for development.

Hampton (1998) tried to highlight a comparatively less popular category of tourism, viz.—backpacker tourism and its contribution to economic development. He compared it to conventional mass tourism and touched on issues like leakage of foreign exchange earnings, issues of local control, ownership and participation etc. Sinclair (1998) had undertaken a survey of the literature on tourism and economic development. The paper considers development in the form of generation of foreign currency, income and employment, simultaneously taking note of the costs involved. It uses mathematical models for estimating the demand for tourism. It shows that while developing countries have obvious potential, they face the risk of deterioration in price competitiveness. It also examines the diverse sectors comprising tourism-based activities and stresses on the importance of cross-country integration. The author was of the opinion that problems relating to the use of environmental resources originated from market failure and suggested means for increasing returns without compromising on sustainability.

Milne and Ateljevic (2001) considered the complex linkages between the tourism industry and the economic development process. The authors emphasized on the fact that the evolving tourism industry needed greater understanding along with the manner in which it influenced the process of economic development at the local level.

Briedenhann and Wickens (2003) addressed the option of using rural tourism as a means of bringing about economic upliftment of rural areas. According to them, this could be particularly suitable for least developing countries, where rural poverty is a major problem. The authors suggested that clustering of attractions and activities along with the development of rural tourism routes can lead to cooperation and partnerships between local areas. They opined that community participation with the support of the public sector can help in the development of small-scale indigenous tourism projects in less developed areas. The paper considered the development of rural tourism routes in South Africa and identified the critical success factors.

Durbarry (2004) looked into the relationship between tourism and economic development with reference to Mauritius. The author tried to go behind the reasons for the success of the Mauritian economy. According to him, the country which was previously dependent mainly on the export of sugar had now become a major exporter of textiles and tourism, the latter obviously being representative of a service. The author proceeded to mathematically support the contention that tourism promotes growth by employing techniques like cointegration and causality tests. He also uses additional evidence to strengthen the claim that tourism has had a substantial impact on the economic development of Mauritius.

The paper by Chi-Ok Oh (2005) relates to the contribution of tourism to the Korean economy. With the help of Engle and Granger two-stage approach and a bivariate Vector Autoregression (VAR) model the study examined the causal relationship between tourism growth and economic expansion. Using cointegration it was revealed that there was no long-run equilibrium relationship between the two data series. Application of Granger Causality shows one-way causal relationship in the form of economic-driven tourism growth, rather than tourism driving growth in tourism.

Kim *et al.* (2006) had studied the causal relationship between tourism expansion and economic development in Taiwan. Like several other similar papers it uses the familiar approach consisting of cointegration analysis followed by the Granger causality test. The results indicated long-run equilibrium relationship accompanied with bi-directional causality, i.e. tourism and economic development in Taiwan support one another.

Based on the sample of existing literature it can be said that there is limited literature relating to tourism and economic development in the North East in general, and Sikkim in particular. Accordingly, the motivation behind this chapter is to throw some light on this area.

Objective of the Study

As mentioned before the objective of the present effort is to identify the inter-relationship, if any, among the different economic variables, GDP, domestic tourist inflow (DTI), foreign tourist inflow (FTI), income from agriculture (income_agri) and income from industry (income_industry).

Database and Methodology

In keeping with the above-mentioned objective, the framework for the methodology is as follows:

1. To examine the data collected for the study in order to evaluate the presence or absence of stationarity.
2. Evaluating the possibility of existence of long-term relationship using the Johansen Cointegration Test.
3. If the long-run relationship is found among the different

economic variables, then to examine the causal relationships among variables utilising Granger Causality Test.
4. If the long-run relationship is not found, to evaluate the exact relationship among the chosen variables.

The data utilised for the purpose includes values of the GDP, DTI, FTI, income_agri and income_industry in Sikkim for the period of 1990-91 to 2009-10.

In order to fulfil the above mentioned objectives we have utilised Unit Root test, Cointegration analysis and Granger causality test. A brief introduction to the three major statistical tools that constitute the bedrock of the present effort would be very relevant here.

(a) Unit Root Test

Whenever a sequence of data is to be used for time series analysis, it is necessary to evaluate whether such data may give rise to spurious phenomena that result in localised short-term effects that die down with time. The property of data that is free from such spurious phenomena is known as stationarity. The difficulty in dealing with a non-stationary time series is that any conclusion regarding the behaviour of such a time series will be applicable only for a limited period of time. In other words, all such conclusions cannot be applied to other time periods. As a result forecasts made on the basis of these conclusions will have little practical value.

As the present work utilises several kinds of time series data, the necessity of unit root tests is self-evident. While a number of tests for stationarity have been proposed, in this work we have utilised the Augmented Dickey-Fuller (ADF) test, which also happens to be the most popular variant of the test. In a few cases, when the ADF test has not proved conclusive, we have opted for the Philips-Perron test.

(b) Cointegration Analysis

For the next step, i.e. evaluation of existence of long-term relationship, we have adopted the cointegration analysis technique proposed by Johansen. The phenomenon of cointegration was introduced by Granger. At a broad level it can be said that cointegration is applicable when several variables are driven by a common stochastic trend; such variables have a particularly strong link that may be of interest. If y_t and x_t are two I(1) variables, then they are said to be cointegrated if a linear combination of these variables is I(0), i.e. if there exists a β such that $y_t - \beta x_t$ is I(0).[4] This can also be denoted as CI (1, 1).

The estimation and testing of cointegration is performed at two levels, viz.—single equation methods and system methods. The simplest form of the single equation is the two-variable model, where each variable is I(1), so that the cointegrating relationship is denoted by

$$y_t = \beta x_t + u_t,\ t = 1,2,.......,T$$

where u_t is I(0). Since the present work involves use of the system methods for estimation and testing of cointegration (besides the disadvantages of the single equation methods compared the system methods) it would be more relevant to look into the cointegration analysis from the system aspect. One of the most popular methods in this respect is the one attributed to Johansen. This method is based on a Vector Autoregressive (VAR) model.

(c) Granger Causality Test

The third component of the analytic portion of the study is made up of the Granger Causality test. This kind of causality study enters into the picture as cointegration analysis cannot throw complete light on the nature of relationship between specific pairs of variables. However, in the light of the present study, the focus is obviously on the latter as we try to examine the interactions between the growth rate with other variables like DTI, FTI, income_agri and income_industry.

At first each data series is to be tested for stationarity using the ADF test. Once it has been ascertained that each of these series is non-stationary, i.e. all of them are I(1), the Johansen cointegration test is carried out to evaluate the existence of a long-term relationship. Lastly, we have again resorted to the Granger Causality test to identify the contours of the relationship.

Results and Discussions

Table 4.1: Results of Unit Root Tests for the Chosen Variables

Chosen Variables	*ADF Test Statistic*	*p value*
ln(GDP)	0.840922	0.9920
ln(Growth rate)	–4.968331	0.0011
ln(DTI)	0.230607	0.9672
ln(FTI)	–1.025504	0.7219
ln(Income_agri)	0.845796	0.9921
ln(Income_industry)	0. 658802	0.9875
ln(Income_tourism)	3.086894	1.0000

From the results of the ADF test Table 4.1 it is clear that with the exception of ln(Growth rate) all other variables are found to be non-stationary. We now proceed to carry out the ADF test with the first difference values of all the variables except ln(Growth rate).

The results of this test are given in Table 4.2 below:

Table 4.2: Results of Unit Root Tests for the DTI, FTI, Income_Agri and Income_Industry after taking the first difference

*Chosen Variables**	*ADF Test Statistic*	*p value*
dln(GDP)	–4.968331	0.0011
dln(Growth rate)	–9.036133	0.0000
dlnDTI	–5.612130	0.0003
dlnFTI	–4.474517	0.0031
dln(Income_agri)	–4.255650	0.0045
dln(Income_industry)	–4.417855	0.0032
dln(Income_tourism)	–3.777445	0.0118

* Here the prefix 'd' indicates the first difference of the concerned series.

This second set of results shows that by taking the first difference the non-stationary series are converted into stationary form. In other words all the series excepting growth rate are I(1). Our original motivation was to examine the relationship between growth rate (as a proxy for economic development) and the income from tourism. However, as the data series for growth rate is originally I(0), so, we substitute growth rate with GDP. The subsequent part of the analysis tries to look into the nature of relationship between GDP and income from tourism. For this purpose we take the help of cointegration analysis and Granger causality test. The variables have been examined as follows:

Results of Cointegration Analysis and Granger Causality Test for the chosen variables are given below:

(i) Results of GDP and DTI Cointegration

Eigen Value (λi)	*Null Hypothesis*	*Value of the Test Statistic (along with the corresponding Probability Value)*	
		λ_{trace}	λ_{max}
0.336090	r = 0	8.626712 (0.4010)	7.372947 (0.4460)
0.067283	r = 1	1.253764 (0.2628)	1.253764 (0.2628)

Note: There is no cointegration at 5 per cent level of significance.

(ii) Results of GDP and DTI VAR

Variable	*dln(DTI)*	*dln(GDP)*
dln(DTI)(–1)	–0.451716 (–1.62349)	–0.035387 (–0.10182)
dln(DTI)(–2)	0.041572 (0.15798)	–0.034480 (–0.10491)
dln(GDP)(–1)	0.4415589 (1.71120)	–0.283326 (–0.87907)
dln(GDP)(–2)	0.342690 (1.23758)	0.093350 (0.26990)
C	0.044670 (0.59747)	0.212511 (2.27566)

Note: t-statistic values are shown in parentheses.
Source: Directorate of Economics and Statistics, Government of India.

As all the absolute values of the calculated t-statistic are within 1.96, the null hypothesis is accepted. In other words, there is no causality.

Results of Granger Causality Test

Null Hypothesis	***F-Statistic***	***Probability Value***
dln(GDP) does not Granger cause dln(DTI)	1.60760	0.2407
dln(DTI) does not Granger cause dln(GDP)	0.00771	0.9923

Source: Directorate of Economics and Statistics, Government of India.

From the preceding results of cointegration and VAR analysis it appears that there is no relationship between GDP and DTI. The results of the Granger Causality Test are also in agreement with the earlier results.

(i) Cointegration between GDP and FTI

Eigen Value (λ_i)	*Null Hypothesis*	*Value of the Test Statistic (along with the corresponding Probability Value)*	
		λ_{trace}	λ_{max}
0.330416	$r = 0$	8.132013 (0.4514)	7.219776 (0.4635)
0.049417	$r = 1$	0.912377 (0.3395)	0.912237 (0.3395)

Note: There is no cointegration at 5 per cent level of significance.
Source: Directorate of Economics and Statistics, Government of India.

(ii) VAR between GDP and FTI

Variable	*dln(GDP)*	*dln(FTI)*
dln(GDP)(-1)	–0.305892 (–0.95151)	0.252447 (0.64778)
dln(GDP)(-2)	0.067853 (0.20242)	–0.034206 (–0.08418)
dln(FTI)(-1)	0.044495 (0.19475)	–0.280582 (–1. 01305)
dln(FTI)(-2)	–0.054715 (–0.26044)	–0.398091 (–1.56311)
C	0.213229 (2.44302)	0.072674 (0.68687)

Note: t-statistic values are shown in parentheses.
Source: Directorate of Economics and Statistics, Government of India.

Once again all the calculated values for the t-statistic are less than the tabulated value of 1.96, indicating that there is no causality.

Granger Causality Test between GDP and FTI

Null Hypothesis	*F-Statistic*	*Probability Value*
dln(FTI) does not Granger cause dln(GDP)	0.06653	0.9360
dln(GDP) does not Granger cause dln(FTI)	0.29289	0.7513

Source: Directorate of Economics and Statistics, Government of India.

The results of the cointegration and VAR analysis suggest the absence of a relationship between GDP and FTI. These are further confirmed by results of the Granger Causality Test.

(i) Cointegration between GDP and Income from Agriculture

Eigen Value (λ_i)	Null Hypothesis	Value of the Test Statistic (along with the corresponding Probability Value)	
		λ_{trace}	λ_{max}
0.305134	$r = 0$	7.695498 (0.4985)	6. 552648 (0.5433)
0.061518	$r = 1$	1.142850 (0.2851)	1.142850 (0.2851)

Note: There is no cointegration at 5 per cent level of significance.
Source: Directorate of Economics and Statistics, Government of India.

(ii) *VAR between GDP and Income from Agriculture*

	dln(GDP)	dln(Income_agri)
dln(GDP)(–1)	–0.338805 (–0.60235)	–0.342335 (–0.55856)
dln(GDP)(–2)	–0.081188 (–0.13754)	–0.145009 (–0.22545)
dln(Income_agri)(–1)	0.040397 (0.07548)	0.071988 (0.12343)
dln(Income_agri)(–2)	0.173176 (0.31903)	0.109086 (0.18443)
C	0.216856 (2.39956)	0.184074 (1.86926)

Note: t-statistic values are shown in parentheses.
Source: Directorate of Economics and Statistics, Government of India.

The absolute values of all the calculated values of the t-statistic being within 1.96, there seems to be no causality.

Granger Causality Test between GDP and Income from Agriculture

Null Hypothesis	F-Statistic	Probability Value
dln(GDP) does not Granger cause dln(Income_agri)	0.16817	0.8472
dln(Income_agri) does not Granger cause dln(GDP)	0.05550	0.9463

Source: Directorate of Economics and Statistics, Government of India.

Following the results of cointegration and VAR analysis there is apparently no relationship between GDP and income from agriculture. The Granger Causality Test results also support the absence of any causality.

(i) Cointegration between GDP and Income from Industry

Eigen Value (λ_i)	Null Hypothesis	Value of the Test Statistic (along with the corresponding Probability Value)	
		λ_{trace}	λ_{max}
0.584464	r = 0	16.85863 (0.0310)	15.80736 (0.0283)
0.056731	r = 1	1.051275 (0.3052)	1.051275 (0.3052)

Note: There is no cointegration at 5 per cent level of significance.
Source: Directorate of Economics and Statistics, Government of India.

Since there is at least one cointegrating equation between the two variables we proceed to the VECM model. As we know, the VECM specification restricts the long-run behaviour of the endogenous variables to converge to their cointegrating relationships while allowing a wide range of short-run dynamics.[5]

Thus the estimated VECM which captures the short-run dynamics involving the two-time series is demonstrated by the following equation:

$$\begin{bmatrix}\Delta y_{1t}\\ \Delta y_{2t}\end{bmatrix}=\begin{bmatrix}\alpha_1\\ \alpha_2\end{bmatrix}\cdot\left\{\begin{bmatrix}\beta_1 & \beta_2 & c\end{bmatrix}\begin{bmatrix}y_{1t-1}\\ y_{2t-1}\\ 1\end{bmatrix}\right\}+\begin{bmatrix}c_{01}\\ c_{02}\end{bmatrix}+\begin{bmatrix}b_{11} & b_{21}\\ b_{12} & b_{22}\end{bmatrix}\begin{bmatrix}\Delta y_{1t-1}\\ \Delta y_{2y-1}\end{bmatrix}+$$

$$\begin{bmatrix}d_{11} & d_{12}\\ d_{12} & d_{22}\end{bmatrix}\begin{bmatrix}\Delta y_{2t-1}\\ \Delta y_{2t-1}\end{bmatrix}+\begin{bmatrix}\varepsilon_{1t}\\ \varepsilon_{2t}\end{bmatrix}$$

Here y_{1t} = ln(GDP) and y_{2t} = ln(Income from Industry)

In our case the VECM results are as follows:

$$\text{The Convergence Parameter}=\begin{bmatrix}-0.726148\\ 1.610688\end{bmatrix}$$

$$\text{The Cointegration Relation}=\begin{bmatrix}1.000000-0.866664-0.015507\end{bmatrix}\begin{bmatrix}y_{1t-1}\\ y_{2t-1}\\ 1\end{bmatrix}$$

Short-term relation captured by VAR$\Rightarrow$

$$\begin{bmatrix}0.010260\\ 0.024825\end{bmatrix}+\begin{bmatrix}-0.760286 & -0.182118\\ -1.642269 & 0.503997\end{bmatrix}\begin{bmatrix}\Delta y_{1t-1}\\ \Delta y_{2t-1}\end{bmatrix}+$$

$$\begin{bmatrix}-0.386596 & 0.44800\\ -1.093234 & 0.345202\end{bmatrix}\begin{bmatrix}\Delta y_{1t-2}\\ \Delta y_{2t-1}\\ 1\end{bmatrix}$$

$$\text{Error correction term} = \begin{bmatrix} \varepsilon_{1t} \\ \varepsilon_{2t} \end{bmatrix}$$

From the preceding cointegrating relation it is clear that the coefficient for β_2 is –0.86664 while the calculated value for the t-statistic is –4.86256. Thus the absolute value of t-statistic (calculated) exceeds its tabulated value (1.96) at 5 per cent level of significance. Hence, the null hypothesis of $\beta_2 = 0$ is rejected and the alternative hypothesis of $\beta_2 \neq 0$ is accepted. In other words, income from industry has a significant impact on GDP.

(i) Cointegration between GDP and Income from Tourism

Eigen Value (λ_i)	*Null Hypothesis*	*Value of the Test Statistic (along with the corresponding Probability Value)*	
		λ_{trace}	λ_{max}
0.310337	$r = 0$	9.916672 (0.2872)	6.687932 (0.5267)
0.164207	$r = 1$	3.228740 (0.0724)	3.228740 (0.0724)

Note: There is no cointegration at 5 per cent level of significance.
Source: Directorate of Economics and Statistics, Government of India.

(ii) VAR between GDP and Income from Tourism

	dln(GDP)	*dln(Income_ tourism)*
dln(GDP)(–1)	–0.606789 [–1.26226]	–0.094855 [–0.19422]
dln(GDP)(–2)	–0.179135 [–0.37431]	–0.161380 [–0.33192]
dln(Income_tourism)(–1)	0.427497 [0.81845]	0.039765 [0.07494]
dln(Income_ tourism)(–2)	0.329726 [0.62515]	0.361698 [0.67501]
C	0.194305 [2.26989]	0.139804 [1.60758]

Note: t-statistic values are shown in parentheses.
Source: Directorate of Economics and Statistics, Government of India.

The calculated values for the t-statistic are less than 1.96. This would suggest absence of any kind of causality.

Granger Causality Test between GDP and Income from Tourism

Null Hypothesis	*F-Statistic*	*Probability Value*
dln(Income_tourism) does not Granger cause dln(GDP)	0.39854	0.6799
dln(GDP) does not Granger cause dln(Income_tourism)	0.05587	0.9459

Source: Directorate of Economics and Statistics, Government of India.

From cointegration and VAR analysis it would seem that no relationship exists between GDP and income from tourism. The results of the Granger Causality Test also indicate the lack of such a relationship.

Conclusions and Policy Implications

From the preceding results it would appear that the long term relationship exists only between GDP and income from industry. This would appear to be surprising considering the fact that the main economic activity for Sikkim is undoubtedly tourism related in nature; yet there is no reflection of this in the results. On the contrary the results indicate the absence of any relationship between GDP and income from tourism based activities. In any case Sikkim is hardly an established industrial centre; so from this viewpoint also the above conclusion does not hold much water. The conclusion itself arises due to the fact that whatever industry is there in Sikkim falls in the formal sector and so has a discernible impact on the GDP values. In contrast, as tourism activities largely come under the informal sector, this effect is not readily measurable.

A possible reason for this could be that the data relating to tourism activities may not be readily reported or published. In this connection it could be pointed out that the tourism activities take the form of hospitality-based activities and transport or logistics-based activities, both of which fall within the informal sector. As a result the actual income is not reported or revealed fully. The government also does not publish reports regarding the impact of the income from tourism on the GDP.

One of the limiting factors for the present work is that it is based on a small sample of 20 observations. A more broad based study could result in more trustworthy results that may be extrapolated for the larger population.

One of the main disadvantages of the economy in Sikkim is that most of the agricultural production of the state is consumed locally. There is no marketable surplus. This situation needs to be rectified at the earliest. The state government could play a major role here.

Another important step on behalf of the government could be to confer the status of a full-fledged industry on tourism and allied activities. This would help to institutionalise mechanisms for developing the resource base for these activities in addition to the establishment of appropriate financing that can undoubtedly strengthen this sector. It would also contribute to government monitoring of these activities and the creation and maintenance of economic data on this area.

A third aspect that needs urgent attention is the development of the infrastructure of the state. The lack of a proper infrastructural base is a serious lacuna that hampers major developmental prospects for the state. Once again the government needs to step in and take concrete steps to resolve this issue. It is worth bearing in mind that tourism is essentially a seasonal activity with the largest tourist inflows occurring in the summer months, followed by a drop in arrivals during the rainy season. The situation is made worse by the dismal infrastructural situation. Development of a proper road network along with proper drainage facilities could minimise the problems during the monsoon. Another relevant area is to work out a solution for the landslides during this season.

Notes

1. Joshi, R. and Dhyani, P.P. (2009). "Environmental sustainability and tourism—Implications for trend synergies of tourism in Sikkim Himalaya", *Current Science*, 97(1), 10 July, 35.
2. Choudhury, M. (2001). *Community Development and Tourism:The Sikkim Experience in the Eastern Himalayas*, Paper presented at the World Mountain Symposium 2001, p. 7.
3. Chakrabarti, A. (2009). "Tourism in Sikkim: Quest for a self-reliant economy", *The NEHU Journal*, VII (1), 96.
4. A time series variable is said to be I(1) if the first difference of its values ($I_t – I_{t-1}$) gives rise to stationary values. On the other hand,

two variables x_t and y_t are said to be I(0), i.e. integrated of the order 0 if for a particular value of β the linear combination $y_t - \beta x_t$ is found to be stationary, though the x_t and y_t themselves are non-stationary or I(1).

5. Sarkar N. and Mukhjopadhyay, D. "Analysis of Long-Run Economic Relationships—The Cointegration Methodology"; Economic Research Unit, Indian Statistical Institute.

References

Briedenhann, Jenny and Wickens, Eugenia (2004). "Tourism routes as a tool for economic development of rural areas: Vibrant hope or impossible dream?", *Tourism Management*, 25(1), 71–79.

Chakrabarti, A. (2009). "Tourism in Sikkim: quest for a self-reliant economy", *The NEHU Journal*, 7(1), 89-104.

Choudhury, M. (2001). *Community Development and Tourism: The Sikkim Experience in the Eastern Himalayas*; Paper presented at the World Mountain Symposium 2001.

Durbarry, R. (2004). "Tourism and economic growth: The case of Mauritius". *Tourism Economics*, 10(4): 389-401.

Ghali, Moheb A. (1973). *Tourism and Economic Growth: An Empirical Study*. Paper presented at the meeting of the Econometric Society 1973, New York.

Hampton, Mark P. (1998). "Backpacker tourism and economic development", *Annals of Tourism Research*, 25(3): 639-660.

Joshi, R. and Dhyani, P.P. (2009). "Environmental sustainability and tourism—Implications for trend synergies of tourism in Sikkim Himalaya," *Current Science*, 97(1): 33-41.

Kim, Hyun Jeong, Chen, Ming-Hsiang and Jang, Soo Cheong Shawn (2006). "Tourism expansion and economic development: The case of Taiwan", *Tourism Management*, 27(5): 925–933.

Milne, Simon and Ateljevic, Irena (2001). "Tourism, economic development and the global-local nexus: Theory embracing complexity," *Tourism Geographies: An International Journal of Tourism Space, Place and Environment*, 3(4): 369-393.

Oh, Chi-Ok (2005). "The contribution of tourism development to economic growth in the Korean economy". *Tourism Management*, 26(1): 39–44.

Sarkar, N. and Mukhopadhyay, D., Analysis of Long-Run Economic Relationships—The Cointegration Methodology, Economic Research Unit, Indian Statistical Institute, Kolkata (Internal Paper).

Sinclair, M. Thea (1998). "Tourism and economic development: A survey." *Journal of Development Studies*, 34(5): 1-51.

Tooman, L. Alex (1997). "Tourism and development", *Journal of Travel Research,* 51(3): 33-40.

Walton, J., Hitchcock, M., King, V.T. and Parnwell, M.J.G. (1993). "Tourism and economic development in ASEAN". In: Hitchcock, M., King, V.T. and Parnwell, M.J.G. (Eds.) *Tourism in South-East Asia,* London: Routledge Kegan and Paul (P) Ltd., pp. 214-233.

5
Expectation of Tourists in Meghalaya and the Effect of Experience on their Visiting Decision

Utpal Kumar De and *Juban Nongbri*

Introduction

The tourism industry is the world largest industry at present and it contributes largely to the income and employment of many countries in the world. Similarly, it is also one of the main suppliers of employment and income to the indigenous people of Meghalaya. A large number of people in the state of Meghalaya are directly or indirectly involved in the tourism sector and earns their livelihood from this industry. Besides, this sector also brings huge revenue to the state exchequer. Thus, the development of the tourism industry will automatically lead to the increase in the income and well-being of the people.

Meghalaya is a land which is extremely beautiful and perfectly blends by Mother Nature. Its moderate climate is perfect for visitors to escape from the scorching heat especially those from mainland India, then its heavy rainfall, the caves, the sacred forest attracted tourist like students, researchers, excavators to visit Meghalaya. The heritage, cultures, rituals and the dances also attracted tourists to come and witness them. According to Richards, the heritage tourism has a great potential to attract tourists and it can also boost local indigenous culture of a country (Richards, 1995). Lately, Meghalaya has become an educational hub of the North Eastern region and every year thousands and thousands of students come from different states of the North East to pursue their higher education here.

But, the development of the tourism industry and for that matter any type of industries depends on the availability a good infrastructure. A good infrastructure will increase the accessibility of the place to tourists and thus many tourists will be attracted to the place which will further benefit the local people. Naturally, when the tourists plan to visit a particular destination they have certain expectations from that destination. These expectations can be increased or decreased, resulting from publicity and marketing efforts of the tourism destination (Aksu *et al.*, 2010).

Expectation can be generally define as the satisfactions a customer expects to receive while buying and consuming a commodity. For a tourist, his expectation can be define as his prior estimation of the satisfaction that he will derived from visiting a place. A tourist who had already visited the place will visit the place again, if he had a good experience of that place. When returning home the tourist will also carry with him the experience he had and such experience will determine whether more or less tourist will visit the place in future.

Therefore, for the tourists having a positive experience of a destination is very essential. A good road, proper communication, hospitality of the people, availability of guide maps and human guide, accommodation and other factors experienced by the tourist will tell them whether to visit the place again or not. It not only the experience of a good infrastructure by the tourists that will decide their chance of revisiting the place, but their expectations of the conditions in their next visit will be also another factor. Hence knowing and understanding the experience and the expectation of the tourist is very essential in order to attract more and more tourists and market the tourist-attracting potential of a place (Stevens, 1992).

Thus, the development of infrastructures like transport, communication, accommodation, accessibility, hospitality etc. is the immediate need so that tourists will have a good experience and high expectation of the place and the possibility of them visiting again will be more. The Meghalaya goverment and the people of Meghalaya should be able to tap the employment and income generated potential of this industry and this is possible by development of infrastructures because it is only a good experience and high expectations had by the tourists, which will make them to visit Meghalaya. Hence, in this chapter we will try to assess how the development and availability of infrastructures increase the experience and the expectation and act as pre-conditions for the variation of tourist inflow to Meghalaya.

Tourism Potential in Meghalaya

The potential of Meghalaya as a tourist spot dated back to the erstwhile Jaintiapur kingdom when the eastern parts of Meghalaya, i.e. present Jaintia Hills district was made the summer capital so that the royals can escape the heat of Bangladesh and enjoy the coolness and pleasant weather of Meghalaya. Informal reports also said that the British like the weather of Khasi-Jaintia Hills so much that compelled them to made Cherrapunjee locally known as Sohra the capital of the North Eastern Frontier and later shifted the capital to Shillong. Thus, the tourist attraction potential of Meghalaya is not new.

Generally comparing to the other North Eastern States of India, Meghalaya is a relatively a peaceful state with less political disturbances, no ethnic violence, a limited militancy problem and people from outside are not required to obtain the Inner Line Permit (ILP) to visit the state as is the case in other states of the region. Meghalaya also boast of a variety of flora and fauna and it has more than 300 varieties of orchids. Moreover, many varieties of medicinal plants are found in Meghalaya. Many tourists who are environment enthusiasts would have like to visit Meghalaya just to experience these vast varieties of floras, faunas and the medical plants.

The overall environment is conducive for the development of the tourism industry, but instead it is sluggish. Tourism industry in Meghalaya is not flourishing as it should be because of wants for the basic necessities such as the various infrastructures like transport, communication, accommodation, hospitality etc. Steps should be taken in order to make their stay a pleasant and memorable one and encourage repeat visit.

Many tourist spots in Meghalaya do not have proper road connectivity which in turn makes the tourist spots inaccessible to the tourists who instead want to visit such spots. Even popular tourist spot like Cherrapunjee where thousands of tourists visits every year do not have a proper hotel, guest house, eateries and restaurants in which the tourists could call in.

If there is a proper infrastructure in different tourist spots then it will result in a larger inflow of tourists as a good infrastructure woo the tourists who had visited the spots and at the same time it will attract new tourists. Study had shown that satisfaction and experience from past visit is an important factor which determines the expectation and intention of tourists to revisit a place (Bowen, 2002).

The tourism industry in Meghalaya was credited by the Indian Brand Equity Foundation (IBEF) of having a high factor advantage, i.e. the benefits which will be derive from this industry is high due to its geographical location and natural beauty. It is also important to note that among the three sectors of Meghalaya's economy, the tertiary sector contributed the highest to the state revenue and tourism industry is one among the main contributor in the tertiary sector. Being a service sector, the tourism industry in Meghalaya must increase its service efficiency and cater to the different needs of the tourists (*www.ibef.org*).

Review of Literature

In a country like India with its huge potential to attract tourists, tourism is considered to be one of the major contributors to the national income, if appropriate steps were taken to harness these potentials. The tourism industry should be able to deliver superior and consistent service to the tourists. The different types of tourists have varieties of needs and requirements, which the place of destination should be able to fulfil. If the place of destination cannot meet the needs and expectations of the tourists then they will not be satisfied with the service provided and from their experience these tourists will not come back to the place in future (Jadhav and More, 2010).

It is widely accepted and argued that there is a great linkage between the level of satisfaction and experience with the frequency of visit a tourist undertake to a place. If the satisfaction level is high then it will increase the loyalty of the tourist and willingness to maintain a long term relationship with the place (Athanassopoulos *et al.*, 2001).

Kozak and Rimmington analysed the satisfaction of tourists with Mallorca in Spain found that satisfaction and experience of the services provided at Mallorca affects the choice of destination and intention to revisit (Kozak and Rimmington, 2000). The satisfaction of a tourist from visiting a place resulted in many benefits and these include the spread of favourable words of mouth acting as free publicity for the tourist site, increased loyalty and a good chance of a revisit by the tourist (Fornell, 1992).

In Thailand Lertwannawit and Anuwichanont conducted a study on the Khao Yai National Park and they found that knowing the tourist perception and expectation such as on pollution, facilities and safety give inputs for the improvement in the management of the Park (Lertwannawit and Anuwichanont, 2011).

Some studies also revealed that environment of the place is critical to the choice of tourists to visit a place hence preservation and proper management of the environment is very essential and this is possible only if expectation of the tourist is known (Hvenegaard & Dearden, 1998; Kim, Borges, & Chon, 2006).

The tourism industry by nature is an information-incentive industry. Therefore, it is very essential to know the experience and expectation of the tourist as it provide vital clues to the marketers and developers to take appropriate course of action. The choice of destination of tourist is driven by sources of information such as recommendations from friends, relatives and colleagues, travel guide books and travel agents (Henderson *et al.*, 2007). And most of this information is the result of experience from past visit. A study on Korean tourists found out that the information they received from the internet determined their choice and expectation from their place of destination (Khumsri, 2006). Castaneda *et al.* were of the opinion that since tourism is an information-incentive industry, hence, the use of internet is necessary to know tourist expectation and the promotion of tourism (Castaneda, Frias & Rodriguez, 2007).

Some authors had also used modern statistical methods to study the satisfaction, experience and expectation of tourist in a site. In their study entitled "Key Issues in Visitor Experience and Tourism Development—A Study of Varanasi" in 2008, Rajeev and Shyju used the factor analysis, the analysis of variance (ANOVA), t-test and descriptive statistics and the results indicate that there is dissatisfaction with various services provided by local tour operators and local tourist guides. Further tests disclose that apart from tour operators and local guide services, tourists have strong apprehensions regarding room service, availability of tourist information, cleanliness, and crowd management (Rajeev and Shyju, 2008).

All the literatures highlighted above prove that the main factors that determine the choice of destination by the tourists depend on their past experience, expectation from the place of destination. Thus, knowing and having information on the tourists' perception and expectation is the most desirable needs in this world of competition. The ways the goverment, people and stakeholders react to the expectation of tourists thus will decide whether the place will attracted more or less tourists.

Method and Material

In this particular study tabular description has been made to have an idea about the experiences and the expectations of the tourists with regard to Meghalaya as a tourist destination and its effect on their visiting decisions. It is done through the examination of the opinion of the visiting tourists obtained by a primary survey on a hundred tourists. Preferences are given to the repeated visitors as their opinion would be more important, who can better explain the changes in those factors over the years. Also their opinion on variation in environmental conditions especially the climate for which many visitors prefer to visit Shillong and its surrounding during the summer time is understood.

Observation

In this particular section we will discuss about the finding that was conducted by surveying on a hundred repeated tourists visiting Meghalaya. Questionnaires were given to the tourists to obtain their opinions regarding the condition of Meghalaya as a tourist destination and their suggestions for improvement. It must also be mention here that in the survey conducted one tourist was found to have visit Meghalaya more than five times and his first visit was in the year 1988. Questions that were asked include such as on the frequency of visits, sources of information about Meghalaya, areas of attractions, conditions of transport and communication, the availability of tourist guides, maps and other requirements that a place of destination should have.

The observation found that main attraction of Meghalaya is its natural beauty as a whopping 65 respondents said they come to Meghalaya because of its natural beauty. It is also worth mentioning here that no tourists visit the state to do shopping and they do not find Meghalaya to be a shopping hub. The number of tourist who came to witness the natural caves is 25 showing that development in this sector is worthwhile. And 10 respondents visit the state just for a stop of itinerary.

Table 5.1: Percentage Distribution of Main Attractions of Meghalaya among the Tourists/Visitors

Natural beauty	*Natural caves*	*Shopping hub*	*Just a stop on your itinerary*	*Total*
65	25	0	10	100

Source: Primary survey.

Table 5.2: Percentage Distribution of Respondent Visitors according to Frequency of Visit by them during last 15 years

Frequency of visit				
Twice	*Thrice*	*Four time*	*More than four*	*Total*
43	27	17	13	100

Source: Primary survey.

Table 5.2 shows that tourist do prefer Meghalaya as a tourist destination. The information in Table 5.2 shows the frequency of visit among the repeated visitors. The number of tourists who had visited Meghalaya twice are 43, those who had visited thrice are 27, 17 tourist had visited Meghalaya four time while 13 tourists had visited this state more than four time.

In the following Table 5.3 given below, the sources of information that the visitors received about Meghalaya was given. Among the different sources of information such as Travel programme in T.V., Magazines and Guidebooks, Newspaper Advertisement, Tour Agents, Friends and Relatives, and Package tour it was found that out of the hundred tourists, 53 of them responded that they got the information from Friends and Relatives. This proves that favourable publicity through words of mouth plays a very important for the promotion of tourism in

Meghalaya. And favourable words of mouth will spread only if the tourists are happy and satisfied with their experience. Thus, the Meghalaya Government must take steps to improve the infrastructures and other requirements in the tourist sites so as to meets the needs of the tourist. Steps should also be taken to increase publicity through other sources like Tour Agents and Package tour which according to the present observation are zero.

Table 5.3: Percentage Distribution of Respondents according to Source of Information about Meghalaya used by them

Travel Programme in T.V.	*Magazines and Guide-books*	*Newspaper Advertisement*	*Tour Agents*	*Friends and Relatives*	*Package tour*	*Total*
13	23	10	0	53	0	100

Source: Primary survey.

Transport and communication are the backbone of any industry and the state as a whole. The availability and condition of transport and communication will determine the growth and development of the area. A good and proper road will reduce the time taken to reach a destination and it will decrease the transportation cost. Similarly, transport and communication will make a destination accessible to the tourist and result in a larger inflows of tourist which will further the income of the local people, stakeholders and the State.

Table 5.4: Percentage Distribution of Respondents according to their Opinion on the Condition of Transport and Communication, Forest and Population in Meghalaya

Items	*Very Good Improve-ment*	*Satisfac-tory Improve-ment*	*Minimum Deteriora-tion*	*Serious Deterio-ration*	*Total*
Transport and Communication	13	27	7	53	100
Forest	0	0	60	40	100
Population	80	20	0	0	100

Source: Primary survey.

Table 5.4 shows the experience of tourist with regards to the conditions of transport and communication, forest and the population in the state of Meghalaya. Table 5.4 indicates that as many as 53 tourists responded that there is a serious deterioration in transport and communication while 7 number of tourists said that it was only a minimal deterioration. The number of tourists who answer with satisfactory improvement is 27 and only 13 think that there is a good improvement in transport and communication in Meghalaya.

It is very heartening to know that the survey found that no tourist is happy with the condition of deforestation in Meghalaya and no one out of the hundred answers with good improvement or satisfactory improvement when asked to on the condition of the state forest. The unanimous answer is that there is either a serious or a minimal deterioration of the forest cover.

Another interesting thing is that when it comes to population it was found that out of the hundred respondents those who said that there is a huge increase is 80 while 20 of them said that there is a satisfactory improvement.

Hence, the goverment and the concerned authority should take measures to improvement the condition of transport and communication so as not to put the tourist in unwanted circumstances. This is because bad transport and communication scare away tourists from visiting Meghalaya. Steps should also be taken to control the rampant falling of trees which act as an eyesore for the tourists.

With regard to the condition of lodges, hotels and guest houses as given in Table 5.5, 17 tourists found them moderately comfortable, 63 think they are good, 7 graded them as excellent while 13 think that there is a need for immediate improvement. This is a good response and positive experience by the tourists, but still more need to be done and there is a lot to be done to improve the services and infrastructures when it comes to lodges, hotels and guest houses.

Table 5.5: Percentage Distribution of Respondents according to their Opinion on the Condition of Lodges and Hotels in Shillong

Moderately comfortable	*Excellent*	*Good*	*Need Improvement*	*Total*
17	7	63	13	100

Source: Primary survey.

The opinion of tourists regarding transportation in the city limit and to the tourist spots was also asked. As the information provided in Table 5.6 39 and 57 tourists think that the condition of transportation in the city limit and to the tourist spots are poor respectively. Those who think that improvement is needed in both the city limits and to the tourist spots are 18 tourists each. Twenty five tourists were of the opinion that the transportation in the city limit is good while only 12 think it is so to the tourist spots. While those who think that the transportation is moderate in the city limit is 18 while 13 said it is moderate to the tourist spots also. Not a single tourist responded that the transportation is good either in the city limit or to the tourist spots.

Table 5.6: Percentage Distribution of Respondents according to their Opinion on Condition of Transportation

	Very Poor	*Moderately Poor*	*Need improvement*	*Good*	*Very Good*	*Total*
In City Limit	39	18	18	25	0	100
To Tourist Spots	57	13	18	12	0	100

Source: Primary survey.

With respect to the availability of local cuisines as given in Table 5.7 below, only 10 tourists think that it is easily available. And 47 said that the local cuisines are not of their types which show the complete lack of knowledge among the local people regarding the taste and preference of the tourists.

Table 5.7: Percentage Distribution of Respondents according to their Experience on Availability of Local Cuisine

Easily available	*Very hard to find*	*Not of their type*	*Have no idea about it*	*Total*
10	15	47	28	100

Source: Primary survey.

It is also very sad that as many as 27 tourists have no idea about the local cuisines and their availability and 15 respondents said though they would like to have but the local cuisines are very hard to find. This also another area where the authority has to work so as the tourists does not face the problem in finding the local cuisines or those that are available should suit their taste and preference.

Table 5.8 below show experience of the tourists with the local guides in Meghalaya. Thirty two respondents said that they are happy with the local guides while 13 were not at all happy with them. As many as 35 number of tourists responded that the service are not at all available and 20 think that the guides need more training.

Table 5.8: Percentage Distribution of Respondents as per their Satisfaction with the Local Guides

Yes	*No*	*Service not available*	*Guides need training*	*Total*
32	13	35	20	100

Source: Primary survey.

When asked regarding the availability and quality of maps and guide books 46 said that these are not at all available while 31 said that the existing maps and guide books are not good and informative and they need immediate improvement and update. But, it is good also to know that 23 think that the present maps and guide books are fine. This is given in Table 5.9 below:

Table 5.9: Percentage Distribution of Respondents according to their Opinion on whether Sufficient Guide Books and Maps are Available

Yes	*No*	*Existing ones not up to standard*	*Total*
23	46	31	100

Source: Primary survey.

Table 5.10 show the most important information receives from the hundred tourists surveyed. A question was asked to them with all their experiences in Meghalaya whether they will visit the state again in the future or not. Out of the 100 tourists, 57 said they like the experiences and they will surely visit this state in future, 33 said they may visit again while 10 said they will not visit Meghalaya in future again. This shows that though with all the drawbacks of

Meghalaya as a tourist destination, but still tourists like the beauty of the state and they are willing to come back to this beautiful state.

Table 5.10: Percentage Distribution of Respondents according to their Opinion on Future Visit to Meghalaya again

Yes	*No*	*May be*	*Total*
57	10	33	100

Conclusion

From the above observation it is very clear that without no doubt Meghalaya is a perfect and favourite destination of the tourists because of its natural beauty and many other attractions, but this survey also highlighted the areas that need improvement. This survey shows the experiences of the tourists and their expectations when visiting Meghalaya which will certainly give an insight to the local people, the stakeholders, the local durbars, NGOs and the goverment to take steps and measures to improve the tourism scenario in the state. This recognition of their roles in the development of tourism is of utmost priority. Moreover, the improvement in the tourism industry need an all round approach since any deficiency would ruin and spoil an otherwise wonderful experience for the tourists.

References

Aksu, A. İçigen, E.T. and Ehtiyar, R. (2010). "A comparison of tourist expectations and satisfaction: A case study from antalya region of turkey", TURIZAM, 14(2): 66-77.

Athanassopoulos, A., Gounaris, S. and Stathakopoulos, V. (2001). "Behaviour response to customer satisfaction: An empirical study", *European Journal of Marketing*, 35, (5/6), 687-98.

Bowen, D. (2002). "Research through participant observation in tourism: A creative solution to the measurement of customer satisfaction/ dissatisfaction (CS/D) among tourists", *Journal of Travel Research*. 41(1): 4-14.

Castaneda, J.A., Frias, D.M. and Rodriguez, M.A. (2007). "The influence of the internet on destination satisfaction", *Internet Research*, 17(4): 402-420.

Fornell, C. (1992). "A national customer satisfaction barometer: The Swedish experience", *Journal of Marketing*, 56(1): 6-21.

Henderson, D., Slaughter, L., and Pegg, S. (2007). "Trust and New Technologies: Looking at Issues from the Perspective of the Young Tourist", Paper presented at The 2007 International Joint Conference on e-Commerce, e-Administration, e-Society, and e-Education, Hong Kong, 15-17 August.

Hvenegaard, G.T. and Dearden, P. (1998). "Ecotourism *versus* tourism in a Thai national park", *Annals of Tourism Research*, 25(3): 700-720.

Jadhav, S.J. and More, V.S. (2010). "Minimum expectations of tourists: An essential factor of tourism companies", *International Journal of Trade, Economics and Finance*, 1(2): 184-188.

Khumsri, P. (2006). "Planning of Internet Marketing Strategy for Wing Travel Chiang Mai Company Limited", Independent Study for Master of Business Administration, Chiang Mai University.

Kim, H., Borges, M.C., and Chon, J. (2006). "Impacts of environmental values on tourism motivation: The case of FICA, Brazil", *Tourism Management*, 27(5): 957-967.

Kozak, M. and Rimmington, M. (2000). "Tourist Satisfaction with Mallorca, Spain, as an Off Season Holiday Destination", *Journal of Travel Research*, 38(3): 260-269.

Lertwannawit, A. and Anuwichanont, J. (2011). "Tourists' Expectation and Perception Towards Environmental Issue Management for Green Tourism of Khao Yai National Park", *International Business and Economics Research Journal*, 10(9): 41-46.

Rajeev, P.V. and Shyju, P.J., "Key Issues in Visitor Experience and Tourism Development—A Study of Varanasi", Paper presented at the Conference on Tourism in India—Challenges Ahead, 15-17 May, 2008, IIMK.

Richards, G. (1995). "Production and consumption of European cultural tourism", *Annals of Tourism Research*, 22(2): 261-283.

Stevens, B.F. (1992). "Price value perceptions of travellers", *Journal of Travel Research*, 31 (2): 44-48.

Websites visited: www.ibef.org/download/Meghalaya_190111.pdf, visited on 9-5-2012.

6
Tourism for Sustainable Livelihood in Meghalaya

P.K. Ryngnga

Introduction

A review of literature identifies weaknesses in the concepts of sustainable development and sustainable tourism and provides legitimacy for using the sustainable livelihood approach to examine the roles that tourism plays in indigenous people's daily lives. Culture is embedded in daily life and the approach allows the researcher to explore the meanings behind people's daily activities. Also, tourism needs to be placed in a broader context in order to identify whether any linkages exist between it and other sectors of the economy and how tourism can better fit in with exiting livelihood strategies.

The research is a collaborative study of the Khasi communities in Cherrapunjee using qualitative research methods. The sustainable livelihood framework is used as a vehicle for guiding research and analysis. Results indicate that Khasi traditional livelihoods and their traditional social structure have been closely linked. The shift of their livelihoods from self-sustaining in the past to being linked increasingly to the global economic market system at present comes from a variety of external and internal factors (e.g., policy, history, politics, macro-economic conditions). The promotion of tourism development and cultural industries by the State Government in recent years has provided aboriginal people with a new opportunity (tourism) in which they can make use of their culture as an advantage (culture as an attraction) to possibly reverse the inferior position. In addition to being an attraction for economic development, culture has many implications for the way things are done and for the distribution of benefits.

In Cherrapunjee, people have realised to employ a wide range of resources and livelihoods strategies to support themselves. Tourism has been incorporated into their livelihoods in forms of employment (regular and occasional) and various collective and self-owned enterprises (e.g., restaurants, homestays, café, food stalls, handicraft stores and campsites). Tourism activities have the potential both to complement and to compete with other economic activities in various forms. Conflicts between tourism-related economic activities and other activities may not be obvious in terms of the use of land, water and time. The benefits and costs of each tourism activity experienced by different stakeholder groups (mainly by age and gender) vary, depending on different personal situations.

The sustainable livelihoods framework was examined and used to assess the context and forms in which tourism might contribute to sustainable livelihood outcomes. Institutional processes and organizational structures are one main factor determining whether different assets, tangible and intangible, are accumulated or depleted on individual, household, and community scales. The study revealed that, the people pursue the maximization of individual interests; which is most likely to lead to sustainable outcome (socio-culturally, economically, and environmentally) in the context of indigenous communities. That is tourism enterprises need to be operated through institutions with a communal mechanism and through efficient operation of the communities' organisations based on collective knowledge guided by the Khasi culture.

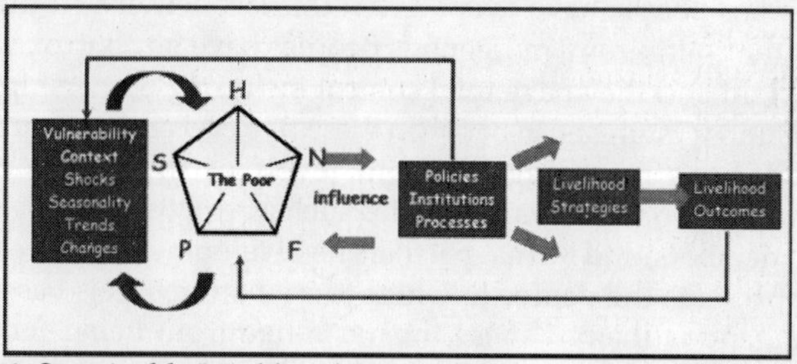

Fig. 6.1: Sustainable Livelihood Framework
Source: Author's Study.

The sustainable livelihood framework is useful because it places the interests of local people at the centre. Such an approach incorporates tourism as one component of development, particularly for indigenous people, and explores how positive development impacts can be expanded and negative ones can be reduced. However, unless supplemented, the framework may not do justice to the importance of culture and the prominent roles played by key individuals.

Indigenous Tourism and Sustainability

Indigenous tourism refers to tourism activities in which indigenous people are directly involved either through control and/or by having their culture serve as the essence of the attraction (Butler and Hinch, 1996). The two key concepts of this phenomenon are illustrated in Fig. 6.2:

<table>
<tr><td></td><td></td><td colspan="2">Indigenous Control</td></tr>
<tr><td rowspan="3">INDIGENOUS THEME</td><td></td><td>Low Degree of Control</td><td>High Degree of Control</td></tr>
<tr><td>Indigenous Theme Present</td><td>Culture Dispossessed</td><td>Culture Controlled</td></tr>
<tr><td>Indigenous Theme</td><td>Non-Indigenous Tourism</td><td>Diversified Indigenous Tourism</td></tr>
</table>

Fig. 6.2: Indigenous Theme and Control in Maghalaya
Source: Author's Study.

The horizontal axis represents the range of control that indigenous people have over a given tourism activity. At the left end of the continuum, indigenous peoples have no control, while at the right end they have total control including ownership and management interests. In between these two ends exists a number of gradations revealing different levels of the influence of indigenous peoples in various roles such as employees, advisory board members, and formal partners in development. The vertical axis represents the degree to which tourist attraction is based on an indigenous theme. These themes range from being focused totally on indigenous culture to a total absence of an indigenous theme (Butler and Hinch, 1996).

The level of control is the key condition in any kind of development. Whoever has control can generally influence the factors of scale, speed and nature of tourism development. Altman

(1993) further defined control as the distinction between the situations where tourism is *invited* and those where it is *imposed,* and indicates that there is some correlation between *invited* and *imposed* tourism and direct and indirect participation in tourism. Other indicators of level of control include direct input into decision-making and ownership of the tourism infrastructure. Similarly, since an attraction is central to tourism activity, the extent to which the attraction is focused on indigenous culture is also an indicator of indigenous tourism. Tourism enterprises that are both controlled by indigenous people and which highlight an Indigenous theme are most likely to lead to positive outcomes for indigenous groups.

The Framework for Indigenous Tourism

Indigenous tourism occurs within the context of a global tourism industry that is dominated by non-indigenous actors. Even this global industry is part of a broader environment which influences and in turn is influenced by non-indigenous and indigencus tourism activities (Butler and Hinch, 1996). This interaction of indigenous tourism industry with the broader environment is also characterised by the temporal (past, present, and future) and spatial (origin, destination, and linkages) dimensions of the environment (Fig. 6.3).

Both of these dimensions provide the context in which causal relationships exist (Butler and Hinch, 1996). The following literature review of indigenous tourism is based on two general contexts One is the issues associated with local control and the synergies and tensions that exist between the indigenous and global tourism industries. The other concern involves relevant issues found in the broader environmental context in which all tourism exists. The factors within this external environment may have particularly strong influences upon outcomes of indigenous tourism, including those associated with the economy, culture, physical environment, social-demographics and politics. These factors are largely beyond the control of either the indigenous or global industry, but help determine the success of the industry (Butler and Hinch, 1996).

Research Approach

This study emphasizes the use of qualitative methods for research

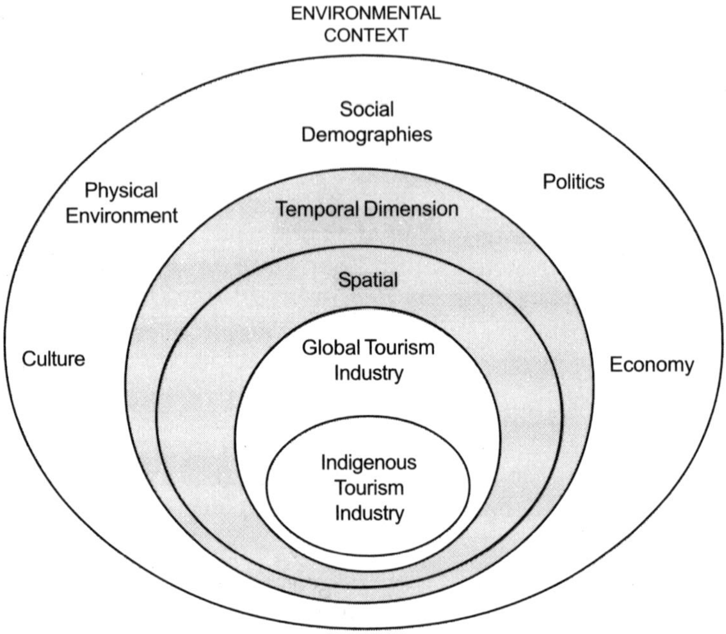

Fig. 6.3: Interaction of the Indigenous Tourism Industry with the Broader Environment

Source: Butler and Hinch, 1996: 12.

and describes the detailed process that was used to gather information in the field and provides a justification for the selection of research sites and the sampling decisions and various qualitative methods of data collection are considered. The following outlined the procedure used:

Quantitative Methods in the Field: Formality, Structure and Utility

Quantitative methods, particularly structured interviews or questionnaires, is used to provide detailed demographic information, which is used both to describe a sample as well as variables for further analysis.

Qualitative Methodology

Qualitative methods, particularly in-depth interviews and participant observation, are emphasized In a culture where oral tradition is still prevalent, subjects are more comfortable with verbal discourse which allows them to explain and illustrate their thoughts and feelings rather than with a structured interview. It enables the researcher to clarify the conceptualisations of the terms under investigation.

Results and Discussion

Tourist Flow: The State of Meghalaya registered 5,91,398 domestic tourists in 2010, while in the previous year (2009) it was 4,49,954. In 2007, the corresponding figure was 4,57,685 as per the statistics

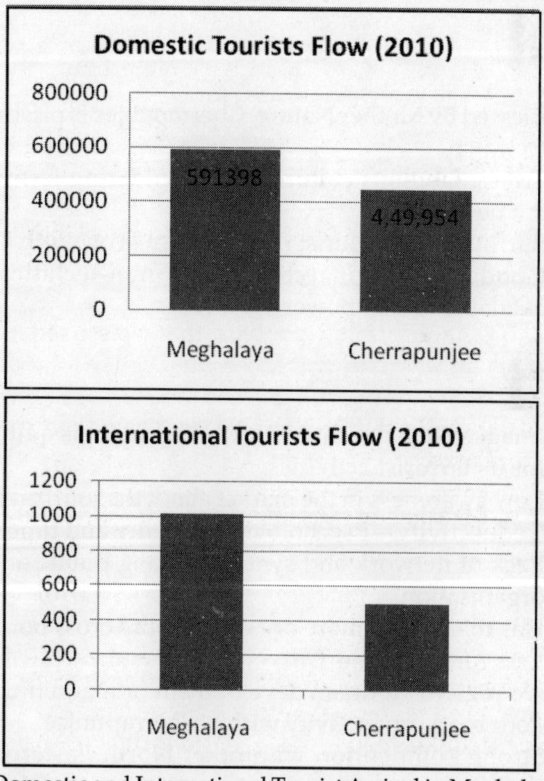

Fig. 6.4: Domestic and International Tourist Arrival in Meghalaya during 2010.

Source: Directorate of Economics and Statistics, Government of Meghalaya.

made available by the state's tourism department, of which the previous year Cherrapunjee registered 5,20,112 domestic tourists and 501 out of 713 international tourists in Meghalaya.

Thus, it can be said that the number of tourist inflow into the State of Meghalaya speaks volume, which indicate that if they do not visit Cherrapunjee their visit to North East India is in vain.

However, it is worth mentioning that SWOT Analysis is used so as to strengthen the impact of tourism in the study area. Therefore, during the fieldwork, careful observations have been made in order to spell out the analysis.

SWOT Analysis of Cherrapunjee Tourism

Strengths

- Blessed by Mother Nature, Cherrapunjee is pristine beauty to watch.
- Tribes, fabulous culture, and bewildering festivals make it a best haunt.
- Surrounded by tourist zones of the rest of North East India.
- Good number of technical and non-technical people available as manpower resource.

Weaknesses

- Image problem—Since North East India is quite popular for its terrorist activities.
- Low awareness in the market about the tourism products.
- Connectivity—Psychological distance and time distance.
- Lack of network and synergy among public and private organisation.
- Has to develop more organised tours cross borders.
- Less funds for tourism.
- No regional tourism development or marketing plan.
- Poor road connectivity within Cherrapunjee.
- Strong competition with other North Eastern states of India.

Opportunities

- Central and State Governments is giving special attention to Cherrapunjee.
- Asian Development Bank is preparing a Sub-Regional Plan for development of tourism covering Bhutan, Bangladesh, India and Nepal, North East Region figures prominently in this Plan because of the Asian Highway.
- Potential for private sector's investment in tourism projects.

Threats

- Strong Competition with other states of India and abroad.
- Terrorism is a major setback of the region.
- Disorganised tourism developement.

Tourism as Livelihood Sustenance

After 2005, tourism development in Cherrapunjee has taken a new turn in which community involvement is highly encouraged with the establishment of Thangkharang Park by the State Forest Department. This Park is under the vigilance of the government however, local services are hired for catering to the tourists. From 2005 onwards tourist spots mushroomed at a faster pace than before in which locals also take initiatives to establish welcoming inn for tourists and slowly by 2010 Sa-I-Mika Park, (a 69 acre plot of land, located in the heart of a picturesque countryside, Cherrapunjee/Sohra. One ambitious and determined woman, Mrs. J.R. Phanbuh started Sa-i-mika Park in the year 2005. She started planning and creating Sa-i-mika with a humble beginning with the help of a few well-wishers and family, and today she is proud to say that she has achieved to a large extent since various facilities are available right from conference hall, which is made available for individuals who seek to have conferences and meetings far from the hustle and bustle of town, traditional Khasi huts as well as conventional rooms for those who love nature and who would like to experience a night or two of this beautiful, breath-taking paradise. There are Picnic huts for those who want to cook by themselves in different areas of the park. A meandering stream flows through the park with small waterfalls and ponds that elaborates the beauty of the park. A guide is also available to take the tourists for hikes in and around Cherrapunjee, and for those who prefer to go sightseeing in luxury and comfort can do so by car.

However, with the government trying to promote tourism in Cherrapunjee, in 2010 the Government declared that every year there should have ***Cherrapunjee Indigenous Festival*** so as to bring awareness about indigenous ideology of local tourism and their contribution to tourism development.

Every year the Cherrapunjee Indigenous Festival showcases the traditional art and culture of Meghalaya. In addition, various competitions will be held for visitors of different age groups. Also one can experience the Archery, a traditional sport in the North East. One can enjoy the colourful performances by various rural artists; the festival highlights include Traditional Khasi Exhibition and sale of various Art and Craft goods, ethnic food stalls, Herbal Medicine stalls etc.

The Sohra Tourism Development Society have also contributed to the development of Tourism in which as an NGO they print pamphlets, carefully sketch down local guide map (*see* Map on next page) indicating tourist spots to ease tourists and are printed along the pamphlets ready for sale to the tourists near tourist spots.

Observations

It is seen that when communities decide to incorporate tourism as one of their livelihoods in order to achieve sustainable development, tourism will be a form of livelihood diversification. Such diversification can have many advantages and tourism can become: (1) a means to enable accumulation (e.g., income) for consumption and investment; (2) a means to help spread risk; (3) an adaptive response to longer-term declines in income entitlements, due to serious economic or environmental changes beyond local control; and/or (4) a means to take pressure of fragile lands and increase household incomes for purchase of additional food or payment of school fees.

Many local individuals are sustained by combinations of livelihood strategies (both subsistence and market-oriented and, rather than specific jobs). Thus, it is found out that tourism

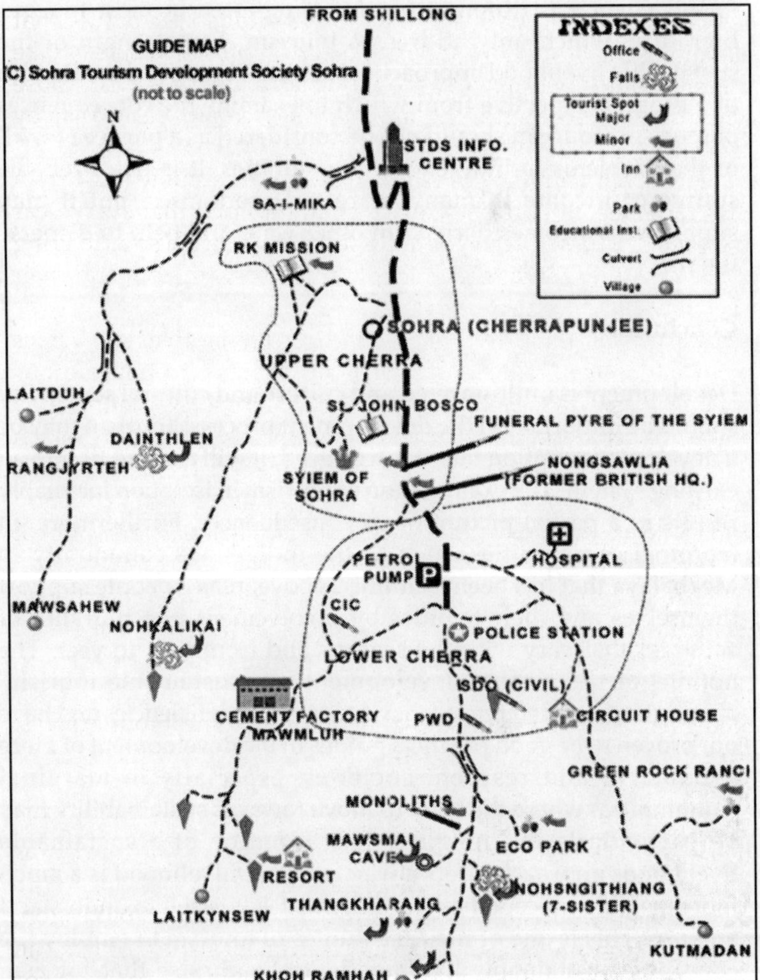

Source: Drawn by Sohra Tourism Development Society, Meghalaya.

complement rather than replace existing livelihood sources leading to diversification of livelihood strategies. Therefore, sustainable development in Cherrapunjee highlights not the maintenance of tourism over an indefinite period of time but the aims would be better served by exploration of how tourism might fit into a suite of livelihood strategies, contributing to the achievement of sustainable livelihood outcomes. The approach that has been taken in this chapter is different from that reported in most tourism literature, which only addresses tourism. The strength of the sustainable livelihood approach is that it encourages the adoption of a broad perspective from which to examine the consequences of tourism. Tourism should not be considered as a panacea for all of the problems in indigenous communities. It is not a reliable source of income in many marginal economies, but it may supplement incomes derived in other ways and help to disperse the risk.

Conclusion

Development is multi-faceted and culture and cultural sensitivity should be important in the development process. Tourism may be a development option but, if introduced, it will need to fit into an existing system. The examination of tourism in isolation inevitably results in a partial picture of its consequences. Furthermore, in marginal communities, such as the indigenous community in Meghalaya that has been examined above, many people support themselves and their families by involvement in a plurality of activities that vary with the seasons and from year to year. The notions of sustainable development and sustainable tourism, although widely referenced, have conceptual deficiencies and have not proven to be good practical guides in the development of more productive and resilient societies, especially in marginal communities where the need to move towards sustainability may be particularly challenging. The adoption of a sustainable livelihoods approach offers a way forward. Livelihood is a much more tangible concept than development: it is easier to understand and use. This is one of the first studies of tourism to employ the concept of sustainable livelihoods, to emphasise that tourism should be understood in the broader economic and cultural context in which it takes place, and to provide a case study to illustrate the kinds of information that can be generated by adopting such an approach.

References

Aronsson, L. (2000). *The Development of Sustainable Tourism*. London: Continuum.

Ashley, C. (2000). *The Impacts of Tourism on Rural Livelihoods: Namibia's Experience*, ODI Working Paper No. 128. London: ODI.

Ashley, C. (2002). *Methodology for Pro-Poor Tourism Case Studies*. London, UK: ODI, IIED and ICRT.

Ashley, C., Boyd, C., and Goodwin, H. (2000). Pro-poor tourism: Putting poverty at the heart of the tourism agenda. *ODI Natural Resource Perspectives, 51*. Retrieved from http://www.odi.org.uk/resources/specialist/natural-resource-perspectives/51-pro-poor-tourism.pdf (Accessed on October 6, 2007).

Ashley, C. and Carney, D. (1999). *Sustainable Livelihoods: Lessons from Early Experience*. Nottingham: Russell Press Ltd.

Butler, R.W. (1998). Sustainable tourism—looking backward in order to progress? In C.M. Hall and A.A. Lew (Eds.), *Sustainable Tourism. A Geographical Perspective* (pp. 25-34). New York: Addison Wesley Longman Ltd.

Chambers, R. (1986). *Sustainable Livelihood Thinking—An Approach to Poverty*. Institution of Development Studies, University of Sussex, Brighton, UK.

Clarke, J. (1997). A framework of approaches to sustainable tourism. *Journal of Sustainable Tourism*, 5(3): 224-233.

Government of Meghalaya, (2010). *The Tourism Policy of Meghalaya*, Shillong.

Hussein, K. and Nelson, J. (1998). *Sustainable Livelihoods and Livelihood Diversification*. Institute of Development Studies, University of Sussex, UK.

International Institute for Sustainable Development (IISD). (1999). Empowering Communities for Sustainable Livelihoods. Retrieved from http://www.iisd.org/casl/default.htm (Accessed on October 6, 2007).

McCool, S.F. and Moisey, R.N. (2001). Introduction: Pathways and pitfalls in the search for sustainable tourism. In: McCool, S.F. and Moisey, R.N. (Eds) *Tourism, Recreation and Sustainability: Linking Culture and the Environment* (pp. 1-15). New York: CABI.

McMinn, S. (1997). The Challenge of Sustainable Tourism. *The Environmentalist*. 17(2): 135-141.

Scoones, I. (1998). *Sustainable Rural Livelihoods: A Framework for Analysis* (Institute of Development Studies, University of Sussex, UK).

Stabler, M.J. (ed.) (1997). *Tourism and Sustainability. Principles to Practice*. CAB International Wallingford.

Teresa, C.H. Tao and Geoffrey Wall (1998). *Tourism for Marginal Groups: Tourism as a Livelihood Strategy in an Indigenous*, Community in Taiwan in Best EN Think tank VII.

UNDP and Wanmali, S. (1999). *Participatory Assessment and Planning for Sustainable Livelihoods*.

United Nations Development Programme (undated). Sustainable livelihoods documents. Retrieved from http://www.undp.org/sl/

Documents/Strategy_papers/Participatory_Assessment_for_SLSW.htm/PAPSL.htm (Accessed on September 10, 2003).

Wall, G. (2002). Sustainable Development: Political rhetoric or analytical construct. *Tourism Recreation Research.* 27 (3): 89-91.

Wall, G. (1997). Sustainable tourism-unsustainable development. In: Pigram J. and Wahab S. (Eds.) *Tourism Development and Growth: The Challenge of Sustainability.* London: Routledge, pp. 33-49.

Wall, G. (1993). International Collaboration in the Search for Sustainable Tourism in Bali, Indonesia. *Journal of Sustainable Tourism,* 1(1):38-47.

Wall, G. (1991). *Tourism and Sustainable Development.* Paper presented at annual meeting,

Kingston, Ontario: Canadian Association of Geographers.

Wheeller, B. (1993). Sustaining the ego. *Journal of Sustainable Tourism.* 1(2): 121-129.

World Commission on Environment and Development (1987). *Our Common Future* (The Brundtland Report). London: Oxford University Press.

Internet Sources on Tourism in Cherrapunjee

http://www.flickr.com/photos/rupak_sarkar/4574018771/lightbox/
http://www.cherrapunjee.com/index.php?mid=81&pid=10
http://saimikapark.com/saimika/saimika.html
http://www.cherrapunjee.com/index.php?mid=78&pid=10

PART 2
Entrepreneurship and Socio-Economic Development

7
Special Economic Zones and Socio-Economic Implications on Rural Population

Sazzad Parwez

Introduction

Land, the basic and long lasting source for production as well as for human inhabitation, is one of the most disputed issues in the public policies in India. Decisions concerning land allocation and land use pattern comprise diverse array of issues that can go beyond the considerations of economic growth. The matter of land-use is predominantly important due to large agrarian population in economies such as India, where access to land, in absence of alternative employment-income opportunities and social security, provide economic security and, therefore, is rendered high in terms of social status. Ideally, diversion of land from agricultural to non-agricultural sectors should be preceded by a considerable shift of workforce and local population. In the absence such provision, diversion to non-agriculture use is most likely to invite resistance from farmers and local communities. The Land Acquisition Act (LAA) has been used to take property for public use without the owner's consent has been practiced since the colonial rule. Growing spatial inequality with economic growth same time only few livelihood opportunities for the rural poor likely to turn issue of land more concerning.

The situation gets further stressed when the Government, being a custodian of land, tends to play the role of a trader as it has come out from the real on ground practices under the LAA.

The enactment of Special Economic Zone (SEZ) Act, 2005 goes a few steps ahead by allowing the Government to transfer the land acquired for public purpose under LAA to the private companies for development. Application of LAA to acquire land is often go along with various kinds of pressure tactics by the corporate by the State to get consent of the land owner because later owing to his low bargaining power. It has been observed that the process of acquisition and conversion of agricultural land reflects failure of the state and the market; in fact largely both of these form a nexus to indulge in 'primitive accumulation' by the state (Chandrasekhar, 2006; Patnaik, 2008).

Question is being asked on processes of obtaining the land rather than the need of acquiring agricultural to promote industrial economic activities such as manufacturing units and infrastructure (Shah *et al.*, 2012). It is also evident from the experience that ambiguous implementation processes generally result in diversion of large tract of land, often more fertile, than what is actually required. It has been also observed that large part of acquired land ends up in the hands of the real estate companies rather than intended productive sectors of industry and infrastructure (Levien, 2011). The absence of land use the policy and federal structure of governance where land is primarily a state subject has been the main culprit for faulty conversion or diversion of land from the agricultural and allied sector. The most critical issue is that of the nexus between the state and the private sector. The extreme nature of these SEZs needs to be analysed through proper policy-making.

Land Acquisition and Rehabilitation

The socio-legal issues such as land acquisition, displacement, rehabilitation and compensation has been the complex subject to deal with. Same time real estate development and land speculation has been the threat as units from other parts of country to take the advantage of SEZ incentives re-locating to various SEZs premises consequent loss of income and rise in regional inequality (Fernandes, 2002). It has been extensively reported that the farmers are protesting against the forced acquisition of agricultural land by using obsolete Land Acquisition Act of 1894 for public purposes.

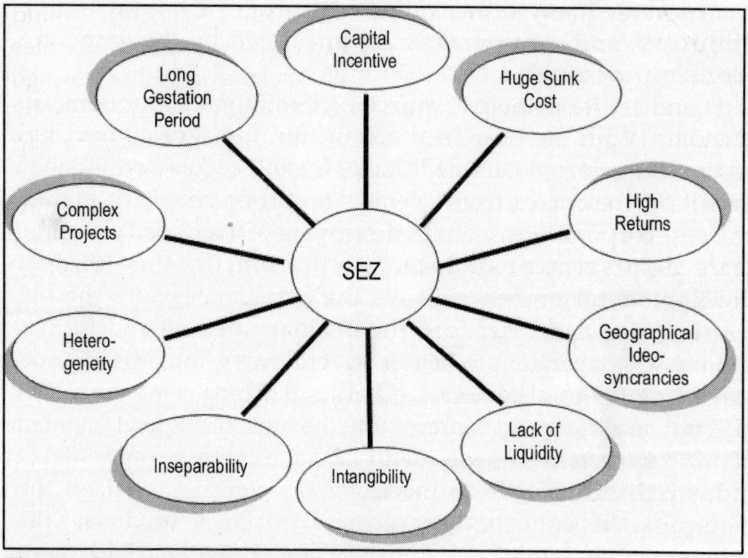

Fig. 7.1: SEZ Hybrid Industrialisation
Source: Conceptualised by the Author, 2015.

The establishment of SEZs countrywide would lead to livelihood losses for farmers and dependent, whose land will be acquired and in reality little job creation, use of advanced technology or network can impact negatively. Gifting the thousands of acres of valuable land to developers in insignificant amount to conduct business by relaxing the laws of the land, including those meant for welfare of labour, environmental protection, taxation etc., in the hope that it will automatically encourage industrialization and solve the prevailing problem of unemployment.

Farmers and peasants in various states such as West Bengal, Uttar Pradesh, Maharashtra, Uttarkhand, Odhisa, Punjab and many more has opposed to the land acquisition for establishment of SEZ is a major growing issue across the country. Water problem due to SEZ is also a major emerging issue as it has been reported from Mundra Economic Zone, it expects to get at least 6 million litres per day by the Sardar Sarovar Project, and same is the case with other operational and proposed SEZ throughout the country. As depicted in the Fig. 7.1, SEZ is a hybrid industry which incorporates many dimensions. All sorts of complex issues, confusions and controversies are attributed by the ignorance about its true nature.

Land is the principal source of livelihood in an agrarian economy. With the time land acquisition for development has become the most obvious medium for forcible acquisition and then transfer of resources from average and poor people to private business corporations, leads to destroying of livelihood and large scale displacement of local population. In this kind of developmental process, always the beneficiaries are the big corporations and losers are the ordinary people and farmer community dependent to land in several ways, the peasants and tenants, agricultural labourers, tribal's and fishing community. The SEZ fast becoming and representing the most outrageous symbol of pro-corporate, anti-people, anti-labour established as model of industrialisation. Due to inaction of government raised the perception that only popular and mass resistance could make the government to re-think and to have a moderate stand. Difference between acquisition land for setting up production industry, and land for mining is very little, so far it is evident that due to inadequate industrial policy and land reform has led to destruction of social auditing, people's livelihoods and displacement.

To understand the impact of SEZ on society and environment following Fig. 7.2 reflects the five different types of impact SEZ can cause at various level and how all these effects are interacting with each other. According to SEZs regulations and guidelines a multi-product SEZ is needed to have 1000 hectares while the single product SEZ can be established in as little 100 hectares of land. Thus, SEZs may incorporate a single manufacturing unit, or a cluster of multi-product industrial units. Guidelines also suggest that 35 per cent of land have to be assigned for the industrial or processing purposes; rest of land can be used for housing purpose, services, institutions, parks, and so on. Only units approved under the SEZ scheme are to establish units in premises of SEZ.

Apprehensions have been expressed about the misuse of the Act for acquiring land and relocating the existing industries into SEZs premises to take advantage of relaxations and incentives. However, so far evidences shows that these apprehensions are untrue to the larger extent, and new investments has been made and some employment opportunities have been generated in the

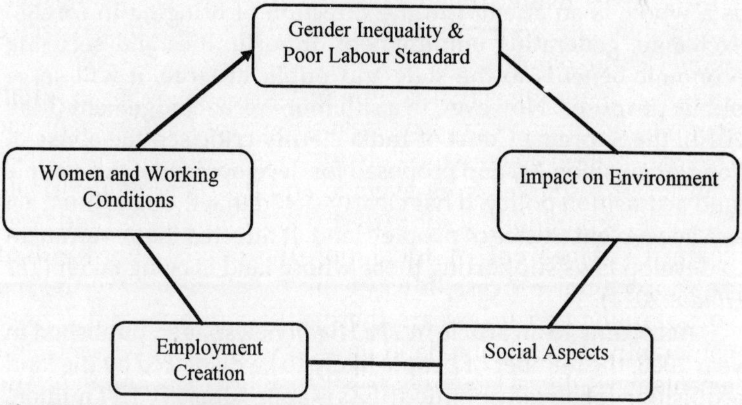

Fig. 7.2: Impact of SEZ on Society
Source: Conceptualised by the Author, 2015.

SEZ units. The subsequent benefits from the spillovers effect of the investments made and acceleration of economic activity in the SEZs, with the creation of employment opportunities is expected to compensate the losses of revenue on account of tax relaxations and exemptions provided under SEZs scheme. These SEZs are supposed to be new industrial enclave as instrument of economic development.

Apprehensions from various corners have been stated regarding acquisition of agricultural land for setting up new SEZs. Even though, there are guidelines by the Central Government to the State Governments for peaceful land acquisition process for setting up of Special Economic Zones, the first targeted land for acquisition should be of waste and barren and, if necessary, single-crop agricultural land could be acquired for the SEZs through lawful acquisition machinery.

Further, it has been said that only if essential than a portion of double-cropped agricultural land can to taken to fulfil the minimum land requirements, especially for the setting up of multi-product SEZ, and acquired land area should not be more than 10 per cent of the total land required for the establishment of SEZ. Many problems related to development of SEZs in the various part of the country, including complex issues mentioned by various political parties has been integrated.

The Supreme Court of India recently ruled, "If the project taken as a whole is an attempt in the direction of bringing in foreign exchange, generating employment opportunities and securing economic benefits to the state and public at large, it will serve public purpose." However, in a still more recent judgement (May 2010), the Supreme Court of India sternly criticised the abuse of Land Acquisition Act and proposed for development of pro-people land acquisition policy. It has clearly stated that the state must act as a benevolent trustee of people's land. It directed the government to develop laws supporting those whose land is being taken (*The Hindu*, 2014).

According to an article in *The Hindu* newspaper, published in year 2008, the number of people likely to be displaced by the land acquisition for already notified SEZs is approximately 1.14 million, which is 18 times higher than the number of people officially claimed to get direct employment in these notified zones. The Commerce Ministry's estimates suggest that 10 new direct jobs and while 14 persons get indirect employment by creation of an SEZ. This estimate lead us to the conclusive numbers as total employment created from SEZs to be just about one-eighth of the loss signified by displacement for land acquisition. This estimate raises many questions on objective and process of establishment of SEZs.

Implications of SEZ on Rural India

Many rural areas are undergoing a process of "de-agrarianization", with younger workers moving out of agriculture because of lack of jobs, low incomes, agro-climatic constraints and most significant one is industrialisation. Increasing numbers of rural people are forced to work in non-agricultural activities in or outside their place of origin in order to diversify their income and reduce risk.

The movement of rural people out of agriculture in order to find jobs in industrial sector is a major ingredient of the development process especially in developing market economies. India is a particularly good example not only because of its large population, history of rural-urban migration and high rates of economic growth, but also because of its experience with economic and political shocks and a large share of the population living in rural areas (Palit, and Bhattacharjee, 2008). The country has developed social protection policies for the poor, but empirical evidence on their success is still sparse and questionable. Migration from agricultural sector to industrial set up does provide a good benchmark for the factors that can determine the success of industrialisation. However, few empirical studies have established the fact that success of industrialisation depends on impact of migration on rural households and the quality of migrant's employment (Bhadra and Brando, 1993). In theory, if migration is successful after several decades of migration one should be able to observe a declining gap in welfare between rural and urban areas. However, as shown in the World Bank's World Development Report (2008), this is not the case, and India remains among the countries with a very high rural–urban divide. Migration opens up more opportunities for the rural population to get into more productive employment opportunities.

SEZs have emerged as one of the most relevant topic in the recent times with diverse dimensions. Most significant and common issues related to the SEZ are relating to the environmental, land acquisition, economic, political and socio-legal issues. These challenging issues are relevant to the entire nation in general. The setting up of SEZs requires huge amount of land (Pandey and Rout, 2004). Consequently, providing of land for the setting up of SEZs will take away the large part of agricultural land. The fixed assets created by the unit in premises of SEZ in the environment of undefined and unrestricted guidelines.

The SEZ policy of Government of India has generated debates that revolve around the trade-off between industrialisation and mass welfare, and towards finding an alternative industrial-development policy. Concerns that received much attention are: (a) optimum compensation for affected people; and (b) impact on livelihood benefits of affected people due to industrial zones.

Thus, it can be maintained that the acceleration of economic growth in general, and the urbanisation of the rural areas in particular provide multiple livelihood strategies. This, in turn, leads to spike in the opportunity cost making agriculture an economically unliveable source of livelihood (Bharati, 1999). The rural people having access to multiple livelihood strategies would be willing to sell land for SEZs at the right offer price without any reluctance. On the contrary, there is a farm economy where agriculture is the only source of livelihood, i.e. the opportunity cost of agriculture as an occupation is zero. Under such situations the landowners and the farmers would exert stiff resistance to sell their land for SEZs development. This is because these farmers consider land as a source of livelihood than just a store of value.

Loss of livelihoods due to establishment of SEZ within the village and growing interaction with labour contractors as well as information and assistance form the colleagues who have migrated outside has been leading to more people seeking labour outside of agricultural horizon.

Impact of SEZ on the Agriculture

A Special Economic Zone (SEZ) is a geographical region which has economic laws that are more liberal than a country's general economic laws. It is a specifically delineated duty-free enclave treated as a foreign territory for the purpose of industrial, service and trade operations, with exemption from customs duties and a more liberal regime in respect of levies, foreign investment and other transactions. In fact, the SEZ is a development tool, with the goal of promoting rapid economic growth by using tax and business incentives to attract foreign investment and technology.

To set up such a large number of SEZs there is a need for huge amount of land to be acquired. The total land area of India is 29,73,190 sq. km out of which 16,20,388 sq. km area is used for agriculture (agricultural area). The share of the agricultural area in the total area is 54.5 per cent and the non-agricultural area in India is 13,52,802 sq. km. The total area for proposed SEZs (formally approved and in principle approved) is approximately. 2061 sq. km which would not be more than 0.069 per cent of the total land area and not more than 0.12 per cent of the total agricultural land in India (Ministry of Agriculture, GoI, 2014).

If SEZs are set up on 'non-agricultural land', especially on barren land, then they play an important role for the social and economic development of the country. They can generate employment, enhance export and attract foreign direct investment (FDI) and technology at low social cost.

On the other hand, if SEZs are set up on 'agricultural land' may create problems for the social and economic development. If fertile land is used for the establishment of SEZs, then the area under agriculture will decline. This will lead to decrease in the production of agriculture. India at present is facing a food problem (leading to on-going import of wheat) and this problem will become more severe if the area under agriculture declines due to the setting up of SEZs.

Setting up SEZ on agricultural land has emerged as major issue throughout India. In case of Punjab, Haryana, Uttar Pradesh, West Bengal, Maharashtra and some other states in the country, SEZs are being set up on fertile land has resistance and subject of controversy. For example, the land of West Bengal is basically good for agriculture, but even then the West Bengal Government is allowing SEZs in Nandigram and Singur. Those SEZs, which are set up on fertile land, adversely affect our agricultural production. The social cost of such SEZs is more than the benefits one gets from these SEZs.

Livelihood Implications: Converting Farmer into Casual Labour

SEZs are noted for their ability to create new employment opportunity. India being the country with a labour surplus, consequently employment creation is a policy priority. SEZs have a dualistic employment generation effect. SEZs create direct employment for individuals employed in Units operating within the SEZ. It create indirect employment for individuals engaged in industries and services, which support the activity within SEZs, such as trucking of goods to SEZs. In all, SEZs have generated substantial employment and are predicted to continue generating employment in increasing volumes.

But on the other side of coin, India's SEZ policy bases their contentions on few unwanted consequences of the policy. SEZ development leads to unjust and inequitable seizure of agrarian land. Second, land acquisition for SEZs promotes underhanded real estate dealing. India may suffer huge socio-economic loss on the SEZ policy, which has been ignored, it is well supported by the estimates of ministry of rural development (2010), which reveals that close to 1,14,000 farming households (each household on an average comprising five members) and an additional 82,000 farm worker families who are dependent upon these farms for their livelihoods, will be displaced due to establishment of SEZ all-over India. In other words, at least 10 lakh people who primarily depend upon agriculture for their survival will face eviction. Experts calculate that the total loss of income to the farming and the farm worker families is at least Rs. 212 crore a year. This does not include other income lost (for instance of artisans) due to the demise of local rural economies. The government promises 'humane' displacement followed by relief and rehabilitation. However, the historical practices does not offer much hope on this count: an estimated 40 million people (of which nearly 40% are Scheduled Tribes and 25% Scheduled Castes) have lost their land since 1950 on account of displacement due to large development projects. At least 75 per cent of them still await rehabilitation. Almost 80 per cent of the agricultural population owns only about 17 per cent of the total agriculture land, making them near landless farmers. Far more families and communities depend on a piece of land (agricultural labour, for work, grazing) than those who simply own it. However, compensation is being discussed only for those who hold titles to land. No compensation has been planned for those who do not own the land but highly depend on the land for their livelihood.

Another concept emerged from special survey conducted by the National Sample Survey Organisation (NSSO, 2003) on farmers reveals that nearly 40 per cent of the farmer households disliked farming and wanted to give up the profession due to its unprofitable nature. These farmers largely belong to the small and marginal category (84% of the farmer households belong to this group), which are characterised by extremely low levels of income and mainly undertake subsistence cultivation. Moreover, with rising costs of cultivation, low remunerations, high risks with crop failure occurring frequently, declining agricultural growth, and mounting debts have led the farmer to a distress-like situation of the kind mentioned earlier.

As SEZ has been established either in outer part of cities or interiors of states, which attract mostly displace local population, agricultural labour, and farmers as prospective manpower, which does lead to creation of few jobs but may destroy thousands of livelihood opportunities. Individuals do get attracted to SEZ related employment opportunities, mainly not due to a better earning opportunity, but main reason has been less productive nature of farming in the country and lack better options.

When land is acquired from the farmers, the farmers and agricultural labourers lose their employment, as they are not skilled labourers to relocate them to other jobs. The problem of displacement and rehabilitation of farmers and agricultural labourers also comes to the fore. Indian farmers are mostly uneducated, so, they cannot get high-rank jobs in SEZs; they can work only as casual labourers in SEZs. If farmers are not ready to work as labourers in SEZs? Already farmers and agricultural labourers are facing a bad situation in India and when there will be no work for them, it will lead to worsening of their economic condition.

On the brighter side, if the farmers invest their compensation money for land in a proper way, they can get more profit. If they spend their money on the education of their children then their future will be bright. The labourers, who work in the agricultural sector, can also work in SEZs when an industry is set up under the SEZ scheme. The wage rate is high in SEZs as compared to the agricultural sector. So, there can be improvements in the economic conditions of agricultural labourers. Thus, SEZs can play an important role for the transformation of labour from the agricultural sector to the industrial sector. Then the burden of the population on the agriculture sector will decline and this will be beneficial for both the development of agriculture and industry. Due to this disguised unemployment in the agriculture sector would disappear and lead to proper utilisation of our manpower.

However, in reality, land as livelihood generates much more complex security and lifestyles, than what the money can offer. Besides the main crop, land provides certain foods, environmental services, wild fodder, and medicinal plants. Thus, those entirely dependent on the land, say artisans, pastoral communities will be at loss. Even today in the villages the common practice is to share grain with the black smith, the potters, and pastoralists. In fact the ones worst affected will be the share-croppers and labourers, the petty traders and service providers. These landless people do not even have a legal basis for compensation. The rehabilitation package offers one job per displaced family, and that also requires the member to have a certain basic educational qualification. For land acquired households, higher likelihood of engaging in salaried or self-employed activities could explain their lower participation rate within SEZ.

Generally, nature of employment at SEZ remains predominantly informal. Such informal positions are "contracted-out" through "contractors"—a term locally used to refer to middlemen who act as agents recruiting on behalf of the SEZ companies. Contractors have a regional/locale presence and bias, it defines their area of operation and expertise. The contractors only source for unskilled labour (casual labour) and are not awarded contracts for "desk jobs" (a local term used to refer to semi-skilled and skilled jobs). Based on the accounts of locals, contractors are primarily used by the companies to pass on responsibility, and take no legal binding on the employment of casual labour. The contracting of work to middlemen also allows companies flexibility on the staffing, as one villager noted "hiring and firing if and when they want". It has been observed that the women are employed rather than men, because they are easy to control and more work can be extracted from them. It has also been noted that contractors have also according to accounts, been advised to always keep young people in the labour pool and discard older individuals and individuals who are deemed not so efficient.

As such, the gains generated by SEZs in terms of employment have not been viewed upon as long-term. According to a study conducted by Society for Participatory Research (2008) on the plight of workers in Indian economic zones, only few workers have long-term employment contracts. Short-term contracts are used for flexible hiring and firing and for avoiding costs such as maternity and redundancy pay (Swaminathan, 2007). Further, with regard to the impact of SEZs on local livelihoods, the opinion is not positive as it has been argued that the SEZs will not create employment for local population, but will instead lead to distress migration of locals since the jobs created will need education and skill levels unreachable for most of the people. Therefore, the communities such as those of the fisher folks, farmers, landless labourers, women, Dalits and other marginalised will remain untouched by all new employment opportunities arising out of the SEZs.

It is important, therefore, that, in addition to suitable financial compensation, the displaced farm labour and allied workers are given preference in employment by the SEZ developer or in the business units in the SEZ. There should be a provision for their subsequent absorption in employment in the SEZ establishment and in the processing units. They should get a preferential treatment. Each SEZ proposal must include a plan for rehabilitation of the workers who would be displaced from their traditional employment. A proper implementation of that plan should be a specific condition attached to the approval of the SEZ and the Development Commissioner of the SEZ should be enjoined to supervise the implementation of the rehabilitation plan.

Given arguments does raise several questions such as, are the SEZs in the interest of the farmers, agricultural and non-agricultural communities who are living off the land? Is the Land acquired in the name of "compelling and overriding national interest" is really for the masses? Actually, in the name of 'development' we are only creating disparities with wealth in a fewer hands and nowhere near making growth 'inclusive' which would be based on the concepts of sustainability, ecological sensitivity and an ingrained understanding of the cultural roots of a people (Levien, 2011). Besides farm size distribution, tenure systems and changing farm types, developments in terms of diversification and pluriactivity, i.e. labour allocation changes, are attributed to the phenomenon of structural change. The effective direction is not always unambiguous: labour markets determine structural change and *vice versa*. Labour allocation decisions are driven by economic incentives such as wage differentials, but non-economic motives may also play a decisive role.

Impact on Employment Pattern in Rural India

Land acquisition has resulted in the disruption of the livelihoods of affected households, lasting several years. Unemployment was a direct result of loss of land, and also of the absence of wage labour in neighbours' farms. Between 2004 and 2007 there was great uncertainty and regular protests. There was very little non-farm activity in the village. Increased unemployment was also due to the large scale conversion of farmland into non-farmland also reduced the scope for work in common lands such as the collection of fruits and fodder for domestic as well as commercial ends. Households engaged in offering services (barbers, washer men, artisans, fishermen, etc.) lost employment with the decline in the economic status of the farmers who were their patrons. Construction work within the SEZ became a major source of labour locally, but only during the early phase of construction. SEZ managers discriminated against those who took part in the resistance and protest agitation and preferred outside labour who are not concerned with the problems of displacement (Venugopal, 2005).

Some women get daily wage work as gardeners, sweepers or as janitors. Long periods of unemployment in some cases led to severe poverty, high indebtedness and the sale of all available assets. Unemployment and poverty has been most intense among those who continued to stick to land-based livelihoods. Although little effort was made in Polepally to offer alternative employment to affected families, some relief has been provided by the National Rural Employment Guarantee Act (NREGA), which was passed in 2005. The NREGA is a national job guarantee scheme that aims to provide the rural poor with a minimum of 100 days employment when none other is available. NREGA work is eagerly sought in the villages, but unfortunately the programme is unable to keep up with the demand for work in the village following the land acquisition.

Studies also suggest that people do get attracted to SEZ related employment opportunities, mainly not due to a better employment opportunity, but main reason has been less productive nature of farming in the country. The impact of SEZ on rural employment can be considered as negative in the sense that it may generate a labour shortage and deprive rural areas of the youngest and best educated people. The impacts, whether positive or negative, vary greatly and depend on a number of factors and variables, which policy-makers and development practitioners need to address. SEZ is hiding behind myths of 'trickle-down' growth to give itself licence to strengthen the hand of corporate elites, thereby contributing at once to accelerated growth for the already enriched and growing poverty for the impoverished (Parwez, 2015). It is thus contributing to rapidly rising economic inequality. Only when the goals and processes of the SEZs, policy are aligned, when evaluation of proposals are based on hard economic criteria and when the government tries to partner with the local community rather than forcing against their will.

Case Study of Mundra Port and SEZ (MPSEZ), Kutch: Impact on Livelihood

Generally, policy-makers assume that industrial development would lead to enhancement in the standard of life of local population. However, they do not understand the fact that diversion of land for industrialisation, though crucial for development, is troubled with contradictions when analysed from the affected rural community's perspective.

A recent study by Institute of Rural Management, Anand (IRMA) based on the impact of industrialisation and land acquisition on rural livelihoods in the coastal villages affected by Mundra Port and SEZ (MPSEZ), in Kutch district of Gujarat, suggests that impact of industrialisation to enable economic development cannot be seen in isolation from the impact of loss of land and other resources and its impact on sustenance of their livelihoods.

In the post-January 2001 earthquake period coastal region of Kutch witnessed massive industrial development. It comprised one of the largest port-based SEZs known as Adani Port and SEZ (APSEZ), it is spread over approximately 3225.68 hectares of land, acquired from 14-15 villages over a period of time.

With the industrialization region has also witnessed protest from local communities and civil society organisations against the potential threat to the livelihood of local population and adverse impact on marine ecology. The study suggests that due favourable policy of government towards industrialisation options for local people shrank (Geevan, 2008). Over a period of time, however, industrialisation has had a direct or indirect impact on the livelihoods of all communities (Hirway and Goswami, 2007). The traditional fishing community is the most marginalised. Fishermen go for fishing whenever the high tide arrives, while fisherwomen sort, grade, and dry the fish caught. They do the vending of dried and fresh fish in the local market at Mundra.

However, with the setting up of the SEZ, high traffic of ships on the port has made it difficult for fishermen with smaller boats to catch fish in the same water. Empirical data of report suggest that with the thinning of intertidal zones due to port activities fish catch has reduced over a period of time. Pollution generated by SEZ units has also damaged both the quality and quantity of fish in the coastal area.

Over a period of time, there has been a decline in the quantity and quality of fish catch due to the deterioration of marine ecology, caused by the destruction of mangroves and industrial pollution.

Report suggest that villagers struggle to survive on their paltry incomes from fishing and working unwillingly as construction workers, agricultural labourers and casual labourers in SEZ units to supplement family income. Due to lack of education and being unskilled, they are unable to take advantage of new economic opportunities.

Agriculture is the one sector which has been most adversely affected due to industrialisation, land acquisition and establishment of SEZs. Agriculture has reported decline in the agricultural productivity of all the crops and also the quality of horticultural crops including coconuts, *chikoos*, and date palms over the last five years. Over a period of time, increased salinity of water due to intensive use of groundwater and sea by the SEZs unit appear to have reduced productivity of the land. In fact, some farmer has reported that agricultural land has become uncultivable.

The main fallout of industrialisation has been damage to the horticultural crops. Fly ash and the chemical content created from the SEZ and thermal power plants located in the contiguous areas settle on the trees, fruit and affect the pollination process causing deterioration in the quantity and quality of the horticultural crops.

Furthermore, it has been observed that the cost of agricultural production has gone up sharply as the costs of agricultural inputs and agricultural labour has increased. There is also huge shortage of agricultural workers as many of them moving towards working as casual labour in the SEZ units and industrial-infrastructural based projects.

As the establishment of Adani Port and SEZ has led to substantial increase in the valuation of land, many local residents and farmers have chosen to sell their land. With given amount they are creating asset in the form of housing and vehicles. With lack of options small and marginal farmers have diversified their livelihood from agriculture to non-farm employment, mostly working as casual labour as construction workers in SEZ or other industrial sites.

Setting up SEZ has also affected animal husbandry in adverse way, which being the important source of livelihood for pastoralists, small and marginal farmers, and poor landless families has resulted in the shortage of pastures for grazing cattle. It has been observed that livestock population has gradually decreased as it become difficult for local population to maintain a large number of cattle. Availability of fodder and fuel wood has also decreased due to deterioration of the quality of land. Besides, small and marginal farmers and landless families pursue livestock rearing as an occupation to supplement their income, have been severely affected.

The benefit of the new economic opportunities has been mainly availed by big and enterprising farmers. As for the others, given the low level of education and vocational skills forced to work as contractual and casual employees as cleaners, labourers, construction workers etc. Gradually, local people are shifting from agricultural activities to non-agricultural activities, working as casual labour in port/industry to better their incomes.

Conclusion

It has been observed that clause of Public Purposes in LAA legislation being used for land acquisition than land is being diverted to private companies. It is evident that thousands of hectares of land lying vacant across the country and it raises question on demand of vast tract of land by corporate. Land has somehow become the most attractive component for companies to be part of SEZ scheme. It is clearly visible that objective of SEZs scheme has lost somewhere and it has become a government instrument for land acquisition for private firms. This chapter also talks about environmental and rural livelihood implication of SEZs across the country. The point is for the benefit of nation at large, there is requirement of a comprehensive policy on SEZ, an optimal use of resources, and leakages needs to be plugged in terms of misuse of allocated land. The government needs to ensure that only large scale manufacturing are allowed in SEZs, regional disparities and potentially located away from the cities in dry-lands so that rural areas may benefit from the industrial development. After several protests over acquisition of agricultural land, there is need of understanding on prime agricultural land and that there would be adequate rehabilitation and compensation to farmers. The development of SEZs may end up destroying employment in rural areas by making farmers landless and population dependent and development of SEZ may just create very little employment for highly skilled and net employment may have negative result.

References

Bhadra, D. and Brando, A.S. (1993). *Urbanization, Agricultural Development and Land Allocation,* World Bank Discussion Paper, 201, Washington D.C.: World Bank.

Bharati, S.B. (1999). Human rights and development projects in India, *The PRP Journal of Human Rights,* 3(4).

Chandrasekhar, C.P. (2006). "Primitive Accumulation", *Frontline,* 23(20), Oct. 7–20, 24-26.

Economic Survey (2008). Government of India, New Delhi.

Fernandes, W. (2002). Displacement and the Land Acquisition Act, 1894: why are tribal areas not considered a part of our history? *Combat Law, 1*(1), March-April. Available at http://www.combatlaw.org/information.ph p?article_id=35&issue_id=1

Geevan, C.P. (2008). *Kutchh Fisheries: Netting livelihood between the Ranns and the Deep.* Centre for Environment and Social Concerns.

Hirway, I. and Goswami, S. (2007). *Valuation of Costal Resources: The Case of Mangroves in Gujarat.* New Delhi: Academic Foundation.

Levien, M. (2011). "Special Economic Zones and accumulation by dispossession in India", *Journal of Agrarian Change,* 11(4): (454–483).

Morris, S. (2007). *Towards Reforms for Land Acquisition Framework in India,* Working Paper No. 2007-05-04, Indian Institute of Management, Ahmedabad.

National Sample Survey Organisation Report (2003). *Employment and unemployment Report,* Government of India, New Delhi.

Palit, A., and Bhattacharjee, S. (2008). *Special Economic Zones in India: Myths and Realities,* Anthem South Asian Studies, Anthem Press (London, New York and Delhi).

Pandey, B. and Rout, B.K. (2004). *Development Induced Displacement in India: Impact on Women,* National Commission for Women, New Delhi.

Parwez, S. (2015). Modified labour welfare measure for Special Economic Zone and Implications. *Indian Journal of Industrial Relations,* Shri Ram Centre for Industrial Relations and Human Resources, New Delhi, 50(3): (386-396), January 2015, ISSN: 0019-5286.

Patnaik, U. (2008). Imperialism, resources and food security with reference to the Indian experience. *Human Geography,* 1(1): (40-53).

Reddy, V.R. (2006). Land alienation from agriculture: use and misuse of land for non-agricultural practice, (Unpublished Report), Hyderabad: Centre for Economic and Social Studies.

Shah, A., Nandani, D., and Joshi, H. (2012). Marginalisation or mainstreaming? Evidence from Special Economic Zones in Gujarat, (210), Gujarat Institute of Development Research, Ahmedabad.

Swaminathan, Padmini (2007). M. Suchitra's, "Economic or exploitation zones", *India Together,* New Delhi.

TOI (2007). The missing dissent: Maoist Salwa Judum and the Orgy violence, Editorial, *Time of India*, (10). Area Production Yield (Various Volume), Directorate of Agriculture, GOG, Gandhinagar. http://masskutch.blogspot.com

Venugopal, P.N. (2005). *Special Exploitation Zone, India Together*, New Delhi.

World Development Report 2008 (2009). *Agriculture for Development*. Oxford: Oxford University Press for the World Bank.

8
Promotion of Micro-enterprises in Rural Areas as a Tool for Rural Development

Sushmita Sharma and *Dipanjan Chakraborty*

Introduction

In India, about three-fourth of the population lives in rural areas. Development process of the country would be hampered if this large section of people is neglected. Hence, economists and policy-makers have given due importance to rural development for solving multidimensional problems like poverty, unemployment, social backwardness etc. In such situation, entrepreneurship in rural areas is viewed as an effective means of accelerating the process of rural development. Self-employment and informal activities in rural areas can address the growing problem of poverty and slow economic growth. Rural microenterprises ensure value addition to rural resources engaging largely rural human resources. Microenterprises contribute significantly to economic growth, social stability and equity. This sector is one of the most important vehicles through, which low income people can escape poverty. With limited skills and education to compete for formal sector jobs, these men and women find economic opportunities in microenterprises as business owners and employees. In India, micro and small scale enterprises account for the majority of firms and a large share of employment. It has been noted that "SMEs constitute the most dynamic segment of many transition and developing economies. They are more innovative, faster growing and possibly more profitable as compared to larger-sized enterprises." Hence, the role of microenterprises in rural development is very significant.

Review of Literature

Deolankar (1984) conducted a study on 264 small-scale units to understand entrepreneurships development in the developed, developing and backward states of India. In spite of the abundant natural resources, industrial development was slow mainly due to untapped entrepreneurial talent rather than due to lack of basic facilities and financial support. The study suggested for timely action of the government to accelerate the process of entrepreneurship development in India.

Giriappa (1996) has analysed the employment as well as income potential from fish as well as cashew, apple processing. He also mentioned that India is among the five major producers of at least a dozen agricultural commodities in the world. These include sugar, tea, tobacco, spices, fruits and vegetables, cotton, jute, milk and milk products, rice and wheat. Yet its contribution to the international trade in farm products is less than 0.5 per cent. Even in domestic market, the agro-processing is not a strong economic activity. It is estimated that 5 per cent increase in the processing of agricultural commodities can help generating 65 million jobs for the rural people. This apart, branded from products can bring more value to the economy.

The study of Kanitkar (1994) aims at understands the emergence of successful entrepreneurs and owners of micro-enterprises in rural India. Based on the case studies of 86 village-based entrepreneurs drawn from different regions of India, the article examines the socio-economic profile of the entrepreneurs, their motivation for shifting from an agriculture-based occupation to a non-farm activity, their approach to raising resources for their enterprises and the factors that facilitated entry of the village based entrepreneurs in to a business activity.

Ramalingam and Gayatri (2006) in their article suggest using Innovation as a strategic tool for development of rural entrepreneurship. Since most of the India populations reside in rural villages, entrepreneurship awareness has to be created among them. The multidimensional aspects of Rural Entrepreneurship are studied with the help of small sample size. The findings suggest that a small innovation in the rural area would definitely catch up the most of the population that would lead to improvement of quality of life of many people in the country.

Andersan (1995) in his thesis attempts to understand what it is that rural entrepreneurs do within the rural context. The central argument of the thesis is that in order to understand the entrepreneur we must place entrepreneurial action in its social context, we must study the process of entrepreneurship. This study, therefore, endeavours to investigate the actions of the entrepreneur in one context, rurality. Consequently, this study is a detailed examination of a rural environment and the interrelationships of this environment and entrepreneurs. Its purpose is to try to establish the nature of the relationships between rurality and to specify the conditions of the entrepreneurial process.

Ram Krishna (2008) in his paper encompasses the present scenario of *Khadi* and Village Industries in the North East States, particularly Arunachal Pradesh, in relation to growth, development, problems and solutions. The author opined that top priority should be given to those small scale industries like KVIs, which need light machine tools and other equipments in order to produce qualitative products because today, a state's progress is measured by the quality of goods it produces.

Khanka (2009) conducted a survey of 248 first generation entrepreneurs in Assam in North East India to understand their entrepreneurial motivation. The study clearly showed that the entrepreneurs were primarily motivated by the need for economic achievement, personal growth, autonomy and recognition. The desire to contribute to the community was not found to be an important reason to become an entrepreneur. The study did not reveal any significant difference in the motivations of men and women entrepreneurs.

Barua and Mali (2011) in their paper on entrepreneurship and its role in the growth of micro and small enterprises: a case study in Assam, found that the MSMEs in Assam had registered an average growth of 20.63 per cent per annum from 1987-88 to 2006-07. This was accompanied by a 45.3 per cent in investment and 89.5 per cent in output. However, there is an element of upward bias in estimates of growth in investment and output as price rise over the years has significantly inflated their values. The whole study is based in secondary data. It can be concluded from the study that entrepreneurial performance indicated by the output is affected largely by the quantum of investment rather than the level of employment.

Need for the Study

The review of literature showed that many studies were conducted on rural entrepreneurship, but no study on management of micro-enterprises for rural entrepreneurship development has been conducted till now in Assam in general and Sonitpur district in particular. There is a need for many more micro-studies because of variations in geographic, social, cultural, political and economic conditions from state to state and from region to region within a state. Further, there is a need to throw light on the performance of rural micro-entrepreneurs and the problems faced by the micro-entrepreneurs in operating their units. Sonitpur district is the industrially backward area when it is compared with other districts. Sonitpur district has been endowed with several facilities beneficial for growth of rural entrepreneurs when compared to other districts in Assam. So, it is felt that this district is ideally suited for a study on rural micro-entrepreneurship.

Objectives

(i) To study the socio-economic conditions of the selected rural micro-entrepreneurs.
(ii) To analyse the performance of rural micro-entrepreneurs in terms of investment, employment and profit.
(iii) To examine the performance of scheduled commercial banks with regard to Micro- and Small Enterprises (MSE) sector advances in Sonitpur district.
(iv) To identify the problems encountered by rural micro-entrepreneurs.

Working Hypothesis

The performance of rural micro-enterprise has a positive impact towards the growth of rural entrepreneurship development.

Methodology

The present study is based on both primary and secondary data. The study was carried out in Sonitpur district of Assam which has 14 blocks. The primary data were gathered through field investigation. Out of the 14 blocks, 2 blocks were selected for study for having the highest number of entrepreneurs. A sample of 60 rural micro-entrepreneurs registered in District Industries and Commerce Centre, Sonitpur was selected by simple random sampling method. The respondents were personally interviewed with the help of a detailed interview schedule. The data so collected was analysed and organised in tabular form wherever necessary and interpreted with the help of percentage and pie diagrams to draw meaningful conclusions. The primary data has been supplemented by secondary data which were collected from DICC Sonitpur, KVIB, banks, research papers, journals, government bulletin, internet etc.

Period of the Study

The study covers a period of two years, 2011-12 to 2012-13.

Limitation of the Study

The study was done with the following limitations:

(i) The study will cover only the rural micro-entrepreneurs who were registered under District Industries and Commerce Centre, Sonitpur.
(ii) The study will only cover a period of two years from 2011-12 to 2012-13.
(iii) The study will give its conclusions from the findings based on only the selected samples.
(iv) Limitations may arise on availability of data, frank submission of the respondent, frank disclosure of the departments etc.

Profile of the Study Area

The Sonitpur district is an administrative district of Assam. The district headquarters is located at Tezpur. As of 2011, it is the third most populous district of Assam. According to the 2011 census, Sonitpur district has a population of 19,24,110. Most of the people live in rural areas. The percentage of people living in rural and urban areas is 90.96 per cent and 9.04 per cent respectively.

Agriculture is the prime occupation of the people of the district; traditional dependence on agriculture is one of the reasons for lack of entrepreneurship among the educated youth. The absence of major industries in the district is also partly responsible for lack of entrepreneurial activities (www.sonitpur.nic.in).

MSMED Act, 2006

In accordance with the provision of Micro, Small and Medium Enterprise Development (MSMED) Act, 2006, the microenterprises are classified into two classes: (a) Manufacturing Enterprises and (b) Service Enterprises.

Manufacturing Enterprises: The enterprises engaged in the manufacture or production of goods, whose investment in plant and machinery does not exceed Rs. 25 lakhs.

Service Enterprises: The enterprises engaged in providing or rendering of services, whose investment in equipment does not exceed Rs. 10 lakhs.

Concept of Micro-enterprise

Since the word 'micro' represents small, the Micro, Small and Medium Enterprise Development (MSMED) Act, 2006 defines it as the enterprise engaged in the manufacturing or production of goods, whose investment in plant and machinery does not exceed 25 lakh, and enterprise engaged in providing or rendering services, whose investment in equipment does not exceed Rs. 10 lakh. Rural micro-enterprises are those industrial and business undertakings where owners, individuals, friends or relatives supply capital; they operate locally, and the size of business as well as management is small. Micro-enterprises such as brick kiln industry, stone crushing industry, bakery, cane and bamboo, washing soaps, food products, mini rice mill, cycle repairing, computer and xerox, jewelry designing, supari processing are some of the examples of rural microenterprises.

Major Findings

The two dimensions of entrepreneurship are the persons (the entrepreneur) and the society in which he or she operates.

Entrepreneurship can improve the economic independence and social status of rural people. The socio-economic origins of the entrepreneurs are considered in micro-enterprises because micro-enterprises usually employ fewer professional specialists, operate with less formality and reflect to a greater degree the personality and attitudes of the entrepreneur. Therefore, it is essential to study the socio-economic background of rural entrepreneur to extract any meaningful conclusions on the entrepreneurial activities and the enterprises, which are run by rural entrepreneurs (*see* Table 8.1).

A large majority of the respondents (73%) were married, while the remaining (27%) were unmarried. It is clear that a majority of the respondents were carrying out the entrepreneurial activity as a means of their livelihood. Forty three per cent of the entrepreneurs have secondary-level of education, while 28 per cent have primary level education, 12 per cent are graduates, while 17 per cent are illiterates. It can be inferred that a sample of 100 per cent educated entrepreneurs could be used for the development of rural microenterprises with skill developing training programmes. Seventy seven per cent of the respondents were males, while 23 per cent of the respondents were females. It should be added that more encouragement needs to be given to women to take up entrepreneurial ventures. Forty eight per cent of entrepreneurs belonged to the general category, followed by 31 per cent belonging to the Other Backward Castes (OBCs), 13 per cent Scheduled Castes (SCs), 8 per cent Schedule Tribes (STs). Thus, it is observed that the weaker section and depressed class of people are less involved in business. It was found that a majority of the respondents, i.e. 68 per cent belonged to joint families while the remaining 32 per cent belonged to nuclear families. It can thus be said that joint family system is still an important determinant of entrepreneurship. A majority 58 per cent of the total respondents were in the age group of 31-40 years, followed by 23 per cent in the age group of 21-30 years and 12 per cent in the age group of 41-50 years. Only 7 per cent of respondents were above 50 years of age. It may be interpreted that microenterprise has facilitated rural entrepreneurs in different age groups. A majority of the respondents (65%) are from service enterprise, while the remaining (35%) are from manufacturing enterprise. It may be interpreted that entrepreneurs like to invest more in service enterprises in comparison to manufacturing enterprises. Seventy two per cent

Table 8.1: Socio-Economic Background of Rural Micro Entrepreneurs

Particulars	*Classification*	*Number*	*Percentage*
Marital status	Married	44	73
	Unmarried	16	27
Educational qualifications	Illiterate	10	17
	Primary	17	28
	Secondary	26	43
	Graduate	07	12
Gender	Male	46	77
	Female	14	23
Caste	General	29	48
	SC	08	13
	ST	05	08
	OBC	18	31
Type of family	Joint	41	68
	Nuclear	19	32
Age	20-30	14	23
	31-40	35	58
	41-50	07	12
	50 and above	04	07
Type of activity	Manufacturing	21	35
	Service	39	65
Sources of finance	Own funds only	17	28
	Own funds and borrowed funds	43	72
Community	Assamese	25	42
	Bengali	18	30
	Marwari	02	03
	Bihari	09	15
	Others	06	10
Form of Ownership	Sole proprietorship	52	87
	Partnership	8	13

Source: Field survey.

of the respondents used their owned and borrowed funds while 28 per cent of the respondents used own funds only. It was found that 42 per cent of the respondents were from Assamese background, 30 per cent from Bengali community, 15 per cent Biharis, 10 per cent represented other communities and 3 per cent belongs to Marwari community. Sole proprietorship was the preferred form of business organisation in the district under reference. Eighty seven per cent of the respondents opted for it, followed by partnership that constituted 13 per cent. The rural micro entrepreneurs preferred proprietorship form of business organisation.

Table 8.2: Classification of Entrepreneurs on the Basis of Employment

Employment	*Number*	*Percentage*
Agro and food based	10	17
Engineering based	8	13
Mineral based	7	12
Beauty parlour	12	20
Shop	12	20
Repairing and service	5	8
Textile	6	10
Total	**60**	**100**

Source: Field survey.

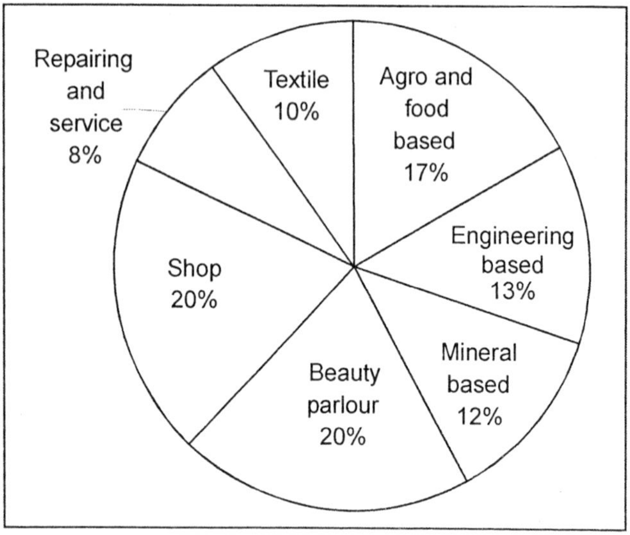

Fig. 8.1: Pie diagram showing Classification of Entrepreneurs on the Basis of Employment

Source: Field survey.

Different types of both manufacturing and service enterprises are found in the study area. On the basis of the type of employment, entrepreneurs are classified accordingly. Seventeen per cent of the respondents were engaged in agro and food based industries. Mini rice mill, *masala* making, spice grinding, bakery products, jam, jelly etc. are some of the examples of agro and food based industries. Beauty parlour and shops were seen as the emerging areas for the entrepreneurs. Twenty per cent of respondents were running each of beauty parlour and shops.

Table 8.3: Capital Investment

Amount	*Number*	*Percentage*
Less than Rs. 10,000	5	8
Rs. 10,001–50,000	12	20
Rs. 50,001–1,00,000	19	32
Rs. 1,00,001–1,50,000	16	27
Above Rs. 1,50,000	8	13
Total	**60**	**100**

Source: Field survey.

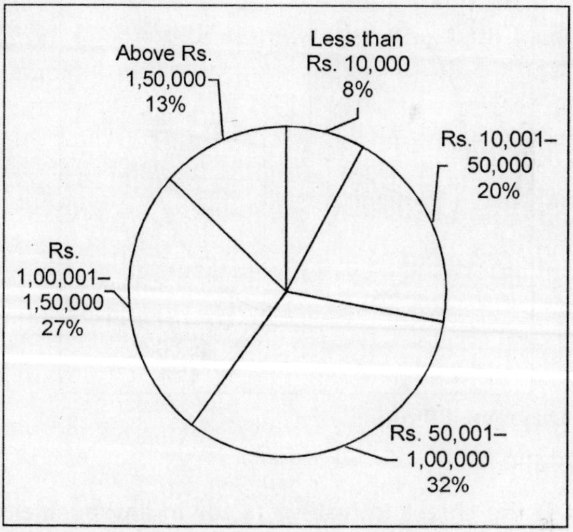

Fig. 8.2: Pie Diagram showing Capital Investment
Source: Field survey.

The capital investment was the major indicator that was taken into consideration while selecting the sample. From Table 8.3, it can be observed that there were 20 per cent entrepreneurs investing in the range of Rs. 10,001–50,000; 32 per cent entrepreneurs who had invested an amount to the tune of Rs. 50,001–1,00,000 to start the business. There were 16 entrepreneurs who made an initial investment of a higher amount in the range of Rs. 1,00,001–1,50,000. Further, 13 per cent entrepreneurs had invested an amount above Rs. 1,50,000 to start the business. Many entrepreneurs pointed out the difficulty in pooling resources, mainly capital, to start the business.

Table 8.4: Profit

Amount per month	*Number*	*Percentage*
Rs. 5,000–10,000	14	23
Rs. 10,001–15,000	27	45
Above Rs. 15,000	19	32
Total	**60**	**100**

Source: Field survey.

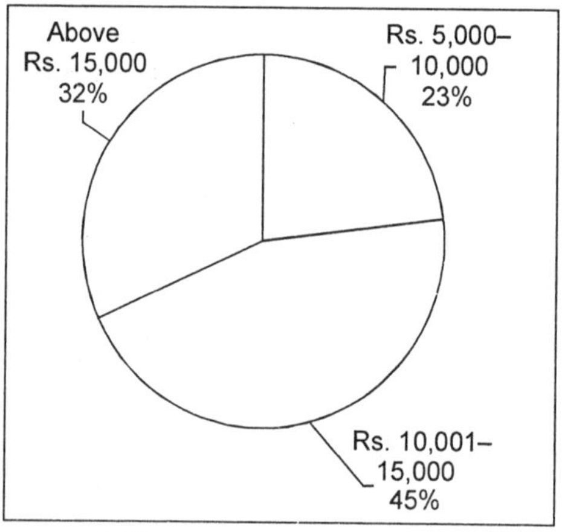

Fig. 3: Pie Diagram of Profit

Source: Field survey.

Profit is the chief motivating factor in any business. Every business activity, be it big or small, public or private, aims at profit. The amount of profit realised by the entrepreneurs is presented in Table 8.4. It was seen that 27 entrepreneurs were earning a profit above Rs. 10,000, but less than Rs. 15,000 per month. These entrepreneurs were mainly those who were running mineral-based, engineering-based, agro-based enterprises and shops.

Table 8.5: Performance of Scheduled Commercial Banks with Regard to MSE Sector Advances, Sonitpur District

(Rs. in thousands)

Year	*Target*	*Achievement*	*Percentage of Achievement*
2011-12	425389	465018	109
2012-13	425660	526875	124
Total	**851049**	**991893**	**117**

Note: Percentages are calculated and figures are rounded off.
Source: Annual Credit Plan, Sonitpur District, 2011-12 and 2012-13.

It can be observed from Table 8.5 that the percentage of achievement of target amount for micro and small enterprises sector advances is quite satisfactory. There was more than 100 per cent achievement of target amount for both the years, which shows a steady demand for advances by the entrepreneurs in the district.

Table 8.6: Outstanding Advances to MSE sector by Scheduled Commercial Banks, Sonitpur District

(Rs. in thousands)

As on 31st March	*Total priority sector advance outstanding (1)*	*Outstanding Advances to MSE sector (2)*	*(2) as percentage of (1)*
2012	6202812	1965138	32
2013	8270512	2055710	25
Total	**14473324**	**4020848**	**28**

Note: Percentages are calculated and figures are rounded off.
Source: Annual Credit Plan, Sonitpur District, 2011-12 and 2012-13.

Table 8.6 shows the credit facility extended by the scheduled commercial banks to micro and small enterprises in Sonitpur district. Table 8.6 also reveals the proportion of MSE sector credit in the total priority sector credit which falls from 32 per cent to 25 per cent in the year ending March 2013.

Problems Faced by the Micro-Entrepreneurs

Table 8.7: Problems faced by the Sample in Operating and Managing their Business

Factors	Percentage	Rank
1. Shortage of skilled workers	60	10
2. Lack of sufficient infrastructural facilities	71	4
3. Insufficient and outdated technology and technical knowhow	64	8
4. Inadequate information on markets	65	7
5. Lack of marketing facilities for their products	67	6
6. Delay in supply of raw materials	59	11
7. Lack of proper training and knowledge	78	1
8. Insufficient demands for products	62	9
9. Lack of sufficient guidelines and counselling by NGOs and from the Government	55	12
10. Inadequate information on source of finance	74	3
11. Absence of credit institutions in rural areas	68	5
12. Too many formalities of banks	77	2

Source: Field survey.

The different problems faced by the respondents are presented in Table 8.7. Ranking was done on the basis of intensity of the problems faced by the entrepreneurs in operating and managing their business. A majority (78%) of the respondents faced the problem of lack of proper training and knowledge. This creates a problem managing their units properly. Seventy seven per cent of the respondents opined that there were too many formalities of the banks for which they had to approach to local moneylenders for financing their units, while 74 per cent faced the problem of inadequate information on different sources of finance. Seventy one per cent of the respondents suffer from inadequate infrastructural facilities in operating and managing their units. Absence of credit institutions in rural areas was one of the major hindrances for 68 per cent respondents. Marketing of products (67%) is another area where the rural microenterprises find themselves handicapped. As the units are resource-constrained, they do not have a separate marketing department. Sixty five per cent of the respondents stated that they did not possess proper information on different markets for marketing of their products. Sixty four per cent of the respondents used outdated technology in manufacturing their products. They mostly suffer from technical knowhow. Sixty two per cent stated insufficiency of demand for their products. Sixty per cent faced the problem of shortage of skilled labour, another important problem faced by 59 per cent respondents was delay in supply of raw materials to the enterprise. Fifty five per cent of the respondents faced the problem of lack of sufficient guidelines and counselling from NGOs and Government. Apart from the problems mentioned above, there are numerous other problems that are faced by the rural micro-entrepreneurs in running and managing their units.

Policy Recommendations

Based on the above study and problems identified, the following recommendations are forwarded:

1. In some rural areas there is absence of banks and other financial institutions to cater to the needs of rural entrepreneurs. The Government and other organisations are needed to come forward and take initiative for establishment of banks in the rural areas at low cost.
2. Training institutions like Institutes of Entrepreneurship Development (IEDs) and Centres for Entrepreneurship Development (CEDs) should be established to organise training programmes in rural areas. There is a need to enlighten the rural entrepreneurs on the various management skills.
3. Proper infrastructural facilities are a prerequisite for the development of entrepreneurship in a particular area. Entrepreneurs in rural areas have to bear additional cost for the absence of proper infrastructural support and this reduces their profitability. So, Government needs to take extensive measures to develop the infrastructural facilities in rural and backward areas.
4. Success stories of entrepreneurs from varied backgrounds should be popularized through text books of schools and colleges. All possible media should be used to project these role models.
5. The adoption of modern techniques must be encouraged. Development and dissemination of appropriate technology to improve productivity and quality should be given due attention.

6. One of the common problems faced by rural micro-enterprises is lack of marketing information and marketing of products. In this regard the government and other agencies have to disseminate the information through database in internet. This can be undertaken by the market research firms and other established institutes. Moreover, by organising trade fairs and exhibitions in home and abroad, new markets for the rural enterprises can be explored.
7. It has been found in the study that there is no system of proper training to develop the efficiency of the workers. In order to improve the efficiency of the workers, it is suggested that recruitment procedure should be modified. Also, management institutes, engineering colleges, universities etc. can take this opportunity to impart technical and managerial consultancy to the students of rural colleges periodically.
8. Appointment of MSME Ombudsman and having one stop centre for needs of rural entrepreneurs to be established.
9. Industrial policy of the state should be strengthened to encourage the unemployed persons to seek entrepreneurial career by providing financial and non-financial assistance.
10. Government agencies should ensure timely supply of raw material, steady flow of Institutional finance relatively lower cost and marketing facilities to the units.

Conclusion

India's villages can be developed by encouraging entrepreneurship in rural areas. Micro-enterprises have an important role to play in the generation of employment opportunities, and also in the promotion of self-employment and entrepreneurship among the youth. In view of this, the Government of India is assigning significant importance to rural industrialisation so that employment can be raised as well as utilisation of local resources can be done to optimum. In fact, if rural development is to be sustained then rural entrepreneurship is must. Understanding the basic characteristics of rural areas and eliminating the inherent constraints, rural entrepreneurs can go a long way in framing proper policies for promoting and developing rural entrepreneurship. Micro and small enterprises can offer much greater service to the nation than their bigger counterparts. These rural enterprises can do miracle if they have greater capital inflows at their disposal. This has been the motive behind MUDRA to ease capital constraints faced by rural micro entrepreneurs and bring much more money at their disposal to grow themselves and make India grow. Micro entrepreneurs can contribute to Mr. Modi's "Make in India" programme through this scheme by making India a manufacturing hub of millions of small items and things and marketing them on a larger scale. However, government policies will be of no use without the participation of people. A combined effort of government, family members and total involvement of the people at the grassroots level will go a long way in bringing about planned development of rural microenterprises.

References

Andersan, A.R. (1995). "The Arcadian enterprise: An enquiry into the nature and conditions of rural small business". Retrieved from www.emeraldinsight.com/Insight/ViewContentServlet?Filename..... html

Barua, A.N. and Mali, A. (2011). "Entrepreneurship and its role in the growth of micro and small enterprise: A case study of Assam". *Small Enterprise Development, Management and Extension Journal, 38*(2): 69-83.

Chakraborty, D. and Borman, R. (2013). Socio-economic impact of rural micro-entrepreneurship in Assam—An empirical study. *Vanijya, 23*: 115-134.

Chellappan, G. (2006). "Marketing products: A great migraine afflicting rural enterprises." *Industrial Economist,* November 15-30: 32.

Deolankar, V. (1984). "Role of entrepreneurship in industrialization". *Southern Economist, 22,* February 19: 14.

Economic Survey, Assam, 2011-12, Retrieved from http://ecostatassam.nic.in/ads_economic%20survey.pdf

Giriappa (1996). *Prospects of Agro-processing Industry,* Delhi: Daya Publishing House.

Kamalakannan, K. (2006). Rural industrialization and poverty alleviation. *Kurukshetra, 54*(7): 3-8.

Kanitkar, A. (1994). "Entrepreneurs and microenterprises in rural India". *Economic and Political Weekly, 29*(9): 25-30.

Khanka, S.S. (2009). "Motivational orientation of Assamese entrepreneurs in the SME sector". *Journal of Entrepreneurship, 8*(2), 209-218.

Kumar, S. (2005, September 29). "Urban IIT goes to rural sector." *HRD Times*, 86.

Kaippachery, S. (2005). "Reforms and its impact on the SSIs: A field appraisal." *Journal on Rural Development*, 24(2): 213-226.

Mali, D.D. (2001). *Micro-enterprise Development—Policies and Programmes*. Guwahati: Indian Institute of Entrepreneurship.

Mandal, R. (2008). *Khadi and Village Industries in North East India with special reference to Arunachal Pradesh: Retrospect and Prospect*. Hyderabad: IUP.

MSMED Act, 2006. Ministry of Small Scale Industries. Notification, July 18, 2006, Government of India.

Nayak, P. and Dey, N.B. (1996). Productivity in small scale industry in Assam. *Yojana*, *40*(5): 48-52.

New Mudra Bank for micro- and small entrepreneurs (2015, June). *Competition Success Review*, 11.

Rajkonwar, A.B., and Neog, J. (2008). "Role of scheduled banks in the development of agricultural entrepreneurship in Karbi Anglong district of Assam". *DGCCS's Journal of Commerce*, *10*(1): 41-53.

Ramalingam, C. and Gayatri, R. (2006). "A Framework for Development of Rural Entrepreneurship in Tamil Nadu using innovation as strategic tool". Retrieved from http://www.indianmba.com/Faculty_Column/FC995/fc995.html

Santana, K.R. and Jegadeesan, G. (2008). *Entrepreneurship and Rural Development in India*. Hyderabad: IUP.

The World Bank Group (2001). "Microfinance and small-and-medium-sized-enterprises. Retrieved from www.worldbank.org/wbi/banking/microfinance.

Thomas, S. and Lavanya, V.L. (2012). "A study on the growth and performance of selected women entrepreneurs in Coimbatore district, Tamil Nadu". *The IUP Journal of Entrepreneurship Development*, *IX*(1): 80-88.

9
Spatial Variation in Private Tuition
An Explorative Analysis in Rural India

Abdul Basith Laskar

Introduction

In recent years, education is being considered as an important driver to create human capital and specially for achieving economic growth in a country. Realizing the importance of education in development of human capital and economic growth, policy-makers in developing countries like India have given substantial attention to education, especially elementary education. In this regard, in the year 2009 Right to Education (RTE) Act has been introduced in India to provide elementary education freely to all children between the age group of 6-14 years. In spite of the introduction of RTE Act, privatisation in education is taking place on two levels in India: on the official or formal level a large number of private schools are being established, while at the same time at the informal level a kind of shadow education (private tuition) system has been evolved which is out of reach of state control.

Private tutoring may be defined as a fee-based tutoring that provides supplementary instruction to children in academic subjects they study in the mainstream education system (Bray, 2006; Dang & Rogers, 2008). Educational institutions are the places where tuition is supposed to take place. The teachers and the students jointly participate in a classroom situation to achieve education. The education provision is such that in majority cases the students require study at home in order to supplement school education. It is done in the form of homework and learning what was asked by the school teachers. Studying at home requires tutoring support, which sometimes the parents, relatives or the household members provide and sometimes do not, so, an external support is often sought for this and such support is sometimes provided free of cost and often on a payment basis. Therefore, private tutoring means payment-based tutoring support to the students outside official school hour (Nath, 2006).

Thus, private supplementary tutoring refers to a kind of extra, fee-paying academic teaching or drilling for full-time students studying in regular school instruction programmes or syllabuses at all levels of education. It can complement and repeat what tutees (full-time students) have learned in their daytime schools. It can help them revise their daytime lessons and deepen their understanding of the underlying concepts or theories through drilling exercises. Its main functions are to help students cope with examinations and improve their academic achievements. There are several possible reasons for the growing phenomenon of private tutoring. First, private tutoring can be considered some form of private supplementary education: it thrives in countries where the public education system fails to satisfy the needs of the students (Kim & Lee, 2004). In this role, private tutoring is also popular in countries where passing examinations becomes the gateway to further education and advancement in society (Bray, 1999). Second, private tutoring can result from corruption in the education system in some developing countries, where teachers require their students to go to their extra classes to supplement their income because they are poorly paid and monitored (Biswal, 1999; Buchman, 1999). Although, there are possible reasons for taking paid tuition by the students, but in Indian context very limited research work has been conducted on the issue of extent and intensity of private tuition. Recognising this urgency, the present chapter makes an attempt to analyse the state-wise and region-wise variation of private tuition in rural India. Given this background, Section II deals with the global scenario of private tuition, Section III reveals data source and methodology of the study, next section analyses the results and findings of the study and the last section concludes the result with the provision of the future research gap.

Extent of Private Tutoring across Countries: An Empirical Overview

Private tutoring is not an issue unique to developing countries only. The prevalence of supplementary tutoring exists around the different countries of the world. Indeed, it is widespread and can be found in countries as diverse economically and geographically as Canada, Cambodia, Egypt, Greece, Japan, Kenya, Singapore, Taiwan, Morocco, Romania, the United Kingdom, the United States, and Zimbabwe. Empirical evidence demonstrates that in Mauritius, almost all senior secondary school students receive private tutoring. In Japan, 70 per cent of students receive such tutoring by the time they complete middle school; 83 per cent students in Malaysia receive tutoring by the time they reach senior secondary school (Bray, 2006; Dang & Rogers, 2008). In South Korea, Kim and Lee (2004) found that parents spent an amount approximately equal to 2.9 per cent of the nation's GDP on private tutoring for primary and secondary students. In Turkey, aggregate expenditure on private tutoring is 1.44 per cent of GDP, and is comparable to total public sector educational spending (Tansel & Bircan, 2006). Dang (2007) conducted a study in Vietnam and noted that supplementary is organised by students' parents, teachers, schools and specialist centres. About 70 per cent of students receiving tutoring at their own schools, 26 per cent receive classes at the tutors' homes, and the remainder attends classes in their own homes or elsewhere. A 2006-07 survey by the Bangladesh Bureau of Statistics identified 5,499 coaching centres in the country with 67,200 full-time and 44,800 part-time employees. Only 7 per cent of the centres had government approval to operate (Nath, 2011). Another report published by Thailand Government, Ministry of Education in 2013 and indicated that 1,964 private tutoring institutions were registered in 2011, among which 77.6 per cent were in Bangkok and the rest were in other parts of the country. In Taiwan, Chou and Ching (2012) indicated that there were around 18,300 registered 'cram schools', 15,248 of which focused on traditional school subjects such as Chinese, English and the Sciences. Elementary and junior high school students were particularly targeted, and comprised 84 per cent of the total enrolment. Most of these schools were "examination-oriented private institutions that focus on drills and practice", but some had curricula which were not directly related to the regular school system. In these institutions the tutor "provides a group of students with a programme designed only for a specific subject or course, such as a foreign language, essay writing, calligraphy, music, art, dancing, and sports, among others."

Methodology

Data Source

The study is based on secondary data collected from various issues of "Annual Status of Education Report" (ASER), 2013. ASER has started its journey since 2005. This report is being published by Pratham in every year and is basically a Non-Governmental Organisation (NGO). It collects data on various issues in connection with education such as enrolment ratio including boys and girls in government and private schools, and judge the quality of education by asking several questions on the basis of their ability to read and write. Today the scale and scope of the reports have widened significantly, but for a first time exercise, it was bold and unparalleled in scale; quite simply, nobody had ever attempted anything like it before. Most striking of all was its intent, captured by the "Preamble" to the report. "We, the people of India, from different states and regions, speaking different languages, sat with our children and looked within, inside our homes, at our villages, into our schools, and prepared this report for ourselves, to build a better India." This was what set ASER apart from donor-funded or government surveys—it was a report of the people, by the people, for the people.

Methods

In order to analyse regional variation of private tuition in rural India, analysis of variance (ANOVA) test has been used which is also popularly known as an F-test. It is to be noted that t-statistic is used for testing whether two population means are equal. The ANOVA test may, therefore, be taken as an extension of the t-statistic for the case of more than two groups. Moreover, to have a clear idea about the variation across major regions of the states, bar diagram has been used.

Results and Findings

Intensity of Private Tuition in India

The empirical study on the issue of private tuition is very limited in India and exact numbers of the students who receive it are not available. Although Sujatha (2014) examines the extent of private tuition in secondary education by collecting the data from Thiruvananthapuram, Pune, Nalgonda and Varanasi districts in four States, viz. Kerala, Maharashtra, Andhra Pardesh, and Uttar Pradesh respectively. Out of the total number of students covered in the study (4,031), around 45 per cent students were seeking private tutoring for one or more subjects at secondary level (Grades IX–X). The extent of private tuition varies among four sampled states, ranging from 55 per cent to 32.26 per cent. Out of four sampled States, Kerala, an educationally progressive state, has the highest percentage of students going for private tuition at secondary level (55%), followed by Maharashtra (49.35%), which is both industrially and educationally developed. In Andhra Pradesh, the percentage of students taking private tuition is the lowest (32.26%), while Uttar Pradesh (46.67%) has been just behind Maharashtra.

However, this study may not be nationally representative as it considers only four districts under four States. Therefore, in order to make the extent of private tutoring nationally representative, we have adapted from Annual Status of Education Report (ASER), 2013. The report reveals that between the age group of 6-14 around 24 per cent students receive paid tuition classes in the elementary level in rural India.

Figure 9.1 demonstrates the state-wise intensity of private tuition in rural India. Intensity of private tuition is observed to be highest in West Bengal (80.53%) followed by Tripura (76%) and Bihar (60%) and Odisha (52%), while it is lowest in Chhattisgarh (1.68%), followed by Mizoram (3.83%) and Rajasthan (3.95%).

Regional Variation of Private Tuition in Rural India

In the present chapter the regional variation in private tuition has been analysed in terms of three categories of school type, viz., Government schools, private schools and all schools, i.e. both government and private schools taken together.

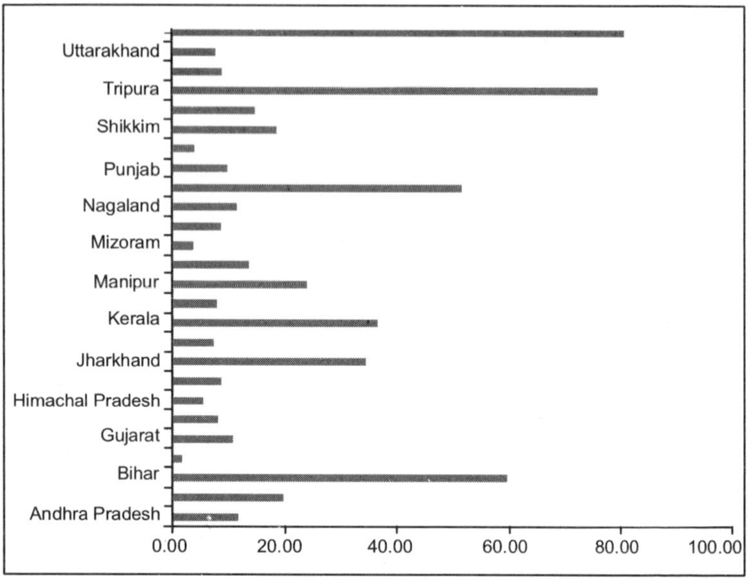

Fig. 9.1: Percentage of Students Receive Paid Tuition Classes
Source: Calculated by Authors.

Regional Variation of Private Tuition in Government Schools

Table 9.1 summarizes the regional variation of PT in government schools only. The F-statistics reflect that the variation across the region is statistically significant. It is noticed that the extent of PT is highest in eastern region followed by NER and southern region throughout the time period. On the other hand, the intensity of PT is lower in central region followed by northern region. However, the variation of PT is quite high in NER followed by eastern and southern region, while the variation is low in central region followed by northern region throughout the time points.

Regional Variation of Private Tuition in Private Schools

Table 9.2 represents the regional variation of PT in private schools. The F-statistic reflects that the variation across the region is statistically significant. It is also depicted from Table 9.2 that the extent of private tuition is higher in eastern region followed by

Table 9.1: Regional Variation of Private Tuition in Government Schools

Region	*2010*	*2011*	*2012*	*2013*	*Average*
NER	24.94 (645.76)	26.66 (597.68)	23.23 (646.27)	21.13 (470.62)	23.99 (568.76)
EAST	57.28 (317.95)	55.93 (382.73)	56.15 (387.90)	56.98 (373.99)	56.58 (363.74)
CENTRAL	7.20 (20.11)	6.13 (17.16)	6.33 (15.41)	6.47 (22.49)	6.53 (17.72)
WEST	9.35 (2.20)	10.55 (3.13)	9.35 (2.20)	8.65 (11.05)	9.48 (4.06)
SOUTH	20.55 (265.04)	18.58 (169.84)	17.30 (138.18)	14.68 (120.07)	17.78 (167.68)
NORTH	8.66 (7.34)	6.77 (5.55)	6.68 (6.78)	7.35 (7.70)	7.37 (4.81)
F- STAT	4.60*	5.43*	5.20*	6.69*	5.66*

Note: (*) indicates significant at the 1 per cent level.
Values in parenthesis represent variance.

Source: Calculated by Authors.

NER and southern region throughout the time periods, whereas the extent of PT is lower in central region followed by northern region. However, the variation of PT is high in NER followed by eastern and southern region, while the variation is low in central region followed by northern region throughout the time points.

Table 9.2: Regional Variation of Private Tuition in Private Schools

Region	*2010*	*2011*	*2012*	*2013*	*Average*
NER	29.68 (372.83)	34.52 (236.09)	32.94 (223.20)	25.40 (221.54)	30.64 (240.38)
EAST	57.70 (111.97)	55.73 (203.44)	59.83 (86.10)	59.37 (283.70)	58.16 (158.19)
CENTRAL	18.83 (75.96)	14.50 (39.63)	14.97 (19.26)	15.37 (34.10)	15.92 (28.61)
WEST	23.95 (198.01)	30.80 (512.00)	28.75 (394.81)	26.25 (356.45)	27.44 (355.78)
SOUTH	28.10 (130.43)	26.78 (75.55)	26.83 (57.04)	20.83 (53.49)	25.63 (73.58)
NORTH	24.40 (30.64)	22.37 (85.87)	22.68 (97.82)	22.45 (104.04)	23.10 (70.81)
F- STAT	3.62**	4.19**	5.92*	5.10*	5.01*

Note: (*), (**) indicates significant at the 1 per cent level.
Values in parenthesis represent variance.

Source: Calculated by Authors.

Regional Variation of Private Tuition in All Schools

Table 9.3 depicts the regional variation of PT in all schools. The F-statistics reflect that the variation across the region is statistically significant. It reveals that the extent of PT is highest in eastern region followed by NER and southern region throughout the time periods. On the other hand, the extent of PT is lower in central region followed by northern region. However, the variation of PT is quite high in NER followed by eastern and southern region, while the variation is low in central region followed by northern region throughout the time points.

Table 9.3: Regional Variation of Private Tuition in all Schools

Region	*2010*	*2011*	*2012*	*2013*	*Average*
NER	31.43 (624.72)	33.81 (555.92)	30.03 (568.66)	25.87 (438.83)	30.29 (538.35)
EAST	57.63 (303.78)	56.18 (362.69)	56.75 (352.06)	57.45 (355.58)	57.00 (341.59)
CENTRAL	9.67 (33.58)	8.13 (30.77)	8.57 (29.10)	9.17 (48.40)	8.88 (33.12)
WEST	12.20 (2.42)	13.85 (6.13)	13.00 (2.00)	12.70 (11.52)	12.94 (4.88)
SOUTH	22.20 (225.52)	20.50 (137.89)	19.90 (120.81)	16.00 (100.05)	19.65 (141.48)
NORTH	13.08 (11.95)	11.45 (17.91)	12.05 (23.46)	12.90 (28.49)	12.48 (17.38)
F- STAT	4.37*	5.37*	5.12*	6.02*	5.31*

Note: (*) indicates significant at the 1 per cent level.
Values in parenthesis represent variance.

Source: Calculated by Authors.

Thus, it is found that there is a high variation in private tuition across all the regions in India. In all categories of schools, viz. private, government and all schools it is found that the extent of private tuition is higher in Eastern region followed by North Eastern Region, while it is lower in central region followed by Northern region in all the time points. However, in all the regions the prevalence of private tuition has been observed to be largest in private schools as seen in Fig. 9.2.

Conclusion

It has been observed that there are large variations in private tuition

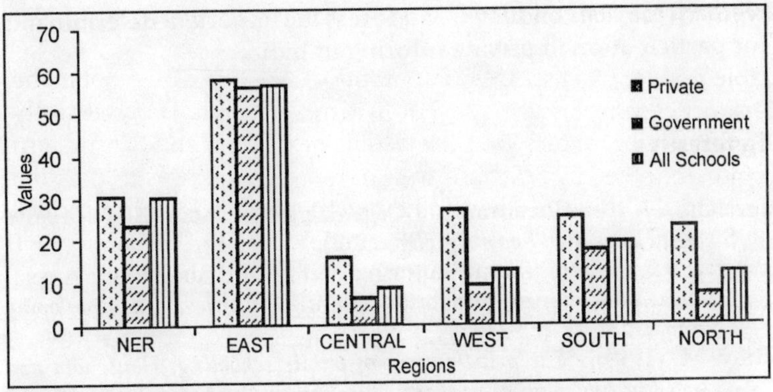

Fig. 9.2: Overall Regional Variation in Private Tuition
Source: Calculated by Author.

across the major states of India. It is observed to be highest in West Bengal followed by Tripura, while it is lowest in Chhattisgarh followed by Mizoram. However, in the context of regional perspective the intensity of private tuition is found to be highest in eastern region followed by northeastern region and it is lowest in the central region. However, section 28 of the RTE Act 2009 states that, "No teacher shall engage himself or herself in private tuition or private teaching activity", banning all teachers, irrespective of whether they work in government or private elementary schools, from taking private tuition. Although the Act does not allow such kind of paid tuition, there is a huge prevalence of private tuition in almost all the states in India. Thus, present study reflects that most of the states are just making mockery to the RTE Act, 2009.

Therefore, the growth of private tutoring should not be ignored in the developing country like India. There may be different factors, including demand and supply that likely to encourage growth of private tuition. They include the value placed on educational qualifications in the global market, high rates of participation in Higher Education, rising educational levels in the population as a whole and parents' increasing affluence. Tutoring is likely to become an important phenomenon with the potential for distorting the education system. It will present a major equity issue, conferring significant disadvantages of those who are unable to afford the cost of tutors. It is time to develop more systematic monitoring and evaluation of the shadow education system. Future research may be conducted to address the important determinants for participation in private tutoring in India.

References

Pratham—A Non-Governmental Organization in India (2013), *Annual Status of Education Report* (ASER, 2013).

Biswal, B.P. (1999). "Private tutoring and public corruption: A cost-effective education system for developing countries." *The Developing Economies*, 37(2): 222-240.

Bray, M. (1999). *"The private costs of public schooling: Household and community financing of primary education in Cambodia.* International Institute of Educational Planning: Paris.

Bray, M. (2006). Private supplementary tutoring: Comparative perspectives on patterns and implications." *Compare*, 36(4), 515-530.

Buchman, C. (1999). "The state and schooling in Kenya: Historical development and current challenges." *Africa Today*, 46(1): 95-116.

Chou, C.P., and Ching, G. (2012): *Taiwan education at the crossroad: When globalization meets localization*. New York: Palgrave MacMillan.

Dang, H.A. (2007). "The determinants and impact of private tutoring classes in Vietnam". *Economics of Education Review*. 26 (6), 1-50.

Dang, H.A., and Rogers, F.H. (2008). "The growing phenomenon of private tutoring: Does it deepen human capital; widen inequalities, or waste resources?" *Oxford University Press*, 23(1): 161-200.

Kim, S., and Lee, J.H. (2004). *Private tutoring and demand for education in South Korea*. Available at http://www.journals.uchicago.edu/doi/pdf/10.1086/648186 (Accessed 25 February, 2015).

Nath, R.S. (2006). *Private supplementary tutoring among primary students in Bangladesh*. Brac Research and Evaluation Division. Available at http://www.bracresearch.org/reports/Private_Supplementary.pdf (Accessed 26 February, 2015).

Nath, S.R. (2011). "Private tutoring". *The Daily Star*, 21 August. Available at http://archive.thedailystar.net/newDesign/news-details.php?nid=199463 (Accessed 26 February, 2015).

Sujatha, K. (2014). "Private tuition in India: Trends and issues". *Revue international ed'éducation de Sèvres*. Available at https://ries.revues.org/3913 (Accessed 26 February, 2015).

Tansel, A. and Bircan, F. (2006). "Demand for education in Turkey: A Tobit analysis of private tutoring expenditures". *Economics of Education Review*, 25 (3): 303-313.

10
Informality in Non-Cultivation Labour Market in India with Special Reference to North East India

Bhaskar Jyoti Neog and *Bimal Kishore Sahoo*

Introduction

Labour informality is a very pertinent issue in the current development debate. Its importance is even more in a developing country like India with a significant section of the population living below the poverty line and meagre public provisions for unemployment insurance. This makes unemployment a very unviable alternative for a common man and he is forced to take up whatever opportunities that comes in his way. In such a scenario looking at the overall unemployment rates does not provide a very informative picture of the labour market in the country as a large section of such employment is likely to be of a bare subsistence nature. Hence, it is important to look at the quality of work of the employed which brings to the forefront the issue of labour informality.

The present study examines the trends and determinants of informality in India. Labour informality as a concept has a history going back to the 1970s. Keith Hart, a British ethnographer is credited with discovering the phenomenon and it was he who coined the term 'informal sector'. At about the same time, International Labour Organisation (ILO) launched a number of studies on the phenomenon in Africa (Jütting, Parlevliet, & Xenogiani, 2008). The early conceptualisation of the concept highlighted the informal economy as a residual sector distinct from the formal economy. In the late 1980s, the structuralist school highlighted the close relation between the formal and the informal economy. Still others have emphasized on the role of institutional bottlenecks in creating the incentives to work informally (Chen, 2012). Although, there is diversified opinion on the drivers of informality, we can put the different views under two broad groups—informality by choice and informality as exclusion (Perry, Maloney, Arias, Fajnzylber, & Saavedra-chanduvi, 2010). The former premise emphasize the voluntary nature of informality as workers engage in informal work to escape burdensome government taxes and regulations involved in working formally (Maloney, 2004). On the other hand, the later premise stress the marginal nature of the phenomenon as workers in the absence of decent jobs and unemployment protection are forced to take up job in the informal sector (Chen, Vanek, Lund, Heintz, & Christine, 2005). Some authors take a more nuanced view contending that both the forms of informality may persist in an economy in varying degrees (Perry *et al.*, 2010). Given the diverging views on the drivers of informality, the present study examines the determinants of the phenomenon over time which can provide us with more information on the factors contributing to the phenomenon.

Although the earlier conceptualisation of informality relies on dividing workers on a dichotomous; workers in reality face varying degrees of informality, the most formal of which enjoy multiple degrees of protection, the least formal none at all (ILO, 2004). In line with the above argument, the study develops an informality index emphasising the phenomenon in a continuous scale.

Finally, we study the macro-determinants of informality by exploring the variation in the rates of informality across states with respect to various state specific macro-variables. The literature on informality ascribes various causes to its prevalence and rise. On the one hand, the proponents of the dualist school highlight the marginal nature of informality associated with poverty and underdevelopment; on the other hand, the neo-liberal school emphasize the role of excessive government regulations and taxes for the rising incidence of informality. Similarly, the structuralist school sees rising contractualisation, casualisation of employment relationships along with a declining role of the public sector associated with the increasing spread of globalisation as one of the drivers of informality (Chen, 2012). Several other studies have also highlighted the role of other factors such as inequality, quality of government services as well as GDP growth in driving informality (Oviedo, Thomas, & Karakurum-Özdemir, 2009; Perry *et al.*, 2010). We investigate the validity of these contradictory hypotheses in India using various state level macro-variables.

The chapter is divided into four Sections. Section 2 discusses the data and the methodology. Section three discusses the results of the study including the descriptive statistics, multinomial logistic analysis and panel econometrics. Section 4 provides the conclusion.

Data Sources and Methodology

The study uses unit level data from the National Sample Survey Organization (NSSO) Employment-Unemployment Survey (EUS) for two time periods 2004-05 and 2011-12. The EUS for the two rounds contains information on the enterprise size and the availability of social security benefits of the workers. It also has information on other variables depicting quality of work, such as union membership, regularity of job etc. We utilise this information to distinguish workers into the formal and informal economy. Further, it provides individual and household level information which we utilize for further analysis. The study also uses data on state-level macro-variables like Gross State Domestic Product (GSDP), total tax revenue, total government expenditure etc. from the Reserve Bank of India (RBI). Similarly, we use data on electricity demand, road infrastructure, and crime statistics from the Reports of respective departments.

The study defines informality in two ways—

1. A sector based definition considering the size of the enterprise as a criterion; and
2. An employment based definition considering the presence of social security benefits as a criterion.

Efforts to generate statistics on the informal economy at a national level led to the definition of the informal sector by the 15th International Conference of Labour Statisticians (ICLS) as consisting of small-scale unincorporated units with low level of capital and organisation and characterised by non-contractual employment arrangements without formal protection. However, such an enterprise based definition of the informal economy was criticised on the ground that it excluded a large and growing section of precarious employment engaged in formal enterprises. Hence, the Delhi Group along with "Women in Informal Employment: Globalizing and Organizing" (WIEGO) concluded that the enterprise based definition needs to be complemented by an employment based criterion. In line with these efforts, the ILO as part of its Report "Decent Work and the Informal Economy" suggested a conceptual framework for defining and measuring the informal economy, which was finally ratified by the 17th ICLS (ILO, 2002). The 17th ICLS defined informal employment as the total number of informal jobs, whether carried out in formal sector enterprises, informal sector enterprises, or households, during a given reference period. A pioneering study on the definitional and statistical issues relating to the informal economy in India was conducted by the 'National Commission for Enterprises in the Unorganized Sector' (NCEUS) using NSSO data (NCEUS, 2008). We have used the NCEUS methodology modifying it suitably for our purpose of classifying workers into the formal and informal economy. We discuss this methodology further in the Appendix I to this chapter. We carry out our analysis excluding the workers engaged in the cultivation of crops in agriculture as information on availability of social security benefits as well as enterprise type or number of workers in the enterprise is not available for such workers. Hence, our analysis is for the non-cultivation workforce in the economy.

The study also develops a labour informality index which helps us to study informality in a continuum. The methodology to develop our labour informality index has been borrowed extensively from ILO, 2004, although we make slight modifications to it to suit our data. The labour informality index has been developed based on five criterions as follows:

(i) *Regularity Status*: A value of 1 is given if a person is in regular wage labour or registered self-employment in the organised sector; 0 otherwise.
(ii) *Contract status*: A value of 1 if the person has a written employment contract (more than 12 months); 0 otherwise.

(iii) *Workplace status*: A value of 1 if the person works in or around a fixed workplace, be it an enterprise, factory, office or shop; 0 otherwise.

(iv) *Employment protection status*: Under this criterion we consider whether a worker is protected against arbitrary dismissal. Due to lack of availability of suitable data, we take eligibility for paid leave as a proxy for this variable. Hence, we impute a value of 1 if the worker is eligible for paid leave; 0 otherwise.

(v) *Social protection status*: A value of 1 if entitled to paid medical care, whether paid by the employer or by medical insurance; 0 otherwise.

The labour informality continuum, obtained by summing up the values of the five criterions, has a range of values from 0 to 5. Each element is given the same weight. The resultant labour informality spectrum is defined as follows: totally informal = 0 (no criteria met); highly informal = 1; moderately informal = 2; moderately formal = 3; highly formal = 4; totally formal = 5 (all criteria met).

We use binomial Logit model to study the determinants of informality. Our model is of the following basic form:

$$y = \alpha + \sum_{j=1}^{k} \beta_j X_j + u,$$

where, y is our dependent variable and y = 1, if the worker is informally employed, and y = 0, if the worker is formally employed. Also, β_j and X_j are the k independent variables in our model.

Let p_i be the probability for y = 1 so that the probability for y = 0 is given by $(1 - p_i)$. Now, the expected value of y is given by,

$$E(y_i) = 0^*(1-p) + 1^*p = pi.$$

Hence, $E(y_i = 1 \mid X_i) = \alpha_t \sum_{i=1}^{k} \beta_i X_i = p_i$.

In the logit model, the functional form of $p_i = E(y_i = 1 \mid X_i)$ is given by,

$$p_i = E(y_i = 1 \mid X_i) = \frac{1}{1+e^{-(\alpha+\sum_{i=1}^{k}\beta_i X_i)}} = \frac{1}{1+e^{-z_i}},$$

where $z_i = e^{-(\alpha+\sum_{i=1}^{k}\beta_i X_i)}$. ... (1)

For ease of exposition, we can write (1) as, $P_i = \frac{1}{1+e^{-z_i}} = \frac{e^{z_i}}{1+e^{-z_i}}$,

Also, $\frac{p_i}{1-p_i} = z_i$,

Taking log we have $L_i = \ln\left(\frac{p_i}{1-p_i}\right) = z_i = \alpha + \sum_{i=1}^{k} \beta_i X_i$

It can be shown that as z_i ranges from $-\infty$ to ∞, p_i ranges from 0 to 1. Also, p_i is non-linearly related to z_i or X_i. The above model is then evaluated through Maximum Likelihood method to yield our estimates. The literature suggests a number of determinants of informality among them being age, years of education, technical education, household income, religion, social group, gender, marital status, sector and industry (Bairagya, 2012; Henley, Arabsheibani, & Carneiro, 2009; Yu, 2012). We consider the impact of these variables on informality in our model. We include both age and its square in our model as we hypothesize a quadratic relation of age with informality. However, taking both age and its square creates the problem with multicollinearity. Hence, we deduct from age its mean and take the demean age and its square in our model which solves our multicollinearity problem. Similarly, in order to bring out the effect of education we utilise the information on the education status of workers. However, rather than taking dummies for different educational levels we derive a continuous variable depicting the mean years of education of the workers. The methodology used to arrive at this variable is discussed in the Appendix II to the chapter. In order to capture the effect of technical education on informality, we take a dummy for the presence or absence of technical education in our model. Monthly Per Capita Consumption Expenditure (MPCE) of the household is taken as a proxy for household income in our model. Rather than taking absolute MPCE levels, we take the natural logarithm of MPCE in our model as it helps to reduce the scale and dispersion of the variable and makes it normally distributed. We also look at the incidence of poverty across various poverty groups. The derivation of poverty groups is discussed in the Appendix III to the chapter.

Among the socio-economic variables included in our model are religion and social group. We consider three broad religions for our study—Hindu, Islam and 'Others', which includes all other religions. We include separate dummies for all the religions except Hindus, which we take as the reference category. Similarly, we create separate dummies for the social groups excluding 'Others' which we consider as the reference category. We also have separate dummies for gender (male/female) and sector (rural/urban) for our study. We interpret our results taking females and urban as the reference categories respectively. Similarly, for marital status we divide the workforce into two groups—never married and married, where all currently married, divorced and widowed workers are clubbed together into a single category. We interpret our results against the base category of never married workers. Finally, we also include dummies for the industrial affiliation of the workers. The industrial affiliation of the workers can be obtained from the National Industrial Classification (NIC) code of the respective workers available in the NSSO data. We divide workers into 7 broad industries, viz. 'Agriculture' (excluding Cultivation workers); 'Mining, Electricity and Water Supply'; 'Manufacturing'; 'Construction'; 'Trade, Hotels and Transportation'; and 'Finance, Insurance and Real Estate'. We create separate dummies for all the above industries except for 'Trade, Hotels and Transportation', which we consider as our reference category.

Finally, we examine the determinants of informality at the macro-level using panel econometrics. The incidence of informality across states is measured by the proportion of the non-cultivation workforce informally employed in each state. We use various macro-level variables as determinants of informality across states. In doing so, the study makes an attempt to examine the strength of alternative hypotheses of different schools of thought in explaining the occurrence of informality in the country. Similar studies have tried to study the relative weight of alternative theories in explaining the cross-country variation in informality (Hazans, 2011; ILO, 2012; Perry *et al.*, 2010; Williams, 2013, 2015). These studies have found do not favour any particular hypothesis, but find multiple factors driving informality. The various macro-level variables used in our study are discussed below:

(a) In order to examine the argument of the dualist school that informality is associated with high poverty and underdevelopment, we consider per capita Gross State Domestic Product (GSDP) as well as Poverty rates at the state level.

(b) In order to examine the soundness of the neo-liberal school that informality is associated with burdensome governmental regulations and taxes, we take into account the Tax-GSDP ratio of the state.

(c) Similarly, the validity of the structuralist view of rising informality associated with lower governmental intervention is examined taking into consideration the Expenditure-GSDP ratio of the state.

(d) Lastly, we also consider the state level Gini co-efficient, last 3-year growth rate as well as an index of government quality to measure the impact of inequality, growth and quality of public services respectively on informality rates.

We collect data on all the variables for the years 2004-05 and 2011-12. We have excluded the Union Territories from our analysis. We also merge the six geographically contagious North Eastern States of Manipur, Meghalaya, Mizoram, Nagaland, Sikkim and Arunachal Pradesh as these states have individually small sample sizes. In all we have data on 23 state regions for two-time periods. The calculation of the different variables used in our macro study is discussed in Appendix IV. Finally, we discuss our panel econometric methodology:

Breusch-Pagan test as well as Hausman test applied on our model suggests that fixed-effects model would be appropriate for our data. Our fixed-effects panel data model is then given by,

$$y_{it} = \alpha_i + \sum_{j=1}^{k} \beta_{jit} X_{jit} + \varepsilon_{it} \qquad \ldots (2)$$

where, i indexes individuals, t indexes time periods and β_j's and X_j's are the k independent variables in our model. In the fixed effects model, we allow the intercept term to vary across individuals so that α_i would capture the unobserved heterogeneity across individuals. Also, we allow α_i to be correlated with the X_j's Averaging (2) over time yields,

$$\bar{y}_{it} = \alpha_i + \sum_{j=1}^{k} \beta_{jit} \bar{X}_{jit} + \bar{\varepsilon}_{it} \qquad \ldots (3)$$

Subtracting (3) from (2), we get,

$$\left(y_{it}-\overline{y}_{it}\right)=\sum_{j=1}^{k}\beta_{jit}\left(X_{jit}-\overline{X}_{jit}\right)+\left(\overline{\varepsilon}_{it}-\overline{\varepsilon}_{it}\right) \quad \ldots (4)$$

The individual-specific effects captured by α_i terms cancel each other as they are invariant over time. Applying OLS to the final model in (3), we arrive at our fixed-effect estimates.

Results and Discussion

Trends of Informality

We first take a look at the overall rates of informality in the country: Labour Informality seems to be quite high in the Indian scenario with around 87 per cent of the non-cultivation workers being employed under informal working conditions in 2004-05. Although, this figure fell to around 85 per cent in 2011-12, labour informality is still significant. Similarly, percentage of non-cultivation workers working in the unorganised sector is also substantial at 75 per cent in 2004-05 which fell down significantly to 68 per cent in 2011-12. Looking at the composition of employment within the organised sector, we find that around half of the organised sector workers are informally employed in 2004-05, a figure which rose to 57 per cent in 2011-12. These figures highlight the rising informalisation of the workforce within the formal sector. Although, the proportion of unorganised sector workers engaged informally is insignificant at around 6 per cent in 2004-05, it still rose slightly to around 7 per cent in 2011-12.

Table 10.1: Labour Informality in India

	2004-05			*2011-12*		
	Formal	*Informal*	*Total*	*Formal*	*Informal*	*Total*
Organised	49.93	50.07	24.82	43.05	56.95	31.58
Unorganised	1.01	98.99	75.18	1.57	98.43	68.42
Total	**13.15**	**86.85**	**100**	**14.68**	**85.32**	**100**

Source: Authors' calculation based on NSSO data.

If we look at the composition of informality across usual status we find that own-account employees, unpaid family workers and casual workers consist entirely of the informally employed in both the periods. Around 87 per cent of the self-employed employers are informally employed, whereas around 55 per cent of the regular workers are informally employed. The picture is similar for 2011-12 with no significant changes in the rates of informality.

Table 10.2: Informality across Usual Status

Year	*2004-05*		*2011-12*	
Usual Status	*Formal*	*Informal*	*Formal*	*Informal*
Own-account workers	0	100	0	100
Employers	13.98	86.02	12.99	87.01
Unpaid family worker	0	100	0	100
Regular Workers	43.97	56.03	44.32	55.68
Casual Workers (Public Works)	4.02	95.98	1.87	98.13
Casual Workers (Other Works)	1.39	98.61	1.21	98.79
Total	**13.15**	**86.85**	**14.68**	**85.32**

Source: Authors' calculation based on NSSO data.

Table 10.3: Informality across Educational Levels

Years of Education	*2004-05*		*2011-12*	
	Formal	*Informal*	*Formal*	*Informal*
Below 6 Years	3.74	96.26	3.41	96.59
6 to 12 Years	15.06	84.94	13.11	86.89
13 Years and above	46.1	53.9	48.86	51.14
Total	**13.15**	**86.85**	**14.68**	**85.32**

Source: Authors' calculation based on NSSO data.

Similarly, the analysis of educational levels of informality can give us some idea on the skills of the workers in the different groups. Looking across educational levels, we find the prevalence of informality falling drastically as one move towards higher educational levels with informality rates falling from a high of above 95 per cent for those with primary education or below to a low of around 50 per cent for those with at least a diploma. Over the period, we see stagnant or rising informality in the lower or intermediate educational levels whereas informality is seen to fall at the higher educational levels (Table 10.3). Informality is also found to be significantly higher among workers without technical education. There is also an evident decline in informality among all workers over the period, especially among those without a technical education.

Table 10.4: Informality across Technical Education

Year	*2004-05*		*2011-12*	
Technical Education	*Formal*	*Informal*	*Formal*	*Informal*
Have	47.58	52.42	55.37	44.63
Don't Have	11.36	88.64	12.54	87.46
Total	**13.15**	**86.85**	**14.67**	**85.33**

Source: Authors' calculation based on NSSO data.

Next, we try to look at the dynamics of informality across ages. Here, we may consider age as an amalgam of the on-the-job-skills of the workers, his experience over the years as well as his social contacts accumulated. Hence, the relation of informality with age might give us an inkling of the possible lifecycle dynamics of the workers as workers move between jobs over the lifetime. The incidence of informality across age groups shows a distinct U-shaped pattern with informality falling from a high level with rising age before rising among the elderly. Probing on it further, we find that the U-shaped patter is evident only for the wage employment category which makes the overall pattern U-shaped. Hence, we presume that the U-shaped pattern may reflect the aggregation of the internal heterogeneity within the informal economy. We hypothesize that informality is higher in lower ages as people queue in the informal sector for better jobs. As they accumulate skills, experience and contacts they get employed in the formal sector. However, as age rise beyond a certain point, informality tends to which may reflect the weight of rising probability of informality among the employers and own-account workers in the higher ages. The incidence of informality is also found to have declined over the period across all age groups (*see* Table 10.5).

Table 10.5: Informality across Age

Year	2004-05		2011-12	
Age	Formal	Informal	Formal	Informal
Below 15	0.58	99.42	0.28	99.72
16–25	4.12	95.88	7.86	92.14
26–35	12.12	87.88	14.56	85.44
36–45	18.68	81.32	16.75	83.25
46–60	24.88	75.12	22.61	77.39
61 and above	1.64	98.36	2.66	97.34
Total	**13.15**	**86.85**	**14.68**	**85.32**

Source: Authors' calculation based on NSSO data.

If we look at the spatial composition of informality, we find that although 56 per cent of workers live in rural areas in 2004-05, it accounts for 60 per cent of informal workers. Labour informality is quite high in rural areas with more than 91 per cent of rural workers working informally in both the periods. The corresponding figures for urban areas are close to 80 per cent. Further, labour informality seems to have declined marginally in both rural and urban areas over the period 2004-05 to 2011-12. The gender composition of informality shows that informality among women to be higher than men in both the the periods. We also see a marginal decline in informality among women, even though it is more or less stagnant among men.

Table 10.6: Informality across Sectors and Gender

Indicators		2004-05		2011-12	
		Formal	Informal	Formal	Informal
Sector	Rural	8.02	91.98	9.03	90.97
	Urban	19.86	80.14	21.37	78.63
Gender	Male	15.04	84.96	15.61	84.39
	Female	8.11	91.89	11.58	88.42
Total		**13.15**	**86.85**	**14.68**	**85.32**

Source: Authors' calculation based on NSSO data.

The incidence of informality across castes and religions should also throw some light as to whether it is restricted to some social groups. The incidence of informality is significantly higher for backward classes like SCs, STs and OBCs compared to the higher classes. We also see informality to be falling over the period for all the social classes. Looking across religions we find informal employment to be higher for Muslims compared to Hindus and other religions over both the periods. Informality is also seen to be falling over the period for all religions except Muslims.

Table 10.7: Informality across Caste and Religion

		2004-05		2011-12	
		Formal	*Informal*	*Formal*	*Informal*
Caste	Scheduled Tribes	11.99	88.01	14.93	85.07
	Scheduled Castes	10.84	89.16	11.07	88.93
	Other Backward Castes	9.83	90.17	11.86	88.14
	Others	18.42	81.58	20.53	79.47
Religion	Hindu	14.19	85.81	16.08	83.92
	Muslim	5.92	94.08	5.93	94.07
	Others	15.73	84.27	18.69	81.31
Total		**13.15**	**86.85**	**14.67**	**85.33**

Source: Authors' calculation based on NSSO data.

Many authors consider informality and poverty as synonymous. On the other hand, others consider incomes to be significantly higher for informal workers especially the self-employed relative to the formal economy. Hence, looking at the poverty rates of the workers across informal categories may give us some insight into the nature of the sector. The incidence of informality is seen to fall drastically as we move towards higher income classes in both periods. However, the incidence of informality is seen to rise marginally over the period in all MPCE classes except in the lowest group where it is more or less stagnant (*see* Table 10.8).

Considering the prevalence of informality across broad industries for 2004-05, we find that the incidence of informality is the highest for agriculture with nearly 99 per cent of the workers working informally, followed by manufacturing and services. Looking across narrow industrial groups, we see high informality in Agriculture; Construction; Trade, Hotels and Transportation; and Manufacturing Industries. It is found to be significantly lower in the other industries. Over the period, informality is seen to be

Table 10.8: Informality across Poverty Groups

	2004-05		2011-12	
	Formal	*Informal*	*Formal*	*Informal*
Very Poor	3.34	96.66	3.74	96.26
Poor	6.97	93.03	5.64	94.36
Marginal	10.94	89.06	8.75	91.25
Vulnerable	20.34	79.66	16.91	83.09
Middle Class and above	41.19	58.81	36.21	63.79
Total	**13.15**	**86.85**	**14.68**	**85.32**

Source: Authors' calculation based on NSSO data.

falling for all industries except for Commercial, Social and Personal Services and Mining, Electricity and Water Supply. The fall is especially significant for Finance, Insurance and Real Estate (*see* Table 10.9).

Table 10.9: Informality across Industries

	2004-05		2011-12	
	Formal	*Informal*	*Formal*	*Informal*
Agriculture	0.65	99.35	1.35	98.65
Manufacturing	10.68	89.32	12.28	87.72
Construction	1.95	98.05	2.25	97.75
Trade Hotels and Transportation	5.71	94.29	8.96	91.04
Finance, Insurance and Real Estate	33.06	66.94	45.44	54.56
Commercial, Social and Personal Services	41.09	58.91	38.98	61.02
Mining, Electricity and Water Supply	44.88	55.12	40.01	59.99
Total	**13.15**	**86.85**	**14.68**	**85.32**

Source: Authors' calculation based on NSSO data.

Informality as a Continuum

So far we have discussed informality as the presence or absence of particular work related benefits such as pensions or medical benefits. The enterprise-based definition, which hinges on the size of the enterprise also divides the workers in a dichotomous scale. However, as discussed earlier, informality can be seen in a continuous scale of the presence of a number of considerations such as job contact, location of workplace, eligibility for paid leave apart from pensions and social security benefits. Considering all these measures we created a scale of informality which measures the magnitude of informality so that lower the value in the scale, higher is the informality.

Looking at this informality scale we find that the more informal a worker is the more likely he is to be working in the unorganised sector. Further, higher informality is more likely to be associated with women and workers from rural areas. Interestingly however, totally informal workers are disproportionally male. Higher informality is also more likely to be associated with lower levels of education. Further, higher castes and Hindus are considerably more formal compared to the other groups. Looking across poverty groups, we find that the more informal groups are markedly more poor compared to the formal groups. Finally, we find that the informal groups have a significantly younger workforce. Moreover, these groups also have a sizeable proportion of elderly among them. The results show that the Informality Continuum Index closely corresponds with other dichotomous measures of informality.

Determinants of Informality

We finally discuss the binomial logit results of our study:

Table 10.10: Goodness of Fit of the Logit Model

Year	*2004-05*	*2011-12*
No. of Observations	137744	116342
Pseudo R^2	0.4061	0.3447

Source: Authors' calculations based on NSSO data.

Table 10.10 shows that the goodness of fit for the Logit models for the two periods given by Pseudo R^2 is decent at around 0.4. The logistic regression results for 2004-05 show that every additional year of schooling decreases the odds of informality by around 13 per cent which is significant at 1 per cent significance level. The relationship is even stronger for 2011-12 where each additional year of schooling decreases the odds of informality by about 14 per cent. Hence, controlling for other factors higher education is associated with lower odds of informality. Labour informality is also found to be significantly higher for those with no technical education. On average, having no technical education raises the odds of informality by about 31 per cent and 88 per cent in 2004-05 and 2011-12 respectively.

Table 10.11: Informality across Industries

Independent Variables	*Coefficients*	
	2004-05	2011-12
Mean Years of School	0.87***	0.86***
Age	0.95***	0.97***
Sq. Age	1.00***	1.00***
Log of MPCE	0.43***	0.52***
Muslim	1.42***	1.59***
Others	1.27***	1.26***
Scheduled Tribes	0.46***	0.44***
Scheduled Castes	0.60***	0.70***
Other Backward Castes	0.98	1.03
No Technical Education	1.31***	1.89***
Agriculture	2.41***	2.56***
Manufacturing	0.30***	0.43***
Construction	1.62***	1.87***
Finance, Insurance and Real Estate	0.34***	0.30***
Commercial, Social and Personal Services	0.10***	0.20***
Mining, Electricity and Water Supply	0.05***	0.09***
Sector	1.29***	1.04
Marital Status	0.81***	1.08
Gender	0.51***	0.74***
Constant	33.24***	8.87***

Note: Significance levels *** 1 per cent, ** 5 per cent, * 10 per cent, Dummy Sector = 1 if Rural, 0 otherwise, Dummy Marital Status= 0 if Never Married, 0 otherwise, Dummy Gender=1 if Male, 0 otherwise, Other variables in our model include Interaction term between Dummy Gender and Log of MPCE; Interaction term between Dummy Gender and Age; Interaction between Dummy Sector and Log of MPCE; and Interaction between Dummy Sector and Age etc.

Source: Authors' calculation based on NSSO data.

Turning to the role of age, we consider a quadratic relation as age shows a distinct U-shaped relationship with informality in Section 1. We find that an additional year of age lowers the odds of informality by around 0.5 per cent. However, the fall in informality is not uniform throughout all ages as given by its significantly positive quadratic coefficient (Table 10.11). Probing into the relationship further, we plot the relation of informality with respect to age through STATA's margins command. We find that the probability of informality fall from a very high level with increasing age until around the age of 45 years. Beyond that age, rising age is associated with lower informality. Looking from a gender perspective, the fall in informality with respect to age is not much significant for females compared to males. There is not much difference in the behaviour of informality between rural and urban areas for both males and females.

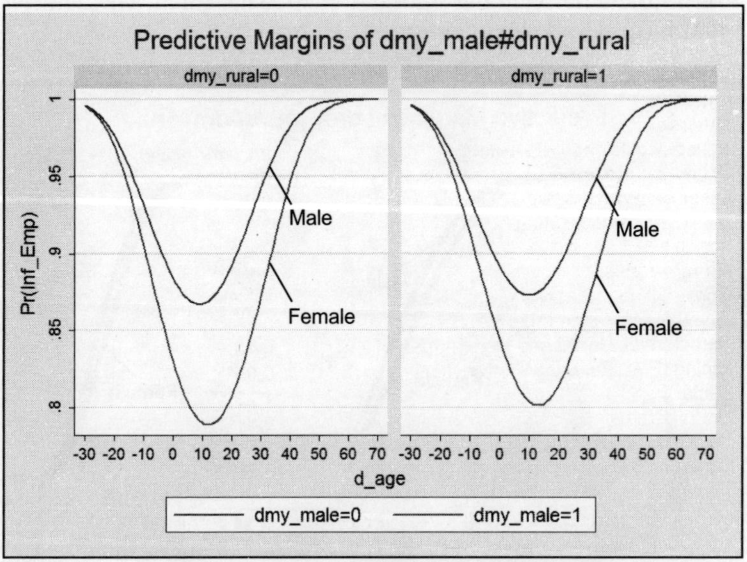

Fig. 10.1: Probability of Informal Employment against Age

Note: (a) As discussed earlier we deduct age from its mean to arrive at d_age. The mean age is found to be around 30 years so that d_age ranges from (–30) to 70.

(b) The two different curves curves depict females and males areas respectively. The left panel shows the relation of informality with MPCE for urban areas whereas the right shows the same for rural areas.

Source: Authors' calculations based on NSSO data.

Informality shows a negative relation with MPCE in both the periods. As seen from the results, a one per cent increase in MPCE lowers the odds of informality by about 0.6 per cent. The relationship is a bit weaker for 2011-12 where every per cent increase in MPCE lowers the odds of informality by around 0.5 per cent (Table 10.11). Further, the graph of the probability of informality with reference to the logarithm of MPCE is quite flat for lower MPCE levels, which becomes steeper as MPCE rises. Hence, we postulate that informality falls marginally with rising MPCE at lower levels of MPCE, but this relation becomes much steeper at higher MPCE levels. Further, informality is also found to be higher among females compared to males for all MPCE levels in both rural and urban areas.

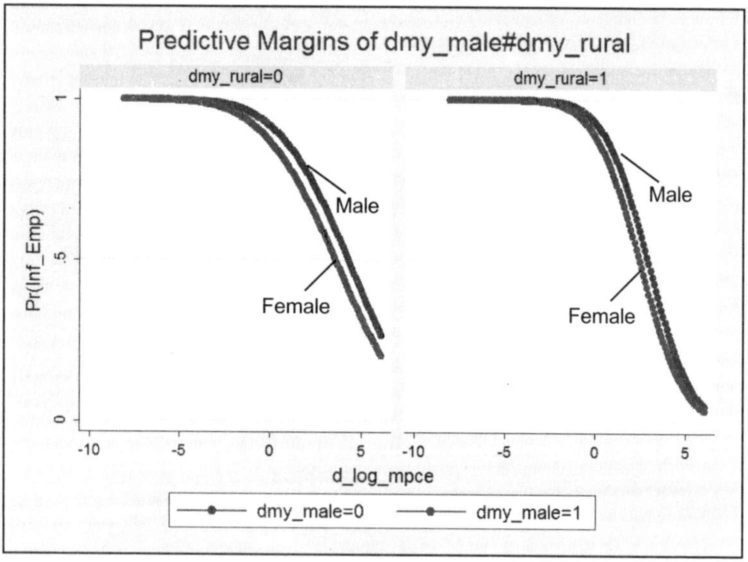

Fig. 10.2: Probability of Informal Employment against MPCE

Note: The two different curves depict females and males areas respectively. The left panel shows the relation of informality with MPCE for urban areas whereas the right shows the same for rural areas.

Source: Authors calculations based on NSSO data.

Looking at informality for different religions, we find that for 2004-05 compared to the reference category of Hindus, informality is higher for Muslims and Others for both the periods. Comparing across social groups, we see that informality is significantly lower for STs and SCs against the reference category of the 'Others' group. The relationship is not found to be significant in the case of OBCs (Table 10.11). Further, we find that informality is significantly higher in rural areas compared to urban areas. For 2004-05, being from a rural area increases the odds of informality by about 30 per cent. However, this relationship weakens down considerably for 2011-12, where the coefficient for rural areas is insignificant. Hence, the odds of informality in rural areas compared to urban areas have fallen considerably over the period. We similarly find a statistically significant negative relationship between being male and being informal. Being male decreases the odds of informality by about 50 per cent and 26 per cent for 2004-05 and 2011-12 respectively. The fall in the coefficient for 2011 implies falling odds of informality among women over the period. Further, being married decreases the odds of informality by about 20 per cent in 2004-05. However, this relation dissipates in 2011-12 as we donot find a statistically significant relationship between informality and being married (Table 10.11). Looking at informality across industries we find that in 2004-05. Informality is found to be significantly higher in the Agriculture and Construction industries with reference to the Trade, Hotels and Transportation industry. Similarly, compared to the base category of Trade, Hotels and Transportation industry, informality is found to be significantly lower in Manufacturing; Finance, Insurance and Real Estate; Commercial, Social and Personal Services as well as Mining, Electricity and Water Supply. The results are similar for 2011-12.

Informality Across the States

The investigation of the determinants of informality at the individual level has given us crucial inputs on its nature at the micro-level. However, in order to comprehend better on its determinants at the macro-level it becomes necessary investigate further the variation in the incidence of informality across states. Looking at the prevalence of informality across states, we find that informality is significantly lower in the North Eastern states, Union

Territories as well as in the Northern states of Jammu & Kashmir Himachal Pradesh.

Table 10.12: Informality Across Industries

States	2004-05		2011-12	
	Formal	*Informal*	*Formal*	*Informal*
Jammu & Kashmir	20.09	79.91	16.71	83.29
Himachal Pradesh	22.05	77.95	21.23	78.77
Punjab	10.98	89.02	10.96	89.04
Uttarakhand	17.24	82.76	17.07	82.93
Haryana	12.28	87.72	19.55	80.45
Rajasthan	8.51	91.49	9.08	90.92
Uttar Pradesh	7.81	92.19	7.57	92.43
Bihar	6.09	93.91	7.64	92.36
Tripura	14.36	85.64	9.72	90.28
Assam	18.93	81.07	16.26	83.74
West Bengal	11.98	88.02	11.63	88.37
Jharkhand	12.70	87.30	12.73	87.27
Odisha	11.26	88.74	11.50	88.50
Chhattisgarh	17.78	82.22	13.46	86.54
Madhya Pradesh	13.41	86.59	14.29	85.71
Gujarat	14.34	85.66	14.51	85.49
Maharashtra	19.94	80.06	22.99	77.01
Andhra Pradesh	10.75	89.25	15.12	84.88
Karnataka	16.34	83.66	23.12	76.88
Goa	33.43	66.57	45.77	54.23
Kerala	12.83	87.17	12.40	87.60
Tamil Nadu	15.03	84.97	16.27	83.73
NE excl. Assam and Tripura	34.08	65.92	35.93	64.07
Union Territories	28.51	71.49	32.76	67.24
India	**13.15**	**86.85**	**14.68**	**85.32**

Source: Authors' calculation based on NSSO data.

We discuss the results of the panel data study on macro state-level variables. Breusch-Pagan conducted on the data yields a χ^2 of 6.30, which is highly significant at 1 per cent level of significance. Hence, the test suggests a panel analysis of the data. Similarly, we conduct Hausman test on our data which reveals a χ^2 significant at 1 per cent level of significance. Hence, we conclude that Fixed Effects Panel method would be appropriate in our study. Hence, we conduct Fixed Effects regression analysis on our data (*see* Tables 10.13 and 10.14).

Table 10.13 shows that our model has an overall R^2 of 0.34. The within R^2, however, is found to be significantly higher 0.71.

Table 10.13: Goodness of Fit and Other Statistics

No. of observations	46
No. of cross-section units	23
No. of time periods	2
R^2: Within	0.71
R^2: Between	0.33
R^2: Overall	0.34
Rho (Fraction of Variation due to individual specific effects)	0.95

Source: Authors' calculation based on NSSO data.

Table 10.14: Macro-Determinants of Informality

Independent Variables	*Coefficients*
Poverty Rate	0.054
Last 5 Year Growth Rate of GSDP	–0.094
Tax GSDP Ratio	0.024***
Expenditure GSDP Ratio	–0.554***
Inequality Rate	–20.934
Per Capita GSDP (in Rs. 1000)	–0.119***
Quality of Public Service Provision	–2.285
Constant	91.528***

Note: Significance levels *** 1 per cent, ** 5 per cent, * 10 per cent.
Source: Authors' calculation based on NSSO data.

Further, the Rho value of 0.95 indicates that a significant part of the total error is due to the individual specific error. The results of our analysis shown in Table 10.14 reveals that a higher per capita GSDP significantly lowers the extent of informality confirming the dualist school hypothesis of higher informality associated with underdevelopment. However, we do not find a significantly, positive relation between informality and poverty. We also find the Tax GSDP ratio to be positively related to informality at 1 per cent level of significance. This vindicates the neo-liberal hypothesis of informality rising with higher government taxes and regulations. Similarly, Expenditure GSDP ratio is also found to have a significantly positive relation with informality rates. This result favours the structuralist view that informality is rising due to falling governmental presence to protect workers from poverty. However, other independent factors such as inequality rate, growth as well quality of public services is not found to have any significant impact on informality. On the whole, our results show that informality is not driven by any single set of macro-factors, but rather there are multiple factors leading to its rising incidence.

6. Conclusions

The study makes an attempt to examine the trends and determinants of informality in India. The chapter finds informality to be significantly higher among the illiterates, youth, females and the poor. It also finds informality to be lower among the Hindus, STs and SCs. Its incidence is also found to be higher in Agriculture and Construction relative to other industries. Although rural dwellers and the married are found to be significantly more prone to be informal in 2004-05, this relation dissipates in 2011-12. The chapter also finds informality to be driven by a multitude of macro-economic factors such as per capita incomes, tax-GDP ratio as well as expenditure-GSDP ratio highlighting the significance of different schools of thought in explaining the phenomenon. Hence, we conclude that efforts to reduce the incidence of informality would need a multi-pronged strategy rather than working on a single front.

References

ILO (2004). *Economic Security for a Better World* (1st ed.). Geneva: ILO. Retrieved from: http://www.socialprotection.org/gimi/gess/RessourcePDF.action;jsessionid=ba5695c9f7bbc9a3a30c5d398728626619fcdcfb08ee9b6437707cd5e3e60929.e3aTbhuLbNmSe34MchaRahaKch90?ressource.ressourceId=8670

Chen, M.A. (2012). *The Informal Economy?: Definitions, Theories and Policies.* Location and Publishers.

Chen, M., Vanek, J., Lund, F., Heintz, J., and Christine, J. (2005). *Progress of The World's Women, Women Work and Poverty.* UN Women Headquarters.

Hazans, M. (2011). What Explains Prevalence of Informal Employment in What Explains Prevalence of Informal Employment in European Countries: The Role of Labour Institutions, Governance, Immigrants, and Growth. *IZA Discussion Papers,* (5872).

ILO. (2012). Statistical update on employment in the informal economy, (June). ILO-Department of Statistics.

Jütting, J., Parlevliet, J., and Xenogiani, T. (2008). Informal Employment Re-loaded Development Centre Working Papers. Retrieved from: URL

Maloney, W.F. (2004). Informality revisited. *World Development, 32*(7), 1159–1178. Retrieved from: http://doi.org/10.1016/j.worlddev.2004.01.008.

Oviedo, A., Thomas, M., and Karakurum-Özdemir, K. (2009). *Economic Informality: Causes, Costs, and Policies: A Literature survey*. Retrieved from: http://www_wds.worldbank.org/external/default/WDS ContentServer/WDSP/IB/2009/09/16/000333037_20090916010012/ Rendered/PDF/503600PUB0Box3101OFFICIAL0USE0ONLY1.pdf.

Perry, G.E., Maloney, W.F., Arias, O.S., Fajnzylber, P., and Saavedra-chanduvi, A.D.M.J. (2010). *Exit and Exclusion. World* (Vol. 57). Retrieved from: http://doi.org/10.1596/978-0-8213-7092-6.

Williams, C.C. (2013). Evaluating cross-national variations in the extent and nature of informal employment in the European Union. *Industrial Relations Journal*, 44(5-6): 479-494. Retrieved from: http://doi.org/ 10.1111/irj.12030.

Williams, C.C. (2015). Cross-national variations in the scale of informal employment. *International Journal of Manpower, 36*(2): 118–135. Retrieved from http://doi.org/10.1108/IJM-01-2014-0021.

Appendix I

The division of workers into the formal and informal sectors is defined as follows—

Enterprise Type	**No. of workers in the enterprise**						
			1	2	3	4	9
Missing	.	****					
Proprietary male	1						
Proprietary female	2						
Partnership with members of same hold.	3						
Partnership with members of different hold.	4						
Public Sector	5						
Public/Private limited company	6						
Co-operative societies/trusts	7						
Employer's hhlds.	8						
Others	9						

1. Cells shaded dark belong to the unorganised sector.
2. Cells shaded light belong to the organised sector.
3. Cells marked with * belongs to the informal sector for all Usual Status except regular and casual workers in government works. Casual workers in public works belong to the organised sector. Similarly, Regular workers belong to the informal sectors if they have Social Security benefits or information on the variable is missing.

The division of workers into the formal and informal employment is done on the basis of presence of social security benefits and informal sector status as follows—

1. Own account workers and unpaid family workers as categorised into informal employment.
2. Casual workers in public works and other works as well as Regular workers are categorised into the formal or informal employment based on the presence or absence of social security benefits.
3. Employers are categorised into formal or informal employment based on whether they belong to the organised or unorganised sector.

Appendix II

The general educational level of a worker is coded as follows in the NSSO data—*not literate*–01, *literate without formal schooling:* EGS/NFEC/AEC–02, TLC–03, *others*–04; *literate:* below primary–05, primary –06, middle –07, secondary –08, higher secondary–10, diploma/certificate course–11, graduate–12, post-graduate and above–13.

The above Education levels refer to the highest level **successfully completed**. For example, if a person has failed in his graduate examination, then his level will be treated only as 'higher secondary'. This is the method followed by NSS.

We derive the mean level of education for a worker as follows—

(a) All persons for who code for education level are from 01 will be allotted 0 years of schooling.
(b) All persons for who code for education level are from 02 to 04 will be allotted 1 year of schooling.
(c) All persons for whom code for education level is 05 will be allotted 2 years of schooling. Below primary means up to Standard 4 (max), so we assume that persons falling under this category will have on an average 2 years of schooling.

(d) All persons for whom code for education level is 06 will be allotted 5 years of schooling.

(e) All persons for whom code for education level is 07 will be allotted 8 years of schooling.

(f) All persons for whom code for education level is 08 will be allotted 10 years of schooling.

(g) All persons for whom code for education level is 10 will be allotted 12 years of schooling.

(h) All persons for whom code for education level is 11 will be allotted 14 years of schooling. Diploma courses are usually for 2 years after completion of Standard 12, so, we assume that persons falling under this category will have 14 years of schooling.

(i) All persons for whom code for education level is 12 will be allotted 15 years of schooling. Graduate courses are usually for 3 years after completion of Standard 12, so, we assume that persons falling under this category will have 15 years of schooling.

(j) All persons for whom code for education level is 14 will be allotted 17 years of schooling. Postgraduate courses are usually for 2 years after completion of Graduate programme, so, we assume that persons falling under this category will have 17 years of schooling.

Appendix III

Our poverty lines are based on the Rangarajan Committee methodology for the year 2011-12. For 2004-05 we deflate the poverty lines from the 2011-12 poverty lines for rural and urban areas using Consumer Price Index for Agricultural Workers and Consumer Price Index for Industrial Workers respectively. We borrow the methodology proposed by Sengupta, Kannan and Raveendran (2008) in classifying households into various poverty categories. Our poverty categories are given as follows—

Poverty Category	*Criterion*
Very Poor	If MPCE ⇐ 0.75 times poverty line (PL)
Poor	If 0.75 < MPCE ⇐ 1 PL
Marginal	If 1 PL < MPCE ⇐ 1.25 PL
Vulnerable	If 1.25 PL < MPCE ⇐ 2 PL
Middle Class and above	If MPCE > 2 PL

It is worth noting that our poverty rates do not coincide with the Rangarajan Committee Report as our poverty rates are based on the Consumer Expenditure information from the Employment-Unemployment Survey rather than Consumer Expenditure Survey data of NSSO as is the norm. Since consumer expenditure derived from the latter is always greater than that obtained from the former, our poverty rates are likely to be larger than the Rangarajan Committee poverty rates.

Appendix IV

The computation of the different variables used in our study is discussed as follows—

(i) For calculation of GSDP per capita we divide GSDP at constant prices of the particular state by its population.

(ii) Calculation of the poverty rates of different states have used the official state level poverty rates given by the Tendulkar methodology.

(iii) In order to calculate the tax-GSDP ratio and the expenditure-GSDP ratio we divide the total tax revenue and total expenditure of the state by its GSDP at current prices to arrive at the figures the tax-GSDP ratio and the expenditure-GSDP ratio respectively.

(iv) For calculating the inequality rate we have used the Lorenz ratio (or Gini coefficient) available from NSSO Reports. Since, these figures are available for rural and urban areas separately we multiply the rural and urban figures by the appropriate rural and urban population weights to arrive at the inequality rate for a particular state.

(v) Calculation of growth rates for the last 5-year period uses the following formula:

$$g_t = (y_t - y_{t-5})/y_t,$$

where y_t is GSDP for year t and y_{t-5} is the GSDP 5 years earlier.

(vi) In order to calculate the index for quality of public services we have used three broad indicators for Crime, Road and Electricity Infrastructure. For the calculation of Road Infrastructure Index we have divided the Total Surfaced

Roads of a state by its respective population. Similarly, for Electricity Infrastructure Index we have used Peak Power Deficit measure for the particular state. Finally, for calculating the Crime Index we have used various measures such as Rate of IPC Crimes, Rate of Violent Crimes, Rate of Cases Completed by Police and Percentage of cases completed by Courts in 0-3 years. We normalize the variable by using the formula—

Normalized Value = (Max. Value – Actual Value)/(Max. Value – Min. Value), for positive indicators like Roads per population, Rate of cases completed by police and courts etc.

= (Actual Value – Min. Value)/(Max. Value – Min. Value), for negative values like Rate of IPC and Violent crimes, Peak Power deficit etc.

We take simple Arithmetic Mean of the indicators of Crime to arrive at our Crime index. Finally, simple Arithmetic Mean of the Crime Index, Road and Electricity Infrastructure yields us the Index for Quality of Public Services.

11
Investigating Expenditure on Tobacco Products
A Study of North East India

Sandip Rudra Paul

Introduction

The epidemic of tobacco use among young people is defined as a major public health problem in developed and developing countries. Smoking is a major worldwide public health problem. It is now by far the largest preventable cause of death in the industrialized world (Jacobson, 1983). In addition to lung cancer and heart disease, smoking causes wrinkles, impotence, strokes, memory loss, a proneness to diabetes, and inflammation of the arteries. The prevention of tobacco use in young Indians appears as the single greatest opportunity for preventing non-communicable disease in the world today as it is home to one-sixth of the global population. Tobacco use is one of the major preventable causes of death and disability worldwide. WHO estimates, 4.9 million deaths annually are attributable to tobacco. This figure is expected to rise to 10 million in 2030, with 7 million of these deaths occurring in developing countries, mainly China and India. India is home for one-sixth of the global population. Currently, about one-fifth of all worldwide deaths attributed to tobacco occur in India, more than 8,00,000 people die and 12 million people become ill as a result of tobacco use each year. It is estimated that 5,500 adolescents start using tobacco everyday in India, joining the 4 million young people under the age of 15 who already regularly use tobacco. Not only the same trend prevails in the

North East India, but certain types of cancers are relatively very high in the region compared to national figures such as oral cancer, mouth cancer, stomach cancer etc.

Global Adult Tobacco Survey India (GATS India, 2009) revealed that more than one-third of adults in India use tobacco in some form or the other. Among them 21 per cent adults use only smokeless tobacco, 9 per cent only smoke and 5 per cent smoke as well as use smokeless tobacco. Based on these, the estimated number of tobacco users in India is 274.9 million. The prevalence of tobacco use among all the States and Union Territories in India ranges from the highest of 67 per cent in Mizoram to the lowest of 9 per cent in Goa.

Tobacco use has economic implications for the society and the nation as a whole. Individual household's economic implications of tobacco include direct cost of tobacco products and indirect cost due to the expenditure arising from the adverse health effects of tobacco use. A health cost study in India revealed that the direct and indirect costs of the three major tobacco-related diseases, namely cancer, coronary artery disease and chronic obstructive lung disease (for the year 2002-03), exceeded the total combined revenue and capital expenditure by the Centre and the States on medical and public health, water supply and sanitation. In order to facilitate the implementation of the tobacco control laws, bring about greater awareness regarding harmful effects of tobacco; it is important to understand the expenditure behaviour of tobacco consumer.

Review of Literature

The World Health Organization predicts that tobacco deaths in India may exceed 1.5 million annually by 2020. There are some authors who found the prevalence rate of tobacco consumption of any form of tobacco consumption, at 47 per cent for men and 14 per cent for women, among them 29.4 per cent men and 2.3 per cent women are current smoker and 28.3 per cent men and 18 per cent women use smokeless tobacco (Rani, Bonu, Jha, Nguyen, & Jamjoum, 2003). Their study also showed that the prevalence of both smokeless tobacco and smoking tobacco was significantly higher in rural, poorer, and uneducated populations compared to urban, wealthier and more educated populations, respectively, both in men and women. Another study conducted by (Mehta, Gupta, Dftary, Pindborg, & Choksi, 1972) among 1,01,761 villagers in Maharashtra, India, where he found 62 per cent of men and 50 per cent women reported using tobacco, women reported using only smokeless tobacco, among men also smokeless tobacco is their main practice and only 8 per cent among men use smoking tobacco, most of this was *bidi*. It has been seen worldwide smoking is still mainly a male problem; overall prevalence was about four times higher in men than women, globally 48 per cent *versus* 12 per cent (WHO, 2003). A study by (Tiwari, Zodpey, 2006) in the Hanumannagar area of Nagpur city, Maharashtra, India, showed that prevalence's of smokeless tobacco in men and women were 28.1 per cent and 12 per cent respectively, but prevalence's varied considerably between states.

The prevalence of both smoking and smokeless tobacco varied significantly among different states in India, smokeless tobacco was relatively more common in the Central, Eastern, Western (except Goa) and North Eastern states (except Meghalaya) compared to in the Northern and Southern states (Rani *et al.*, 2003). It has been found that the smoking habit differs in different states of India; a study in Bhopal region of India showed that the habit of *bidi* smoking and '*zarda*', a form of smokeless tobacco, is peculiar to this region (Dikshit & Kanhere, 2000). It has been found in New Delhi, India the prevalence's of *bidi* usage among men and women aged 25–64 years were 21.3 per cent and 6.7 per cent respectively, while of cigarettes they were 23.7 per cent and 0.03 per cent, respectively (Rahman, Fukui, 2000).

However, the association between level of education and prevalence of tobacco use is quite vague. A study by (Vaidya, Vaidya & Naik, 1992) in Goa, reported that there is an inverse association between level of education and prevalence of tobacco use. The same inverse association was also found by (Gupta, 1996), but interestingly, he found a strong positive association between cigarette smoking and level of education. Another study by (Sinha, Gupta, Ray & Singh, 2012) in South-East Asia showed that the prevalence of smokeless tobacco is higher among India male than in the female, and prevalence of smokeless tobacco use is higher in groups with less education and lower socio-economic condition and it is more commonly practiced in rural areas. Similar study by (Corci *et al.*, 2013) in Andhra Pradesh,

India showed that the prevalence of current smoking and smokeless tobacco use was higher in men compared with women, and higher among older age groups. They also found that illiterate individuals were more likely to be current smokers of any type compared to those with secondary/higher education, although cigarette smoking was higher in men of high socio-economic status. Similarly, a study by (Narayan *et al.*, 1996) in New Delhi, India found 45 per cent of men and 7 per cent of women were smokers and among smokers, 52.6 per cent of men and 4.9 per cent of women smoked only cigarettes while the others also smoked *bidi* or cheroot. They also found that men with no education were 1.8 times more likely to be smokers than those with college education, and women with no education were 3.7 times more likely.

Methodology

The study is based on secondary data collected from National Sample Survey Office (NSSO) 2011-12, Household Consumption of Various Goods and Services in India 20ll-12, NSS 68th round.

In order to analyse data, the study has mainly used graphical technique, bar diagram. Besides I have also used Analysis of Variance to examine the mean difference of a variable among the different states of the region.

Results and Analysis

State-wise Variation in Expenditure on All Tobacco Products

In this section an attempt has been made to see the state-wise variation in expenditure on different tobacco products. The different tobacco products include *pan*, tobacco and intoxicants.

From Table 11.1, we see that the per capita spending on all kinds of tobacco among North East is highest for Mizoram, rupees 53.57 per month while the least spending state is Manipur, spending rupees 16.36 per month only. Now, if we see the variation among the spending on *pan*, tobacco and intoxicants within state, it is seen that the highest variation is also in Mizoram (1754.22) and the state with least variation is Manipur (40.15). It may be noted that F statistic is 0.71, which is statistically

Table 11.1: Expenditure on All Tobacco Products (*in Rs. per month*)

States	*Pan, Tobacco and Intoxicants*
Arunachal Pradesh	39.52 (1662.41)
Assam	20.44 (67.11)
Manipur	16.36 (40.15)
Meghalaya	38.58 (382.58)
Mizoram	53.57 (1754.22)
Nagaland	25.48 (164.21)
Sikkim	27.29 (817.07)
Tripura	24.47 (197.52)
F-Value	0.71

Notes: 1. The test statistic used for ANOVA is the F-statistic and is calculated by taking the Mean Square (MS) for the variable divided by the MS of the error (called Mean Square of the Error or MSE).

2. Numbers in parentheses are variances; expenditures are in rupees per month.

Source: Computed by author using data from Household Consumption of Various Goods and Services in India 2011-12, NSS 68th round.

insignificant, indicating that on an average all the states spend same amount of money on different tobacco products, there is hardly any variation.

Variations in Expenditure on Pan Product in North Eastern States

In this section we have noticed the variations in expenditure on *pan* products in North Eastern states. The *pan* products include *pan* leaf, *pan* finished and ingredients for *pan* (Table 11.3).

It has been found that the highest per capita spending pan product in North East is pan finished, on an average Rs. 20.39 are spend on pan finished, while the lowest spending pan product is pan leaf, Rs. 5.18. Whereas, the variation among different states of North East in spending on *pan* products is also high in case of pan finished (577.96), and least in *pan* leaf (41.93). It may be noted that

Table 11.2: Expenditure on Pan Products *(in Rs. per month)*

Pan Products	*North East*
Pan; leaf(No.)	5.18 (41.93)
Pan; finished(No.)	20.39 (577.96)
Ingredients for *pan* (gm)	7.59 (125.89)
F-Value	2.15

Notes: 1. The test statistic used for ANOVA is the F-statistic and is calculated by taking the Mean Square (MS) for the variable divided by the MS of the error (called Mean Square of the Error or MSE).

2. Numbers in parentheses are variances; expenditures are in rupees per month.

Source: Computed by author using data from Household Consumption of Various Goods and Services in India 2011-12, NSS 68th round.

the F-statistic is 2.15, which is statistically insignificant, indicating that the variation in spending on different pan products in north east is negligible.

Variations in Expenditure on Tobacco Products in North Eastern States

In this section an attempt has been made to see the variations in expenditure on tobacco products in North Eastern states. The tobacco products include *bidi*, cigarettes, leaf tobacco, snuff, *hookah* tobacco, *cheroot*, *zarda*, *kimam*, *surti*, and other tobacco products.

From Table 11.3 we observe that the per capita spending on different tobacco products among North Eastern states is highest in cigarettes, Rs. 17.27 per month, while the lowest spending on tobacco product is cheroot rupees 0.01 per month. Whereas, the variation among different states of North East in spending on tobacco products is also high in case of cigarettes (261.59) and least in cheroot and snuff (0.00). It may be noted that the F-statistic is 6.53 which is statistically significant, indicating that variation so observed in spending on tobacco products in North East is meaningful.

Table 11.3: Expenditure on Tobacco Products

(in Rs. per month)

Tobacco Products	*North East India*
Bidi (no.)	6.07 (34.73)
Cigarettes (no.)	17.27 (261.59)
Leaf tobacco (gm)	1.99 (3.03)
Snuff (gm)	0.06 (0.00)
Hookah tobacco (gm)	0.21 (0.06)
Cheroot (no.)	0.01 (0.00)
Zarda, kimam, surti (gm)	1.00 (0.72)
Other tobacco products	5.73 (38.54)
F-Value	6.53*

Notes: 1. The test statistic used for ANOVA is the F-statistic and is calculated by taking the Mean Square (MS) for the variable divided by the MS of the error (called Mean Square of the Error or MSE).
2. Numbers in parentheses are variances; expenditures are in Rs. per month.
3. * denotes significance at 1 per cent levels.

Source: Computed by author using data from Household Consumption of Various Goods and Services in India 2011-12, NSS 68th round.

Variations in Expenditure on Intoxicant Products in North Eastern States

In this section an attempt has been made to see the variations in expenditure on intoxicants in North Eastern states. Intoxicants include *ganja,* toddy, country liquor, beer, foreign liquor or wine and other intoxicants (Table 11.4).

It has been found that the highest per capita spending intoxicant in North East is foreign liquor or wine, Rs. 10.63 per month, while the lowest spending intoxicant is *ganja,* Rs. 0.01 per month. Whereas, the variation among different states of North East in spending on intoxicants is also high in case of foreign liquor or wine (132.74) and least in *ganja* (0.00). It may be noted that the F-statistic is 2.65 which is statistically significant, indicating that

Table 11.4: Expenditure on Intoxicant Products

(in Rs. per month)

Intoxicants	*North East India*
Ganja (gm)	0.01 (0.00)
Toddy (litre)	0.15 (0.02)
Country liquor (litre)	6.98 (41.67)
Beer (litre)	4.74 (58.19)
Foreign liquor or wine (litre)	10.63 (132.74)
Other intoxicants	4.14 (68.40)
F-Value	2.65**

Notes: 1. The test statistic used for ANOVA is the F-statistic and is calculated by taking the Mean Square (MS) for the variable divided by the MS of the error (called Mean Square of the Error or MSE).

2. Numbers in parentheses are variances; expenditures are in Rs. per month.

3. ** denotes significance at 5 per cent levels.

Source: Computed by author using data from Household Consumption of Various Goods and Services in India 2011-12, NSS 68th round.

the variation so observed in spending on intoxicants in North East is meaningful.

Percentage Share of Expenditure on Tobacco and Related Products in Non-food Expenditure

In order to see the share of spending on tobacco and related products in total non-food expenditure we have drawn the bar diagram. The percentage share of spending is found to be highest for Mizoram 15.45 per cent and lowest for Manipur 7.04 per cent. However, it is visible from the Fig. 11.1 that more or less the percentage share of expenditure in all the states of North East are more or less same.

Relative Expenditure on Different Dimensions of Tobacco Related Products

In this section we have tried to see the relative expenditure state-wise, i.e., out of total tobacco expenditure in a state how much is spend on pan product, tobacco product and intoxicants (Fig. 11.2).

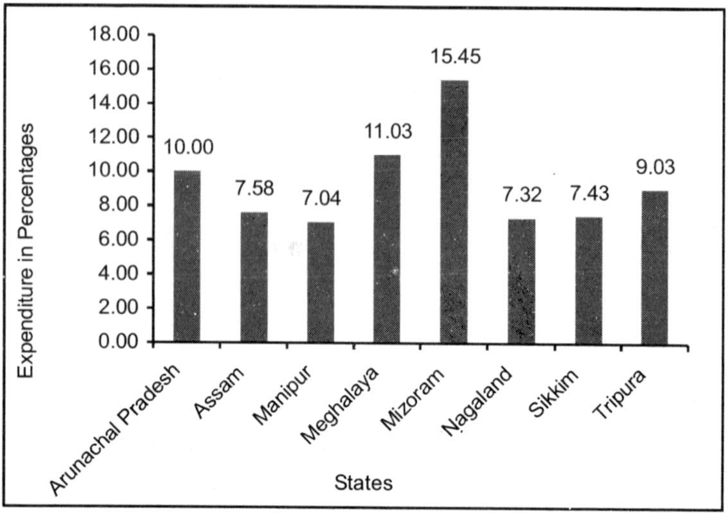

Fig. 11.1: Percentage share of expenditure on tobacco and related products in Non-food expenditure

Source: Computed by author using data from Household Consumption of Various Goods and Services in India 2011-12, NSS 68th round.

It has been found that Sikkim and Arunachal Pradesh are the two states where the relative expenditure is very high on intoxicants 73.30 and 72.91 per cent respectively and lowest in Mizoram and Tripura 3.33 and 11.98 per cent respectively. On the other hand Mizoram and Tripura are the states with higher relative expenditure on tobacco products 50.29 and 48.95 per cent respectively and lowest in Arunachal Pradesh and Sikkim with 16.32 and 17.97 respectively. In case of *pan* product the relative expenditure is high in Assam and Meghalaya with 48.70 and 47.80 per cent respectively and lowest in Sikkim and Arunachal Pradesh with 8.73 and 10.77 per cent respectively.

Conclusion

We observed that the expenditure on tobacco related products is relatively higher in North Eastern region compare to all other regions of India. However, there exists considerable variation in such expenditure across states within North East India. Second, the per capita expenditure on all kinds of tobacco products is found to be

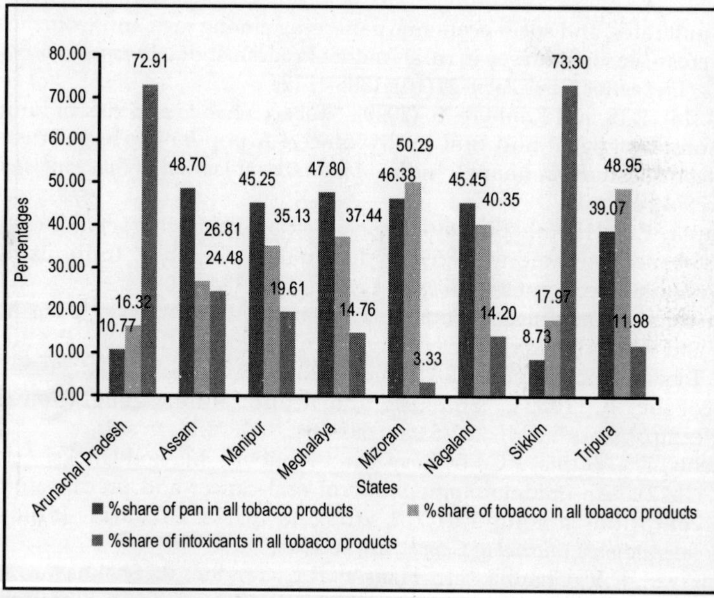

Fig. 11.2: Relative expenditure on different dimensions of tobacco related products

Source: Computed by author using data from Household Consumption of Various Goods and Services in India 2011-12, NSS 68th round.

highest in Mizoram, while such expenditure is observed to be lowest in Manipur. Third, Speaking in terms of expenditure on specific tobacco products, Assam has been observed to be the highest consumer of the *pan* product and Mizoram as tobacco product, while Sikkim is reported to have the highest consumer of intoxicants. Fourth, viewed from North East as a whole, *pan* product shares the highest expenditure followed by tobacco product. Fifth, within the broad category of tobacco related products "finished *pan*" contributes the highest share in respect of *pan* products, among tobacco, cigarette shares the highest expenditure, while spending on wine is identified to be the highest among intoxicants.

References

Corsi, D.J., Subramanian, S.V., Lear, S.A., Teo, K.K., Boyle, M.H., Raju, P.K., Joshi, R., Neal, B., and Chow, C.K. (2014). Tobacco use, smoking quit rates, and socio-economic patterning among men and women: a cross-sectional survey in rural Andhra Pradesh, India. *European Journal of Preventive Cardiology, 21*(10): 1308-1318.

Dikshit, R.P., and Kanhere, S. (2000). "Tobacco habits and risk of lung, oropharyngeal and oral cavity cancer: A population-based case-control study in Bhopal, India". *International Journal of Epidemiology,* 29(4): 609-614.

Gupta, P.C. (1996). "Survey of socio-demographic characteristics of tobacco use among 99,598 individuals in Bombay, India using handheld computers". *Tobacco Control,* 5(2): 114-120.

International Institute for Population Sciences: (IIPS), Ministry of Health and Family Welfare, Government of India (2009–2010). Global Adult Tobacco Survey India (GATS India), 2009–10, India.

Jacobson, B. (1983). "Smoking and health: A new generation of campaigners". *BMJ,* 287(6390): 483-484.

Mehta, F.S., Gupta, P.C., Daftary, D.K., Pindborg, J.J., and Choksi, S.K. (1972). "An epidemiologic study of oral cancer and precancerous conditions among 1,01,761 villagers in Maharashtra, India". *International Journal of Cancer,* 10(1): 134-141.

Narayan, K.V., Chadha, S.L., Hanson, R.L., Tandon, R., Shekhawat, S., Fernandes, R.J., and Gopinath, N. (1996). "Prevalence and patterns of smoking in Delhi: Cross sectional study". *BMJ,* 312(7046): 1576-1579.

NSSO (2014): Household Consumption of Various Goods and Services in India 2011-12, Report 558 (68/1.0/2), National Sample Survey Office, Ministry of Statistics and Programme Implementation, Government of India, New Delhi.

Rahman, M., and Fukui, T. (2000). "*Bidi* smoking and health". *Public Health,* 114(2): 123-127.

Rani, M., Bonu, S., Jha, P., Nguyen, S.N., and Jamjoum, L. (2003). "Tobacco use in India: prevalence and predictors of smoking and chewing in a national cross sectional household survey". *Tobacco Control,* 12(4), e4-e4.

Sinha, D.N., Gupta, P.C., Ray, C.S., and Singh, P.K. (2012). "Prevalence of smokeless tobacco use among adults in WHO South-East Asia". *Indian Journal of Cancer,* 49(4), 342.

Tiwari, R.R., Zodpey, S.P. (2006). "Use of smokeless tobacco: a community-based study of behaviour, attitude and beliefs". *Regional Health Forum WHO Southeast Asia Region,* 3: 1–4.

Vaidya, S.G., Vaidya, N.S., and Naik, U.D. (1992). Epidemiology of tobacco habits in Goa, India. *Control of Tobacco Related Cancers and Other Diseases,* Oxford University Press, Bombay, pp. 315-323.

PART 3
Agricultural and Environmental Perspective of Development

12
Effect of Plant Density on Economic Return from *Thysanolaena maxima* (Roxb.) *Kuntze* (broom grass) Plantation in Jaintia Hills, Meghalaya, India

Etiban Lapasam and *B.K. Tiwari*

Introduction

Thysanolaena maxima (Roxb.) *Kuntze* (family—Poaceae), popularly known as broom grass, is an important NTFP that grows in almost all parts of South and South-East Asia up to an elevation of 1,600 m and climatic conditions ranging from tropical to sub-tropical. The inflorescence of *T. maxima* is used as broom in South and South-East Asia. It grows wild in the hills of the North Eastern region of India and in Darjeeling and Sikkim Himalayas. In Meghalaya broom grass is collected from the wild as well as cultivated. In Garo Hills region of Meghalaya broom grass is collected from the wild, whereas in the Khasi and Jaintia Hills region it is cultivated in large areas, though a small quantity is also collected from the wild (Tiwari and Kumar, 2008). The broom made from inflorescence of this grass species is of high quality and the grass is considered as multipurpose, non-perishable cash crop that can withstand harsh environmental conditions and grow in steep rocky mountain slopes in shallow soil as well as in drought and high rainfall conditions. It is immensely important both ecologically and economically for the hill dwellers (Shankar, Lama, Bawa, & Shankar, 2001).

Prior to planting of broom grass, first the vegetation are cleared off the fields and the debris is burnt usually in the month of March or April. Rhizome or root slips are either collected from the wild or from plantation in the month of April-July. The rhizomes are removed from the ground with the help of spade and hoe. In the plantation site the rhizomes are then split in to proper sizes and planted immediately. The plants start producing panicles (broom sticks) in the month of November and majority of the panicle mature in the month of February. The panicles are harvested immediately before maturity. After harvesting of brooms the culms are cut 10-20 cm above ground. The culms and leaves are then either left in the field to rot or burnt or collected for other uses. New culms emerge at the onset of rainy season in the month of April-May.

Even though *T. maxima* has emerged as a very important cash crop of Meghalaya (Tiwari, Shukla, Lynser & Tynsong, 2012), no experimental research is available on the effect of plant density on growth and yield. This chapter is an attempt to fill in this gap in our knowledge about this important cash crop of South and South-East Asia.

Materials and Methods

The experiment was laid out at Mynska village situated at 25°26′32.09″ N latitude and 092°25′17.84″ E longitude at 1158 m asl. located in West Jaintia Hills District of Meghalaya with annual average rainfall of 310 cm and the average minimum and maximum temperature of 11°C and 21.6 °C respectively. The planting was done in July 2012. The vegetation was cleared off the field during May 2012 and the plants debris was burned after they were fully dried. The rhizomes were collected from the forests in the month of July 2012 and brought to the site where they are split into required sizes of four tillers per root slips. The root slips were then planted immediately after splitting. Weeding was done twice times in a year using hand held hoe. No fertilizer and pesticides were used in the experiment.

The experiment was conducted using random complete block design (RCBD) with four replicates and five treatments. The size of each treatment plot was 8.0 × 8.0 m = 64m^2. The experiment was of a single factor treatment. The treatments were: 10000 plants ha^{-1} (1.0 × 1.0 m spacing), 5000 plants ha^{-1} (1.0 × 2.0 m spacing), 3333 plants ha^{-1} (1.5 × 2.0 m spacing), 2500 plants ha^{-1} (2.0 × 2.0 m spacing) and 2000 plants ha^{-1} (2.5 × 2.0 m spacing).

Data were collected from five inner plants selected randomly from each plots and recorded continuously up to three harvests. The mean yields from each plant were then multiplied by the number of plant ha^{-1} to get the yield ha^{-1}. The cost of setting up of plantation was taken into account by adding the cost fencing materials, root slips, transportation, digging of pits, weeding, harvesting, labour charges, etc. ha^{-1}. Benefits was calculated from the average price at which the farmers sold their produce, i.e. Rs. 56 kg^{-1}.

Economic Analysis

The economic analysis was carried out using benefit-cost ratio, net present value and internal rate of return. Benefits and costs are linked to the age of the crops. At the early stages, there are high establishment costs which are then followed by annual benefits that are non-linear over the life of the crops (Nkang, Ajah, Abang & Edet, 2007). Due to the time value of money, futures cost and benefit values that were discounted to enable comparison with present values. This required discounting and compounding. The costs and benefits were discounted using the appropriate interest rate and the Net present Value was calculated on a ha^{-1} basis.

$$\text{Net Present Value} = \sum_{t=1}^{n} \frac{(Bt - Ct)}{(1+r)^t}$$

Benefit Cost Ratio was used to measure the present value of returns per rupee invested. The Benefit Cost Ratio (BCR) was worked out by using following formula:

$$\text{Benefit Cost Ratio} = \sum_{t=1}^{n} Bt(1+r)^t \Big/ \sum_{t=1}^{n} Ct(1+r)^t$$

Internal rate of return was worked out by using following formula:

$$\sum_{t=1}^{n} \frac{Bt - Ct}{(1+r)^t} = 0$$

where,

Bt = Benefits ha^{-1} in each year, $t = 1, 2, \ldots, n$

Ct = Costs ha^{-1} in each year, $t = 1, 2, \ldots, n$.

n = Number of years, and

r = Discount rate.

Results and Discussion

The analysis revealed that 60-80 per cent per cent of the total cost was incurred during the first year depending upon the density of plants, the major expenditures being plantation establishment (site preparation, cost of root slips and planting) and fencing. The expenditure on establishment of broom grass plantation varied with density of plants (Table 12.1). The highest expenditure was incurred in treatment of 10,000 plants ha^{-1} with Rs. 95,700 and the lowest in 2000 plants ha^{-1} treatment with Rs. 28,740. In Jaintia Hills the cost of root slip for collection and transportation to the site of planting is higher as compared to other regions of the State, viz., in Ri Bhoi and War areas where root slips are available locally.

During the second year, the expenditure was about 7.5–15 per cent of the total cost, which consist of labour charges only on weeding, harvesting and drying of broom panicles and the remaining 11–23.5 per cent was incurred during the third year which also consist of labour charges for weeding, harvesting, drying of broom panicles and also maintenance of fencing. The total cost over a period of three years worked out to be highest in 10,000 plants ha^{-1} treatment with Rs. 1,27,120 and the least was in 2000 plants ha^{-1} with Rs. 61,120.

Rearing cattle and goats is an important economic activity in this part of the State, therefore, fencing of the plantation against grazing is an important component of expenditure for protection of plantation especially during the initial stage of broom grass plantation. An amount of Rs. 10,800 ha^{-1} was spent as cost of fencing which included the cost of labour charges and buying of fencing material like bamboos and wood logs, which were the cheapest material available locally.

The expenditure includes both family member's contribution as well as payment to labourers, therefore, the farmers get more cash than the amount shown in Table 12.1. In most cases the farmers employ labourers only for harvesting of broom panicles as the broom panicles have to be harvested within a short period otherwise the quality of broom panicles degrade and command less price in the market as compared to those harvested in time.

The expenditure incurred on weeding was highest during the first year and dropped with age. This was due to the fact that weed density were very high during the initial year and it involved more

Table 12.1: Expenditure Incurred during Three-Year Cultivation of *T. maxima* at Different Spacing

Particulars	10000 plants ha^{-1}			5000 plants ha^{-1}			3333 plants ha^{-1}			2500 plants ha^{-1}			2000 plants ha^{-1}		
	1st year	2nd year	3rd year	1st year	2nd year	3rd year	1st year	2nd year	3rd year	1st year	2nd year	3rd year	1st year	2nd year	3rd year
Clearing	1200			1200			1200			1200			1200		
Fencing	10800		1200	10800		1200	10800		1200	10800		1200	10800		1200
Digging of pits	37200			18600			12399			9300			7440		
Cost of root slips	46500			23250			15498			11625			9300		
Weeding	7600	6100	4420	7600	7000	4200	8600	7200	4200	8600	7200	4200	8600	7200	4200
Harvesting	1000	4500	4800	600	4000	4800	600	4000	5500	600	3600	5500	600	3000	5500
Drying of panicles	300	600	900	300	600	900	300	600	1200	300	600	1200	300	600	1200
Total	**104600**	**11200**	**11320**	**62350**	**11600**	**11100**	**49397**	**11800**	**12100**	**42425**	**11400**	**12100**	**38240**	**10800**	**12100**
Total expenditure		**127120**			**85050**			**73297**			**65925**			**61140**	

Source: Primary Survey.

man-days for weeding but due to weeding and closing in of broom grass canopy the weed density decreased and so also the cost of weeding. The cost of weeding in the lower density of plants was higher as the densities of weeds were still higher as gaps between plants were higher, which provided space for weed growth.

The cost of harvesting increased with age of the plantation. In the first and second year harvest, treatment with 10,000 plants ha^{-1} required maximum money for harvesting and the cost decreases as the density of plant decreases but in the third year, the treatments with plant density of 3333 plants ha^{-1}, 2500 plants ha^{-1} and 2000 plants ha^{-1} incurred maximum expenditure for harvesting. This was due to the higher panicle production ha^{-1} in the lower plant density than in the higher density plantations. Plant density treatment of 3333 plants ha^{-1} produced the maximum panicles over a period of three years with 4734.30 kg ha^{-1} followed by plant density of 2500 plants ha^{-1} and 2000 plants ha^{-1} with 4509 kg and 4150.13 kg respectively (Table 12.2).

Table 12.2: Yield of Broom Panicles kg ha^{-1}

Year	*Plants density*				
	10000 plants ha^{-1}	*5000 plants ha^{-1}*	*3333 plants ha^{-1}*	*2500 plants ha^{-1}*	*2000 plants ha^{-1}*
1	109	50.95	36.12	26.6	23.22
2	1937.776	1522.971	1405.77	1109.70	865.92
3	2103.376	2121.504	3292.40	3372.70	3260.98
Total	**4150.15**	**3695.42**	**4734.30**	**4509**	**4150.13**

Source: Primary Survey.

The income from sale of broom panicles in the first year was negligible. The break-even was obtained in the second year, when maintenance and protection cost was offset by the income from broom panicles sales. It was found that up to three years, Plant density treatment of 3333 plants ha^{-1} gave the highest net present value of Rs. 1,26,199.8 ha^{-1} year^{-1} followed by treatments of 2500 plants ha^{-1} and 2000 plants ha^{-1} with Rs. 1,23,055 and Rs. 1,12,271 respectively. Treatment 10,000 plants ha^{-1} gave the lowest return of Rs. 61,173. The low net present value in the higher density of plant was due to the high investment and low production of broom panicles in the third year.

Benefit Cost Ratio is an important parameter in which farmers are interested to see the gain in net returns with a given increase in total cost (Rehman, Qamar & Qamar, 2014). It is seen that plant density treatment of 2000 plants ha^{-1} gave the highest benefit to cost ratio with a value of 3.6 followed by plant density treatment of 3333 plants ha^{-1} with 3.15. The lowest benefit to cost ratio was found in plant density of 10,000 plants ha^{-1} with 1.71 (Table 12.3). The findings are similar to those reported by Tiwari, (2014) who recorded a benefit cost ratio of 3.46. Shankar *et al.* (2001) in their benefit to cost ratio analysis reported a return of 1.7 from six-year harvest. Singh, Rai and Pradhan (1989) found a ratio of 6.84, which is substantially higher than the present study. The variation in benefit cost ratio can be attributed to the locally prevailing factors such as soil fertility, labour charges, selling price and plantation management. Similarly, the internal rate of return revealed that broom grass plantation with 2,500 plants ha^{-1} gave the best rate of return (79.8 %), followed by 2000 plants ha^{-1} (78.4 %).

Table 12.3: Economic Analysis of *T. maxima* Cultivation in Jaintia Hills, Meghalaya at Discount Rate of 12 per cent $Year^{-1}$

Sl. No.	*Parameters*	*Plants density*				
		10000 plants ha^{-1}	*5000 plants ha^{-1}*	*3333 plants ha^{-1}*	*2500 plants ha^{-1}*	*2000 plants ha^{-1}*
1.	Net Present Value (Rs. ha^{-1} $year^{-1}$)	61173.5	73544	126199.8	123055.9	112271.3
2.	Benefit to Cost Ratio	1.71	2.12	3.15	3.05	3.6
3.	Internal Rate of Return %	35.15	50	76.46	79.8	78.4

Source: Primary Survey.

The data reveal that lesser spacing limits the growth and production of broom tillers, which reduces the production of broom panicles. The production of broom panicles increased slightly in the narrower spacing whereas in the wider spacing the production increased by almost three times between the second and third harvest. Even though 2500 plants ha^{-1} treatment gave the highest internal rate of return and 2000 plants ha^{-1} gave the highest benefits to costs ratio, but 3333 plants ha^{-1} gave the highest net present value of 1,26,199.8 ha^{-1} $year^{-1}$, therefore, it can be concluded that 3333 plants ha^{-1} is the best treatment for broom grass plantation in Jaintia Hills, Meghalaya.

A return of more than three times the amount invested from the sale of broom panicles excluding leave and stems is lucrative enough for the farmers. The maximum expenditure was incurred on labour charges where, mostly the farmers and their family members are involved, therefore, the total return is much higher than the amount calculated. The maximum expenditure was incurred on the establishment of the plantation and from the second year onward only minor expenditure was incurred on labour charges such as weeding, harvesting and protection. In a situation where labour is available in the family, the income is very high and growers get very high return. This is the reason for continuous growth in area and production of broom grass in Meghalaya and it has occupied almost all the land previously used for shifting cultivation (Tiwari & Kumar, 2008). Cultivation of broom grass on the unproductive *jhum* fallows should be encouraged as this prevents soil erosion. This is already replacing the practice of shifting cultivation and also reducing the excessive dependence of people on forest (Bhuyan, 2014).

References

Bhuyan, L.R. (2014). Viable practice of broom grass cultivation in Arunachal Pradesh. *Manjari*, 1(1), 9.

Nkang M., Ajah, E.A., Abang, S.O., and Edet, E.O. (2007). "Investment in cocoa production in Nigeria: A cost and return analysis of three cocoa production management systems in the cross river state cocoa belt". *Journal of Central and European Agriculture*, 8 (1): 81-90.

Rehman, A., Qamar, R. and Qamar J. (2014). "Economic Assessment of Sugarcane (*Saccharum officinarum* L.) through Intercropping". *Journal of Agricultural Chemistry and Environment*, 3: 24-28.

Shankar, U., Lama, S.D., Bawa, K.S., and Shankar, U. (2001). "Ecology and economics of domestication of non-timber forest products: An illustration of broomgrass in Darjeeling Himalaya". *Journal of Tropical Forest Science*, 13: 171–191

Singh, K.A., Rai, R.N. and Pradhan, I.P. (1989). "Grow amliso grass in the NEH region". *Indian Farming*, 38(10): 43-44.

Tiwari, B.K. and Kumar, C. (2008). *Forest products of Meghalaya: Present Status and Future Perspective*. Shillong (India): Regional Centre

National Afforestation and Eco-Development Board, North Eastern Hill University (pp. 47-57). Shillong, Meghalaya.

Tiwari, B.K. (2014). "Broom grass: Its cultivation and production economics in Meghalaya". *Manjari*, 1(1): 7-8.

Tiwari, B.K., Shukla, R.P., Lynser, M.B. and Tynsong, H. (2012). "Growth pattern, production, and marketing of *Thysanolaena maxima* (Roxb.) Kuntze: An important non-timber forest product of Meghalaya, India". *Forests, Trees and Livelihoods*, 21 (3): 176–187.

13
Economic Viability to Resource Conservation Farming Systems and Rural Livelihood in India

Anil K. Srivastava

The National Commitment—

"To all we give assurance that—

- *It will be our endeavour;*
- *To end poverty and squalor; and its companions—hunger and diseases;*
- *To abolish distinction and exploitation; and*
- *Ensure decent condition of living".*

Dr. Rajendra Prasad,
Constituent Assembly, India, 1949.

Introduction

The fast growing Indian Economy is being highlighted the world over. However, the status of farm sector continues to be a matter of serious concern. The economic viability of Indian Farm sector, is crucial not only for economic development for country, but also the livelihood and economic well-being of almost 50 crores population of the country. However, the livelihood security in Rural India is faced with several constraints, expressed in terms of uncertainty, increasing climate variability, infrastructural limitations, economic disadvantages and dependence on several factors beyond the control of farming community. Livelihood security in Rural India is faced with several constraints, expressed in terms of uncertainty, increasing climate variability, infrastructural limitations, economic disadvantages and dependence on several factors beyond the control of farming community, which are outside the systems. This has led to poor growth, uncertain profitability and unsustainability. Most of these factors get aggravated in the hill region. The relevance and urgency can only be highlighted by the MDGs, 1 being eradication of poverty and hunger followed by 3. Gender equality and women empowerment and 7. Being the protection of environment.

Deeper understanding of hill farming, farmer's perspective and their response is needed to provide basis for sustainable development in the Mountain Region. These have often suffered isolation from main stream development (Srivastva, 2006). Lack of livelihood security to majority of rural population particularly in hill region, along with the issues of economic viability, social equity, environment degradation, natural resource conservation and climate resilience; are predominantly responsible for resulting farming into far less preferred livelihood option.

Economic viability and livelihood security supported by resources, knowledge, skill, enhanced productivity, loss prevention and market infrastructure with complementary policy support is expected to make significant impact on poverty reduction. Let us attempt sustainable transformation of agriculture aiming at generating farm income and providing sustainable livelihood security.

Status, Concept—Approach

India continues to face the challenges of environment and food security, which are also major factors related to poverty. In our country today, the number of poor's equal to the national population at independence. If we get to understand the canvas of Indian Agriculture, the total gain is as well intimately linked to the prevention of losses and its different dimensions. Be it total photo syntheses or the efficiency of resource use including energy. At the same time the declining quantity and quality of produce directly affecting the profitability are major manifestation. The Indian Himalayan Region (IHR) spreads to 5.3 lakh km^2 and it comprises 16 per cent of India. Due to lack of general economic development, agriculture remains predominant livelihood in hill region. The population pressure on farm land is very high in hills, being 1,047/km^2 compared to national figure of 704/km^2. Mountain regions can be characterized by positive attributes like diversity, human adaptation, niche advantages, largely nature based farming, whereas negative attributes include marginality, in accessibility fragility. These have often resulted in larger isolation from main stream development (Jodha, 1990; Srivastava, 2006). The recent ranking of India at 135 by the UNDP's Human Development Index among 187 countries speaks of the gigantic task ahead for all of us, without any excuses.

Hill Agriculture is characterised by fragmented, small terraces on sloping land, with very little area under irrigation. Accessibility is very poor and often necessary infrastructure is absent. Use of purchased inputs is very low, except in pockets of valley and irrigated terraces. Hill agriculture is predominantly carried out by farm women, who constitute 70 per cent and more of the work force. Almost 88 per cent of the farming community consists of small and marginal farmers who own 55 per cent of agriculture land. An average holder of 0.95 ha land may be having more than 10 plots dispersed in over 5 km radius with minimum vertical separation of 170 m. Slopes of agricultural land vary up to 60° in hills. This is one of the main reasons behind alarming rate of soil erosion. In the Himalayan Region, the hill agriculture is faced with challenges of low productivity, economic unviability, unsustainability due to exploitative natural resource management and lack of alternate livelihood available to mountain people. These challenges of the hills, mountains and its people have evoked concerted efforts on research, technology development thereby offering knowledge based management of hill agriculture to impart sustainability and livelihood security.

The Indian Himalayan Region (IHR)

Geographical area is 5.37 lakh km^2 consisting, 16.2 per cent of India. The location is 21° 59′–37° N Latitude and 72°40′–97°25′ E Longitude. The region has 41.5 per cent forest cover. The **North-West Himalaya Region (NWHR)** consists of the states of Jammu & Kashmir, Himachal Pradesh and Uttarakhand. The **North East Himalaya Region (NEHR)** consists of Sikkim, Arunachal

Pradesh, Nagaland, Manipur, Mizoram, Tripura, Meghalaya and Part of Assam state.

Hill region can thus be characterized by:

Ecosystem :	Extreme variation, harsh climate, increasing weather risk.
Land scape :	Steep slope, orientation to sun.
Technical :	Pest and diseases, soil sickness, nutrient management
Economic :	Poor investment, lack of infrastructure and market.
Social :	Lack of skill, awareness, often-orthodox traditions.
Remoteness :	Lack of organizational Infrastructure, implementation, week input Service delivery and governance.

Let us consider what is at stake: food, environment, employment, economic and livelihood security. Farm-based livelihood in mountains cannot be seen in isolation from surrounding forest areas. Only 0.4 to 0.6 ha of cultivable land is available per family in North West Himalaya (Baseline Survey, NAIP, VPKAS, 2009). Thus, whereas 1 ha of cultivable land is available in the region which needs to support 10 persons, it is for only 5 persons for the country. Consequently, serious ecological degradation occurs across the mountain region due to deforestation, excessive grazing and cultivation of marginal lands.

The Vicious Cycle of Rural Poverty

- Low producing, high risk farming, with poor knowledge and input base.
- Rich traditional knowledge with limitation to adapt to the challenges.
- This leads to poor production, increase in cost and uncertainties.
- Economic insecurity leading to over exploitation of natural resources and out migration.
- Low producing exploitative farming further leads to

resource degradation, subsistence farming aggravating poverty issues.

The National Agricultural Policy has placed high priority on raising agricultural productivity so as to raise the farm growth and control poverty. Sustainable development of hill ecosystems could be achieved by integrated farming systems, thereby transforming hill agriculture into a vibrant and viable livelihood enterprise. Addressing to these concerns, some of the major initiatives include:

(i) **Rio + 20 Conference:** The concerted Indian efforts resulted priority to poverty reduction in addition to green economy.
(ii) **National Council on Climate Change—India 2009**. It includes National Action Plan on Climate Change, leading to integrated approach on climate management.
(iii) **National Environment Policy, 2006.** It includes mitigation and adaptation measure effectively addressing the development objectives and climate change. The National Missions included the National Mission for Sustaining the Himalayan Eco-system.
(iv) **International Year of Mountains: Bishkek Global Mountain Summit, 2002.** Bishkek, Kyrgyzstan. It provided Bishkek Mountain Platform, a framework to improve the livelihood, protect eco-system and judiciously use the mountain resources.
(v) **The Millennium Summit-2000.** Four of the eight goals (MDGs) to be achieved by 2015, were in direct context of the present discussion: **MDG-1** eradicate extreme poverty and hunger, **MDG-3** promote gender equality and empower women, **MDG-7** ensure environmental sustainability, and **MDG-8** global partnerships for development.
(vi) **United Nations Conference on Environment and Development, 1992**. Agenda- 21: Chapters 13, 14 and 15 were directly related to mountain development.

Thus, in our attempt to make hill agriculture economically viable, the following issues and challenges have to be managed:

(i) Low productivity, economic unviability, unsustainability due to over exploitation of fragile natural resources and lack of available alternate livelihood.

(ii) Development and adoption of agro-ecosystem specific integrated farming systems, for sustainable transformation of hill agriculture as vibrant and viable livelihood enterprise.

(iii) Large volume of useful farm research information developed by several institutions need to be integrated on farm scale addressing to the needs of farm families and appropriateness to the ecosystems, resources and the market.

(iv) Similarly, the aspects of their scaling up and replicability were rarely attempted. This was observed to be a major constraint by Srivastava (2013) and Gupta *et al.* (2006).

Thus, the key management factors included realisation of the potential eco-system productivity, natural resource conservation and improvement, optimising the management of arable and non-arable land and providing livelihood security, inclusive of the farming community, the farm holding, infrastructure and the market. This realisation led to the presently reported cluster of studies having large share of on-farm studies by the author and his team carried out in North West Himalaya.

Objectives and Strategy

The objective of ensuring economic viability should involving the farming community and their resource status, the possible integrated farming systems and secondary agriculture, allied activities and other off-farm livelihood options. Thus, approach for meeting the goal of economically viable farming has to be realistic, holistic, knowledge based, inclusive and comprehensive, keeping farmer, farming and market at the centre place. These have to commensurate with the market needs, ecosystems potentials and the knowledge support. There has to be a complete budgeting approach so as to identify potentials, deficiencies and surpluses in the system. These aspects become important in view of growing competition for natural and developed resources from other sectors of the economy.

Major Challenges

Persistent poverty, high migration due to absence of alternate employment, degradation of resources, poor productivity, insufficiency of knowledge and skill, and poor market infrastructure in addition to remoteness are major challenges. Since, the prevailing farming has largely been traditional; the limitation of the indigenous knowledge was also a major constraint.

Thus, the poverty reduction, environment conservation, productivity enhancement and ensuring economic security were main concern, which have been addressed in this chapter.

The Region

The NWHR are characterised by extreme terrain variability, high attitude (1,000 m to >3,500 m msl), steep slopes (15% to >100%), high intensity rainfall (>100 mm/hr), dominance of shallow and gravelly soil (7.5–15 cm depth and > 40% gravel), severe degradation, loss of forest cover and poor accessibility (only 8.6 km length of roads compared to 37km/100km^2 in India). The region spreads over 33 million ha across Jammu & Kashmir, Himachal Pradesh and Uttarakhand in North West Himalaya. Twenty five million people and nineteen million livestock inhabit this region, which are supported by only 2.14 million ha of cultivable land, with an average land holding of less than 0.1 ha in NWHR. The mountain ecosystem impacts almost half of the world population, as about 10 per cent live in mountain area and nearly 40 per cent occupy downstream low land area.

Base Line

Five identified districts included 15 clusters, having more than 3,700 farm families. These families consist of 5 to 12 members with holding ranging from 0.21 to 1.62 ha. Cropping intensity was only 146 per cent. The selected area consisted of 2,427 ha of cultivable and 1,312 ha of non-cultivable land. Dominant farming system families were 2,158 for food crops, 808 for livestock and 771 families for fruits, respectively.

Land and water degradation is a growing challenge to food

production and secondary agriculture and more so in hill and mountain regions. The relation between resource degradation and food security is strongly inverse. Often the farm operations required for agriculture aggravates the runoff and erosion problem. It is estimated that a family size of 6 members and livestock of 4, needs 800 litre of water/day, 1.2 t of food/yr, 0.66 t of fruits and vegetables/yr, 2 t of fuel wood/yr and 36.5 t of fodder/yr, respectively.

Strategy

The Indian Council of Agricultural Research (ICAR) envisages food and nutritional security in the country by inclusive growth. Enhancement of natural resources, better employment, value addition, profitability and augmentation of farm family's income are considered to be the key interventions (ICAR, 2010). The eco system constraints, infrastructural limitations and socio-cultural preferences provide a situation where, integrated hill farming along with secondary agriculture and allied enterprises are considered natural options for livelihood security. Livelihood security can be defined as "the capabilities, assets (including both material and social resources) and activities required for a means of living" (Carney, 1998).

Productive performance of hill farming essentially depend on the ecosystem specificity, natural resources, biological material, skill and market. The agro-ecosystem is defined as "An ecological unit that is managed for the purpose of producing food, feed, fibre and other economic products. The functional component consists of fluxes of energy, nutrients, matter and biological species (Altieri, 1995). "Ability of an agro-ecosystem to maintain production through time, in face of long-term ecological constraints and socio-economic pressures" (Altieri and Anderson, 1986). Thus, sustainable agriculture must be economically viable, socially acceptable and ecological sound. It should enable meeting present needs without compromising the needs of future generation.

Approach and Methodology

The approach of raising farm profitability starts with enhancement of natural resources and management of agro-ecosystems in the hill region. Ecologically, a hectare of farm land needs around five hectares of forest land to support sustainable hill agriculture (Singh, 2004). The efforts involved systematic scaling up from farm holding to village scale and then to regional scale in North West Himalaya. Innovative approach inclusive of base line, ecosystems, production systems, entire community and alternates were adopted. The entire programme was build-up on the basic needs of the farm families, resource potentials and projected demand of the market. The site and family specific knowledge input, skill development and service delivery were the highlight in achieving the success. The study at farm holding level involved evaluating the promising farming system the terrace level. It was then scaled up accommodating, the needs and potentials at the village level. The greater ecosystem variability at the regional level offered the option of greater range of farming systems and secondary agriculture.

Need based integrated farming systems addressed to domestic and market priorities further improves the profitability. The inclusion of ecosystems components of: (i) The sink capacity of soil; (ii) The moisture, temperature and sun-shine regime of the land-scape; and (iii) The overall impact of the terrain on the growing condition; enhanced the efficiency and performance of the production systems. This was also most important factor in profitability of the farming. It is the appropriate utilisation of the land and aquatic resources, then the farming systems with its components of crops, live-stocks, fisheries and others and the post-harvest-marketing management, which were attempted for higher productivity and economic sustainability. The entire watershed including non-arable and arable land, has to be managed in totality (Srivastava, 2003).

Thus, it is the reorientation of Research and Technology Development from being the scientists, development projects and agencies centric to the farm families and farms, natural resources and eco-systems; stakeholders and other end users; and domestic and market needs centric, which can ensure the economic viability of the farm sector. Subsequently, it is the efficient management of entire production systems, resources and the community adopting the inclusive approach, supported by efficient delivery mechanism, which decides the basic profitability of agriculture.

Development Efforts

The five essential components of economic viability include:

(i) Status of Natural resources and ecosystems specific farming systems. (ii) Integrated resource management farming systems. (iii) Knowledge, community skills and service delivery. (iv) Resource sufficiency, and (v) loss prevention, marketing, infrastructure and enabling policy.

The developed knowledge was stage-wise integrated for further site specificity. Then the same was accommodated to farm holding needs, and the agro-ecosystem specificities and technical potential developed. In this regard, the results from the field experiments and the available knowledge of components were well integrated with the projected needs of a farm family. Well laid out studies, under divergent ecosystems at farm holding level were conducted, which were further scaled up to village and regional level.

Socio-Economic, Farm Profitability and Productivity Issues

When we are dealing with a community organisation, it essentially addresses to a group of individuals and families having certain or a set of communities:

(i) The community level gives larger dimension of area variability of farm families, their holding and their dominant farming systems. Pooling of resources is common for operations, e.g. Land preparation, weeding, harvesting and threshing.

(ii) The losses to the farming at community level goes beyond the farm holding level. It involves water, flood, erosion, pathogens, insect and nutrient related losses. A well-organised community imbibes the spirit of sharing the resources and the benefits, thereby complimenting both the efforts made and the gains accrued.

(iii) The management of loss prevention has to be necessarily seen in terms of the space, time and community dimension.

(iv) Out-migration of skilled farmers and workers is a major social problem.

Research and Technology Development Efforts

Research: Agro-ecosystem specific study by the author in NWHR, spread on three widely divergent sites, with orientation of 90, 140 and 200° to sun, having with terraces located on 35, 30 and 25 per cent slopes, respectively. These sites were representative of the majority of cultivated area in North West Himalaya. Growing conditions specific to the three sites were characterized. The area under sunshine at respective sites includes 48, 72 and 61 per cent. The annual moisture regime varied from 9.4 to 12.6 and 11.5 per cent, respectively. The nitrogen content ranged from 0.213 to 0.270 and 0.223 kg N/m^3. However, when it was adjusted to the gravel content in soil (40, 23 and 17%), the respective value of N was 0.134, 0.207 and 0.285 kg N/m^3 only. Similarly, strong relationship with the siting of the terraces was observed.

Characterization of High, Medium and Low Productivity Conditions

Characterization and grouping of cultivable terraces under high, medium and low productivity conditions was made. These were primarily based on aspect influencing sunshine hours, soil volume (considering the depth and gravel content), organic carbon, soil nitrogen and soil erosion including runoff and soil loss. The details are presented in Table 13.1.

Table 13.1: Characterization of High, Medium and Low Productivity Conditions in Mid Altitude Hill Agro Ecosystems

Productivity Conditions	*Characterization*
High productivity	High coverage of sunshine at 08.00 hrs: 80%. Soil Volume: 0.5m^3, (depth × gravel). Organic carbon: 2.4 kg/m^3, soil N: 0.207 kg N/m^3. Soil erosion: Runoff: 23%, soil loss:< 12 t/ha/yr.
Medium productivity	Sunshine cover at 08.00 hrs: 68% Soil Volume: 0.4 m (depth × gravel) Organic Carbon: 2.1 kg/m^3. Soil N: 0.185 kg N/m^3 Soil erosion: Runoff: 31%, Soil loss: 17 t/ha/yr.
Low productivity	Sunshine cover at 0.8.00 hrs; 28% Soil volume: 0.3 m (depth × gravel) Soil erosion; Runoff 37%, Soil loss 23 t/ha/hr.

Source: Author's Survey.

Based on the ecosystem and related factors of land productivity were worked out for the region and provided in Table 13.2.

Table 13.2: Factors for Land Productivity Classification in NWHR

Factors	*High*	*Medium*	*Low*	*Quantification*
Slope	Moderate steep	Steep	Moderate steep Steep Very steep	<15% 15–33% >33%
Soil Depth	Moderate deep	Moderate deep Shallow	Moderate deep Shallow Very Shallow	22.5–45cm 7.5–22.5 cm <7.5 cm
Gravel Content	Low	Low Moderate	Low Moderate Heavy	10–30% 33–50% >50%
Landscape Siting	Lower Slope, Valley Middle Slope	Lower Slope, Valley Middle Slope	Lower Slope, Valley Middle Slope Upper Slope	1/5 – 1/3rd 1/3–1/2 Upper 1/2

Source: Author's Survey.

The Technology Development

Invariably the research results which are either based on Research Farms or the Laboratories studies, are taken as technology. This prevailing fact has been greatly limiting the up-scalability and replicability of the farm technology. Integration of research results into an efficient appropriate and feasible technology needs consideration of: (i) Range of time options, to suit farmers' resources, on one hand and, resource status and market demand pattern, on the other hand; (ii) Accommodating the weather risk pattern of a given agro-eco-region to farming systems, choice of crops, varieties and fine matching the harvest pattern and market needs; (iii) The harvest schedule of farm produce *vis-à-vis* quality and quantity of produce, energy availability, market demand and income demand pattern of the producing farmers; and (iv) Appropriate knowledge for nutrients, water, and harvest scheduling. The quantity of nutrient removal, status and availability have to be factored in. Similarly, we have considerable information on nutrients, but how about nutrient translocation back and nutrient content of grains and vegetation.

Protected Cultivation

In this region, where the temperature during winter drops to –3 to –4°C (much below the plant tolerance limit), optimal growing condition could be obtained using the greenhouse. On the contrary, during the summers, air temperature in the region rises to +35°C, it needs aeration and suitable cropping. Although mean total production under squash-frenchbean-tomato-spinach sequence was highest (1,585 kg/100m^2 and Rs. 11,636), the highest B:C ratio was observed in the plots under capsicum-tomato-spinach(963 kg/100m^2 and Rs. 12,113).

Off-season Vegetable Based Cropping System

Garden pea-squash-baby corn-radish cropping sequence was found giving the highest garden pea equivalent yield (575 q/ha) and net returns (INR 228 thousand/ha. Broccoli-squash-rice cropping sequence gave REY (660q/ha) and net returns (INR 229 thousand/ha). Rice-wheat traditional cropping sequence recorded lowest REY (135 q/ha) and net returns (INR 45 thousands/ha). Broccoli-squash-rice cropping sequences was found to be the best thereby giving the highest REY (660 q/ha) and net returns (Rs. 229 thousand/ha).

Diversified Farming Systems

Diversification of traditional farming, which consisted of 63 per cent cereals and pulses followed by only 30 per cent vegetables and 7 per cent fruits to diversified integrated farming system consisted of 50 per cent under cereals and pulses, 36 per cent under vegetables, 12 per cent under fruits, 1.3 per cent under protected and 0.3 per cent under fisheries. This could be achieved in a phased manner over three to five year's period. A broad matrix of farming systems and agro-eco system is provided as a result of studies conducted by the author in Table 13.3.

Thus, integration of modern knowledge has been successfully possible with the principles and practices of traditional hill farming. As it has been presented in previous sub-sections, the integrated hill farming system consisting of resource management, utilization and synergistic integration proceeds to ensuring sustainably and profitability (*see* Table 13.4).

Table 13.3: Farming System Synergy Matrix for a Given Agro-Eco-systems in a Watershed

Agro-eco system	*Farming system suitability matrix*				
	Perennial vegetation based	*Field cropping based*		*Commercial cropping based*	*Livestock farming based*
		Intensive	*Mono*		
High altitude Low temperature Low rainfall	VH	VL	M	H	M
Mid altitude Moderate Temperature High rainfall	H	VH	VL	VH	VH
Mid altitude Moderate temperature Low rainfall	H	L	M	M	H
Low altitude Moderate rainfall	H	M	L	H	M
Valley ecosystem	H	VH	NA	VH	VH

VH = Very high, H = High, M = Medium, L = Low, VL = Very low, NA = Not applicable
Source: Author's Survey.

Integration of Agriculture, Livestock, Horticulture and Forestry Components of Hill Farming System

Natural resource management on micro- watershed scale could raise integrated farming system productivity from 2.9 t/ha/yr to 4.3 under appropriate to that of 7.3 t of food, 11t of fruits and 12 t/ha/yr of fodder from micro-watershed. Improved farming system included the components of traditional crops, plantations of *kharif* and *rabi* season vegetables including French bean, tomato, capsicum, squash, okra and cabbage, vegetable pea and cauliflower resulting INR 13 lakh income from 7.5 ha area (INR 1.95 lakh/ha) from vegetables alone, averaging around INR 2 lakh/ha. Thus, it was possible to raise the carrying capacity of one hectare of land in hill region to 15 humans and 1 unit of livestock against the existing level of only 8 and 0.3, respectively.

Table 13.4: Site Specific Modules for Integrated Hill Farming System in NWHR

Components	*Production*
(i) High Producing Agro-Ecosystem (Rainfed):	
(a) Field crops: Rice, finger millet, wheat, lentil, *toria*	45 q/ha/yr (wheat equivalent)
(b) Fodder crops: Hybrid napier, *Morus alba*, Winter rye	800 q/ha/yr
(c) Land use ratio Field to fodder crops (a:b)	3:1
(d) Agri-horti-pastoral systems integrated on terrace risers Fruits (by fifth year of plantation) Pear, peach, plum, citrus (36 trees/holding of 0.4 ha) Leaf fodder trees (by fifth year of plantation) *Alnus, Bauhinia, Grevia, Quercus*	8.0 q/0.4 ha 6.5 q/ha/yr
(e) Integration of Mushrooms and apiary at household level Mushrooms (white button and Oyster mushrooms) wheat straw was utilized as main synthetic component Apiary: Integrated as pollinators@ 30 boxes of at least 4 frames	2 crops of 1 q each (Rs. 5,000/yr) 20-25 Kg/box (Italian) 8-10 Kg/box (Indian)
(ii) Medium producing agro-ecosystem (rainfed)	
(a) Field crops: Rice, finger millet, horse gram, wheat, lentil, *toria*	35 q/ha/yr (wheat equivalent)
(b) Fodder crops: Hybrid napier, *Morus alba*, Winter rye	745 q/ha/yr
(c) Land use ratio Field to fodder crops (a:b)	3:1
(d) Agri-horti-pastoral systems integrated on terrace risers Fruits (by fifth year of plantation) Pear, peach, plum, citrus (36 trees/holding of 0.4 ha) Leaf fodder trees (by fifth year of plantation) *Alnus, Bauhinia, Grevia, Quercus*	5.9 q/0.4 ha 6.0 q/0.4 ha
(e) Integration of Mushrooms and apiary at household level Mushrooms: wheat straw was utilized as main synthetic component Apiary: Integrated as pollinators@ 30 boxes of at least 4 frames	2 crops of 1 q each (Rs. 5,000/yr) 20-25 g/box (Italian) 8-10 Kg/box (Indian)

(Contd.)

Components	*Production*
(iii) Low producing agro ecosystem	
(a) Field crops: Rice, finger millet, horse gram, sesame, wheat, lentil, *toria*	40 q/ha/yr (wheat equivalent)
(b) Fodder crops: Hybrid napier, *Morus alba*, Winter rye	700 q/ha/yr
(c) Land use ratio Field to fodder crops (a:b)	1:1
(d) Agri-horti-pastoral systems integrated on terrace risers Fruits (by fifth year of plantation) Pear, peach, plum, citrus (36 trees/holding of 0.4 ha) Leaf fodder trees (by fifth year of plantation) *Alnus, Bauhinia, Grevia, Quercus*	 4.5 q/0.4 ha 5.0 q/0.4 ha
(e) Integration of Mushrooms and apiary at household level Mushrooms: (white button and Oyster mushrooms) wheat straw was utilized as main synthetic component Apiary: Integrated as pollinators@ 30 boxes of at least 4 frames	 2 crops of 1 q each (Rs. 5,000) 20–25 g/box (Italian) 8–10 Kg/box (Indian)

Source: Author's Survey.

Village Scale

Vivekananda Parvatiya Krishi Anusandhan Sansthan (VPKAS) of ICAR, Almora has developed technologies for different micro-climate and different situations of North-Western hills. This has transformed the scenario of agriculture in the village Bhagartola located 50 km from Almora (Uttarakhand). Diversification was pursued by the author and his team to enhance the farm income along with production of sufficient food grain through village level diversification and intensification of hill farming by improved crop varieties, water, natural resource management, farm machineries, protected cultivation, allied activities and skill improvement. This was supported by resource conservation, water harvesting and protected cultivation. The shift from traditional farming, which consisted of 63 per cent cereals and pulses followed by 30 per cent vegetable and only 7 per cent fruits to diversified integrated farming system consisted of 50 per cent under cereals and pulses, 36 per cent under vegetables, 12 per cent under fruits, 1.3 per cent under protected and 0.3 per cent under fisheries.

Thus, scaling up of IHFS to village scale has helped to improve resources, productivity and profitability. This could be achieved in a phased manner over five years' period. Improved farming systems included the components of traditional crops, plantations of *kharif* and *rabi* season vegetables including French bean, tomato, capsicum, squash, okra, cabbage, vegetable pea and cauliflower resulting Rs. 13 lakh income from 7.5 ha area (INR. 1.95 lakh/ha). The income of average farm family increased by 95 per cent from INR 24,960 to >INR 48,000. The village domestic product increased to >INR 17 lakh from INR 8.7 lakh. At the same time land diversion from food crop did not reduce the total food production because of introduction of high yielding varieties and 26 per cent higher yield as compared to the local varieties grown earlier. The income from average farm family was increased by 95 per cent from INR 24,960 per annum (Fig. 13.5). About 39 per cent increase in man-days was observed due to Increased cropping intensity, diversification of activities for incomes etc. About 4,000 man-days was observed in the village earlier which increased up to 6,120 man days due to increased investment. Moreover, the economic indicators like Net Present Value of the investment was estimated at INR 121.06 lakh showed that investment was done correctly. Benefit cost ratio (1.6) indicated that the target group is being benefited with the investment made. And most importantly, high internal rate of return indicates that the investment is sustainable and bankable.

Integrated Hill Farming System (IHFS) Development across the Five Districts in NWHR

The challenges of ensuring livelihood security was addressed in 5 selected disadvantaged districts of Kupwara, Doda, Chamba, Tehri Garhwal and Champawat of NWHR states of Jammu & Kashmir, Himachal Pradesh and Uttarakhand. Large scale adoption of integrated farming system was undertaken as a major strategy while working with 3,737 farm families of 15 clusters of villages of the region. The project had allocation of INR 30 crore for the period of 2007-2012. The major thrust included: Diversification, intensification of farming, fruits, livestock, mushrooms, fisheries, perennial, vegetation, processing, community skill and capacity building, women drudgery reduction and knowledge empowerment.

Baseline Survey

Five identified districts included 15 clusters, have 3737 farm families. These families consist of 5 to 12 members with holding ranging from 0.21 to 1.62 ha. Cropping intensity was only 146 per cent. The selected area consisted of 2,427 ha of cultivable and 1,312 ha of non-cultivable land. Major farming system families were 2,158 for food crops, 808 for livestock and 771 families for fruits, dominant.

Enhancement of Productivity

The cropping intensity and productivity has resulted in > 60 per cent enhancement, diversification to vegetables and fruits. Cultivation of vegetables has raised farmers income to Rs. 2.7 lakh/ha. Plantation of fruits includes 1,25,125 of tropical and temperate crops. The interventions led to improvement in productivity from 1.5 t/ha of food to > 2 t/ha and from 2.79 t/ha of vegetables to > 5 t/ha, respectively. The largest area (2,410 ha) was under food crops, of which 368 ha was diverted to vegetables and fruits. This was possible due to increased production of food. The area under food was reduced to 64 per cent and under vegetables and fruits increased to 22 and 14 per cent as compared to 70, 18 and 8 per cent in pre-project period, respectively. The sustainability to farming system was incorporated by water harvesting (305 ponds), 331 ha area under perennial vegetation and 6,763 numbers of bio-engineering measures. The scaling up of protected cultivation involved 296 polyhouses growing high value vegetables, seedlings and floriculture. This led to an earning of INR 23,68,000 resulting the employment generation of 14,800 human days a year to 3,700 farm families.

Livestock Management

Breed upgradations, health care and nutrition management were major efforts. Backyard poultry has become a run-away success. Introduction of improved breed—cattle + poultry + innovating housing cattle, poultry; better housing-better cow dung added to higher assured income. It positively impacted the farmer's nutrient management-vermi composting-nutrient management in vegetables farming and protected cultivation. The improvement in milk production by 8,000 l/day over 10,800 l/day and 565,000 eggs/yr from backyard poultry was significant component imparting diversification, climate change resilience and economic sustenance. Integration of feed, fodder and meal demand of livestock, poultry and fish in the production cropping+ high value crop, flowers and fruits was highlighted in Doda, Makot and Majhgaon clusters.

Environmental Security

Perennial vegetation including fodder grasses have covered 1,046 ha of non-arable land across selected 5 districts. Multipurpose trees were planted on 105 ha area. Water harvesting and protected cultivation with a total of 268 poly tanks and 296 poly houses were completed. These measures improved moisture regime, vegetative cover and imparted better environment for farming system productivity.

Employment Generation

Natural Resource Management

Non-Arable Land: 485 ha × 50 human days/year = 24,250 human days/year

Arable Land: 570 ha × 30 human days/year = 17,100 human days/year

Water Resource Development: 168 ponds, 296 poly-houses; 108 ponds under fish,

Employment: 14,800 human days/year

Farm Power and Machinery: 2,400 ha, 11,700 human days/year

In addition; saving of 6,000 human days/year

Total human days generated: 67,850 human days/year

Inclusive of the selected 3,700 farm families of North West Himalaya.

The performance of the farm sector in country greatly depends on the availability of labour and energy; both on account of sufficient extent and time of availability. The invariably narrow window of peak demand increases the cost otherwise affects the productivity thereby the profitability. Establishing the values of economic threshold for productivity under a given farm situation and stage-wise attempted to achieve the same.

Climate Change Management and Carbon Sequestration

The aggregate increase in farm production has been 482 t of food grains and 1,831 t of vegetables from 3,054 ha of cultivated area. The estimated additional biomass including grain, stalk and root mass was 1,446 t from food crops and 3,662 t from vegetable crops. This has resulted in total additional carbon trapped being 1,092 tonnes. Carbon sequestration of 0.35 t/ha/year, was obtained due to higher production. Reduced tillage in >250 ha prevented losses of carbon to atmosphere. This was achieved directly by reducing tillage and indirectly by plantation of perennial vegetation.

Thus, to summarise: the production of food and vegetables increased from equal to 9.5 months to 11 months and 6.8 months to 19.0 months of human consumption for more than 3,700 farm families, respectively. Employment raised from 234 human days to 362 human day/family/year. This resulted increase in income from INR 59,600 to INR 98,340/family/year.

Overview: Learnings and Lessons

The task of ensuring the economic security cannot be achieved just at the individual farm family level. The task has to be inclusive of village farming community, the natural resources-both terrestrial and aquatic with full support of market, policy and credit facilities. The Action Plan leading to economic viability include:

(i) Natural Resource Management and Agro-eco-systems: Conservation and enhanced dependence on natural over purchased resources, better performance of production systems due to site specificity.
(ii) Raised productivity: quantity and quality.
(iii) Niche production of high value commodities linked to market demand pattern—organic farming, protected cultivation with advantage off seasonality.
(iv) Resource sufficiency including energy and efficient

operational management, with skill upgradation of farmers.

(v) Loss prevention, value addition, market and credit support.

(vi) Highly efficient knowledge based diversified farming systems, secondary agriculture, and allied activities.

(vii) Service delivery, credit, policy and continued hand holding.

(viii) Targeting decent living standard, resource conservation and self-esteem to farming community.

Thus, the knowledge based robust farming system for risk minimisation and loss prevention has to involve: Pre-Production, Production and Post-Production aspects on a time scale and Field, Farm holding, Village and Regional scale.

The efforts made by the author, his team of farmers and scientists have shown the success of phase-wise scaling up and replicability of a mega effort towards sustainable productivity and profitability. However, the marketing, as well as service delivery in the region continue to be matter of great concern. This needs synergy and complimentary such as the provisions for marketing for example; provision of refrigerated van, made by the Government of West Bengal for marketing of perishable commodities and making available the Cooperative Building by Government of Uttarakhand for the integrated farm women community led processing and marketing outlets at Dharaunj, Disrict Champawat.

Agenda for Future

Let us look for intelligent technology and smart decisions.

Repositioning, reorienting, the priorities, emerging issues:

- There has to be a strong component of non-arable land management for enhancing the natural resources and ensuring fodder, fuel and minor produce adding the income and improving the resilience of the farming.
- Knowledge based smart agriculture. Climate resilient farming systems ensures minimum assured production and higher profitability.
- Economic compensation for the ecosystem services and carbon credits for hill regions.

- Stablishing producer-consumer chain reducing the middlemen.
- Strategic advantage of the community and development in the region.
- Processing and market supported repositioning the farming ensuring minimum assured income.
- Prioritisation of factors for losses and enhanced profitability to the systems. The farm sector has to be quickly transformed to meet the aspirations and needs of the ambitions and growingly modern younger generation. Transformation of the community and farming to a knowledge based, modern and viable livelihood enterprise.
- Inclusive approach to rationalisation of Integrated farming system, secondary agriculture and allied activities for secured livelihood and ensured profitability.
- National initiative for economically viable and sustainable farming aimed at food, fodder, fuel, environment, livelihood and economic security.

Conclusion

The agenda of ensuring the economic security supported by food, livelihood and environment security faces the issues of productivity, marketability, profitability and sustainability of the country's farm sector. The economic security and welfare of the farming community goes far beyond productivity and environment security to loss prevention, remunerative pricing and employment security. The sectors external to farmers and farming are equally important players including marketing, infrastructure, intelligent information and policy interventions. It needs a strong backward linkage including seed, energy and necessary resources as well as forward linkage from harvest stage onward including processing, branding and transparent marketing and pricing.

The present state involving almost 20 crore of farm families need inclusive and holistic approach on mega scale. These are not beautiful words, but have to be part of any effort to alleviate poverty.

Profitability has reference to increasing the gains with maximum efficiency both with respect to resources as well as the market. The losses to and individual crop entire farming and the village has to be dealt with not only from the perspective of direct damages to crops and commodities but, also to the sustainability of natural resources. Thus, the total production, environment, nutrition efficiency, profitability and livelihood are directly affected due to crop losses in one form or the other. It has been achieved in the North Western Himalaya, where at the Farm Holding Scale, compared to the base annual productivity of only 25 q/ha and some 3-5 q/ha of fodder, fuelwood and fruits, the concerted efforts of agro eco-system specificity, improved resource management and integrated farming systems, could raise the total production up to >200 q under medium productivity and > 240 q/ha under higher productivity conditions. At the Village Scale, in Bhagartola, Almora, with 35 farm families, the output in terms of increased income from INR 61,000 ha/yr, to INR 130,000. At the Regional Scale, this experience was scaled up to over 3,700 farm families in 15 villages across 5 districts of North West Himalaya. The employment could be raised from 234 human days to 362 per family and income from INR 62,000 to 98,340 per family per year in addition to meeting their domestic needs. The food production could be raised from 9 months to 11 months, vegetables from 6.8 to 19 months of consumption. Thus, sincere efforts are needed. Let us recall our memory about the CD Blocks and the superb role played by them in ushering green revolution. It has to be taken up as campaign.

Reorienting and repositioning the research and technology development efforts made by the author have convincingly shown the possibilities of imparting economic profitability and competitiveness to the Indian farm sector. Thus, in the hill region, the farm based economic well-being of farm families could be ensured by appropriate farming and allied activities. This could be achieved by enhancing productivity, employment and profitability. This could be a major path for ensuring economic security and tool for poverty reduction in hill region.

References

Altieri, M.A., Anderson, M.K., (1986). An ecological basis for the development of alternative agricultural systems for small farmers in the Third World. *American Journal of Alternative Agriculture*, 1: 30-38.

Altieri, M.A., (1995). *Agroecology: The Science of Sustainable Agriculture.* 2nd Ed. West View, Boulder, CO, USA.

Carney, D., (ed.) (1998). *Sustainable Rural Livelihoods: What Contribution can we make?* London: Department for International Development.

ICAR-2010. ICAR-2030, *Visioning Future challenges ınd harnessing opportunities.* ICAR, Krishi Bhawan, New Delhi, India.

Jodha, N.S. (2004). High land-low land linkages in the globalised world. In: N.S., Jodha, B., Bhadra, N.R., Khanal, Richter Jurgen, (Eds.), *Poverty Alleviation in Mountain Area of China.* ICIMOD, Kathmandu, pp. 167-183.

National Commission on Agriculture, 1976. *Report of the NCA, Part XIII.* Rural Employment and Special Area Programme. Ministry of Agriculture and Irrigation, Government of India, New Delhi, p. 191.

Pandey, S.C., Srivastava, A.K., Murty, N.S., Bhatt, J.C. and Gupta, H.S. (2012). *Climate and Crop Planning in mid hills of North West Himalaya,* Vivekananda Parvatiya Krishi Anusandhan Sansthan, (ICAR), Almora.

Jodha, N.S. (1990). Mountain Agriculture: Search for Sustainability. Mountain Farming Systems, Disc: Paper No. 2. ICIMOD, Kathmandu, Nepal.

Singh, J.S. (2004). "Sustainable development of Indian Himalayan region-linking ecological and economic concerns". Pt. Pant Memorial Lecture-X. GBPIHED. Kosi-Katarmal, Almora, 28 p.

Srivastava, A.K. (2003). *Watershed research in NW Himalaya—An overview.* VPKAS, Almora (UA), p. 12.

Srivastava, A.K., Mishri, B., Singh, B. (2003). Resource Management in silvi-pasture in Shiwaliks. *Indian Forester,* 129 (4): 446-456.

Srivastava, A.K. (2006). Sustainability of hill agriculture agro ecosystem and watersheds. pp. 22- 49. In: H.S. Gupta, A.K. Srivastava and J.C. Bhatt, *Sustainable Production from Agricultural Watersheds in North West Himalaya.* VPKAS, Almora, India.

Srivastava, A.K. (2009). *Challenges of Hill Agriculture in North West Himalaya, Hill Agriculture in SAARC Countries: Constraints and Opportunities,* SAARC Agriculture Centre, Dhaka, Bangladesh, pp. 53-66.

Srivastava, A.K. (2013). *Sustainable and Replicable Hill Faming for Secure Livelihood in North West Himalaya Region.* VPKAS, Almora. p. 183.

14
Adaptive Measures of Agricultural Sustainability between two Agro-Climatic Zone of Rajasthan

Parthsarathi Dehury and *Jagdish Jadhav*

Introduction

Sustainable agriculture is an important movement today; it is provided for the future of farming and may prevent the collapse of the world's food system (Cindy, 2007). But, it is not a bonus; when an agricultural resource base erodes beyond a certain point, the civilization it has supported collapses or changes rapidly. There is an increasing worldwide perception that the trends in agricultural production are neither sustainable nor environmentally sound (Conway and Barbier, 1998). The major crop, such as wheat, is no longer increasing at the rate it has, and excessive soil erosion remains an ever present threat to sustained crop production. Potential climate change associated with increasing atmospheric carbon dioxide may strengthen the problems of sustainability.

Climate change will have a profound impact on human and eco-systems during the coming decades through variations in global average temperature and rainfall according to the Fourth Assessment Report (FAR) of the Inter-governmental Panel on Climate Change (IPCC). Agriculture and livestock sectors are highly sensitive to climate change. It would also effects on agricultural sustainability, which is a major threat to human well-being. Consequently, the interaction between agricultural performance and weather, which has been an important area of research since the last few decades, has gained momentum due to the awareness of the adverse effects of climate change on agriculture and livelihood. In the context of developing nations, such as India, where agriculture continues to support the livelihoods of more than two-third of the population, a study of the nature and impact of climate change on agriculture and people's livelihood assumes importance.

It is observed that 'climate change' is one of the serious environmental issues that the modern world is going to face multi-dimensional problems on agriculture in the 21st century. The earth's climate is frequently changing and leading to degradation of biodiversity, water and soil resources, desertification, coastal, erosion, decrease in agricultural productivity etc. As per the IPCC, climate change refers to any change in climate over time, either due to natural variability or as a result of human activity (IPCC, 2007). The UN Framework Convention on Climate Change (UNFCCC, 2007) refers to climate change as a change that is attributable directly or indirectly to human activity that alters the composition of the global atmosphere in addition to the natural climate variability observed over comparable periods of time (IPCC, 2007). It refers to a statistically significant variation in either the mean state of the climate persisting for an extended period, usually decades, or in its variability (GoI, 2008). Climate change occurs due to natural internal processes, external forces, and persistent anthropogenic changes in the composition of the atmosphere or in land use (GoI, 2008). The world community faces many risks from climate change.

India is a large country with 15 agro-climatic zones, diverse seasons, crops and farming systems. For a majority of the people in India, agriculture is the main source of livelihood. Agriculture is also most vulnerable to climate change because it is inherently sensitive to climate variability. So, it has an impact on Indian agriculture in various direct and indirect ways besides affecting the lives and livelihood of millions of Indians. Agriculture and allied activities, such as livestock and fisheries, constitute an important component of India's Gross Domestic Product (GDP) contributing nearly 25 per cent of the GDP and providing employment opportunities to two-third of the population. The South-West monsoon, which brings most of the region's precipitation dominates Indian climate and is critical for the availability of irrigation for agriculture. Agricultural productivity is sensitive to two broad classes of climate-induced effects: (1) direct effects from changes in temperature, precipitation, and carbon dioxide concentration; and (2) indirect effects through changes in soil moisture and the distribution and frequency of infestation by pests and diseases.

Agriculture will be adversely affected not only by an increase or decrease in the overall amount of rainfall, but also by shifts in the timing of the rainfall. For instance, over the last few years, the Chhattisgarh region received less than its share of pre-monsoon showers in May and June. These showers are important to ensure adequate moisture in fields being prepared for paddy cultivation. Agriculture will be worst affected in the coastal regions of Gujarat and Maharashtra, where agriculturally fertile areas are vulnerable to inundation and salinization. Standing crops in these regions are also more likely to be damaged due to cyclonic activity. In Rajasthan, a rise in temperature by 2°C was estimated to reduce production of pearl millet by 10-15 per cent. Madhya Pradesh, where soybean is grown on 77 per cent of all agricultural land, could ironically benefit from an increase in carbon dioxide in the atmosphere. Soybean yields could go up by as much as 50 per cent if the concentration of carbon dioxide in the atmosphere doubles (Lal *et al.*, 1999).

However, if this increase in carbon dioxide is accompanied by an increase in temperature, as expected, then soybean yields could actually decrease. If the maximum and minimum temperatures go up by 1°C and 1.5°C respectively, the gain in yield comes down to 35 per cent. If maximum and minimum temperatures rise by 3°C and 3.5°C respectively, then soybean yields will decrease. Changes in the soil, pests and weeds brought about by climate change will also affect agriculture in India. For instance, the amount of moisture in the soil will be affected by changes in factors such as precipitation, run-off and evaporation. Scientists predict that because of global warming, this already erratic weather system could become even more undependable. Semi -arid regions of western India are expected to receive higher than normal rainfall as temperatures soar while central India will experience a decrease of 10 to 20 per cent in winter rainfall by the 2050s (Rupakumar *et al.*, 2003).

In India, climate change will put additional stress on ecological and socio-economic systems that are already facing tremendous pressures due to rapid urbanization, industrialization and economic development. With its huge and growing population, a 7500 km long densely populated and low-lying coastline and an economy that is closely tied to its natural resource base, India is considered to be especially vulnerable to the impacts of climate change. Various studies conducted in the country have shown that the surface air temperature in India is rising at the rate of 0.4°C per hundred years, particularly during the post-monsoon and winter season. Models project that mean winter temperatures will increase by as much as 3.2°C in the 2050s and 4.5°C by 2080s. Summer temperatures will increase by 2.2°C in the 2050s and 3.2°C in the 2080s (GoI, 2008).

Rajasthan is the largest state of India with an area of 3,42,239 km^2 and a population of 56.47 million, of which 76.6 per cent is rural area and their main occupation are agriculture (Census, 2001). The state have different agro-climatic zone. The climate of Rajasthan signifies the annual rainfall of the study region varies from 500 to 600 mm^3. Summer and winter temperatures are not as extreme as in the arid west, but the summer temperature may reach around 45°C. In winters, minimum may reach 8°C. The groundwater varies from 15 to 25 metres but the annual fluctuations are high, especially in the years when the south-west monsoon fails and the yearly replenishment rates are low. Surface water sources are scarce and so harnessing of ground water resources has been going on at an accelerated pace. A very common feature of the area is drought, which appears in regular cycles and continues to exert a toll on production. Climate change, the greatest global challenge, is already a reality for the farmers of Rajasthan. It is increasing the pressure on already scarce resources and if proper measures are not taken, migration towards the cities will soon reach new heights. Rajasthan has a livestock population of about 49.1 million and ranks among the top three states for having the highest livestock population. Though contribution of animal husbandry to the state GDP is about 9.16 per cent, it is also one of the biggest methane emitters contributing almost 9.1 per cent to the total methane emissions in the country [Rajasthan State Action Plan on Climate Change (RAPCC) Report, 2014].

Low rainfall coupled with erratic monsoons makes Rajasthan vulnerable to drought which directly influence on agriculture. A recent report of the Indian Institute of Tropical Meteorology analysed the rainfall patterns all over the country and indicated an overall decreasing trend in the rainfall in Eastern Rajasthan. The study, analysing more than 100 years of regional rainfall data found decreasing trends in overall, winter and summer-monsoon rainfall, while pre- and post-monsoon summer rainfall showed increasing trends (Sontakke *et al.*, 2008). The instability of the resource base in much of Rajasthan, agriculture is a high risk activity. Climate change poses formidable challenges to the animal husbandry sector as well. Rajasthan is the second highest producer of milk in the country (amounting to nearly 17 lakh kg per day). But, its annual loss in milk production due to heat stress in Rajasthan is 98.65, 40.55 and 29.74 litres per animal per year in crossbred cows, local cows and buffaloes respectively (*Times of India*, 2012).

Apart from good seeds, agricultural productivity depends on soil health, irrigation water quality and quantity, clean atmosphere of proper composition of carbon dioxide, nitrogen and oxygen, in addition to diverse micro-organisms, pollination insects, birds, earthworms, farm animals and other non-domesticated flora and fauna (Swaminathan, 1983). Most long-term (>50 year) studies indicate that crop productivity is rising with the adoption of new varieties and appropriate management inputs and appears sustainable. Genetic controls repressing or stimulating the cascades of gene expression that move a plant through stages in its life cycle, facilitating the morphogenesis of vegetative and reproductive tissues and organs. The new technologies are permitting the identification of key gene activity responses to the range of biotic and abiotic challenges experienced by plants. The effects of technology improved weed control, disease suppression, and crop varieties, which is highly visible and confirmed by long-term harvest trends (Leigh and Johnston, 1994). Some introduced agricultural crops, livestock and trees have become invasive species, spreading beyond their planned range and displacing native species (Matthews and Brand, 2004). Concerns about genetically modified crop varieties include their potential to become invasive species or to hybridize with wild relatives; leading to the loss of biodiversity (Jackson, 1990). Intensive agriculture practiced without adherence to the scientific principles and ecological aspects has led to loss of soil health, and depletion of freshwater resources and agro-biodiversity. Further, even with food availability through production, millions of marginal farming, fishing and landless rural farmer families have very low or no access to food due to lack of income generating livelihoods. Approximately 200 million rural women, children and men in India alone fall in this category (Kesavan and Swaminathan, 2008).

Sustainability in developing countries may be placed at increased risk when partial adoption of modern technology is strongly established (Rasmussen *et al.*, 1998). The effectiveness of the coping mechanisms adopted the intra-household sharing of the burden of coping and the appropriate state and non-state interventions to strengthen the survival mechanisms adopted by the families (Sathaye, 2006).

Research Design

The study employed mixed methodology. The goal of the study was to gather data about the coping patrons regarding agricultural sustainability of farmers and agricultural workers on climate change and its impact on their livelihood. The measure of agricultural components was explored in both qualitative and quantitative approach. Two agro-climatic zones Fagi and Shahbad blocks from Rajasthan were selected for the study purpose. Both zones have certain quality in different geographical locations. The study was conducted from ten villages, five from each zone by simple random sampling method. Hundred samples were taken from farmers and agricultural labours through semi-structured interview and ten Focus Group Discussion (FGD) were conducted to justify the objective. Using descriptive statistics, the data were analysed in terms of frequency distribution and percentage using excel sheet as raw data were difficult to understand for meaningful conclusions to be made. The data were presented using tables, frequencies, and percentages. All the necessary statistical formats like tables, graphs, means and median were calculated from the programme. The exploratory data were concluding by thematic analysis.

Result

As described in research methodology section, primary data are collected from the rural community's framers of Fagi and Shahbad blocks of Rajasthan. All interviews and focus group discussions have been conducted to focus on agricultural sustainability as per the changing pattern of climate. Change in climate and its effects to the agriculture and livestock are experienced differently in different aspects. It also gathers information regarding perception of village farmers about how climate change influences to agriculture and the various coping mechanism. Acquired information and their interpretation are presented below, and now the situation is becoming harder each year for farmers.

Impact of Climate Change on Agricultural Production

Majority of people were depending on agriculture and it heavily depends on seasonal rainfall. Due to less and irregular rainfall adverse effect on agriculture has been noticed. Unseasonal rainfall, irregular and erratic rainfalls have resulted in excess water and drought in Rajasthan. This has adverse impact on crops production (food and crops), which is threatening food security, and well-being of the people. People have to work harder to meet their necessary food needs. Less rainfall and increasing temperature, water resources are drying up slowly. Wet-land is decreasing and becoming arid. The most common crops are cultivated in the study area are *bajra* (pearl millet), *jowar* (sorghum), pulses and soybean in the *Kharif* (Rainy) season, and wheat, barley, gram, mustard and coriander in the *Rabi* (Winter) season. The effected crops are presented below.

Table 14.1: Impact of Climate Change on Agricultural Crops

Effected crops	*No. of Respondent*		*Frequency (%)*	
	Fagi	*Shahbad*	*Fagi*	*Shahbad*
Mustered and Soybean	6	17	12	34
Decrease in production of all crops	27	15	54	30
Stable production	3	0	6	0
Inset, weak and premature crops	14	2	28	4
Decrease wheat and coriander	0	3	0	6

Source: Field survey, 2014.

According to collected data unseasonal rain influence the production of crops which has been decreased. Soybean and wheat destroyed due to excess rain and hailstone. Whereas, 30 per cent of respondents lost all crops from Shahbad and 54 per cent of respondents from Fagi have been facing same problem. Various Insets have been influenced to week and premature crops which leads to less agricultural production.

Impact of Climate Change on Water-level

According to the collected data from two agro-climatic zone there are huge difference between levels of water resources. Ninety per cent respondents from Shahbad are in the perception that water level has increased, which was not earlier as unexpected rainfall have experienced in last five year. At same time another zone of Rajasthan where 54 per cent respondents told the level of water decreasing and the quality of the water also decreased, which is effecting on crops. Even from last five year the vegetable production has decreased because the water is not useful for producing vegetables.

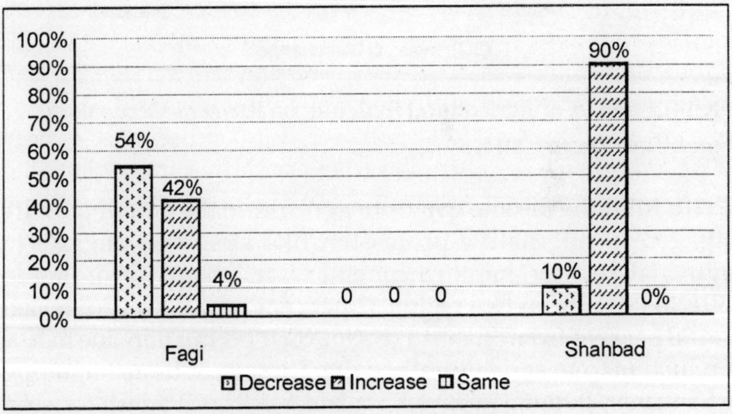

Fig. 14.1: Impact of Climate Change on Water-level

Source: Field survey, 2014.

Influence of Agro-Activities on Farmers Occupation

Livelihood can be measured from the dependency of household on which they are depending. Economic status is also measured from the dependency and occupation. Most of the households were depending on agriculture on the study area. It indicates that if there is threat on agriculture the direct impact falls upon livelihood of the people. Impacts of agricultural activity influence on income and overall economy slow down also marked. As agriculture is main sources of income, the loss or degradation in agriculture threatens the income level of the household.

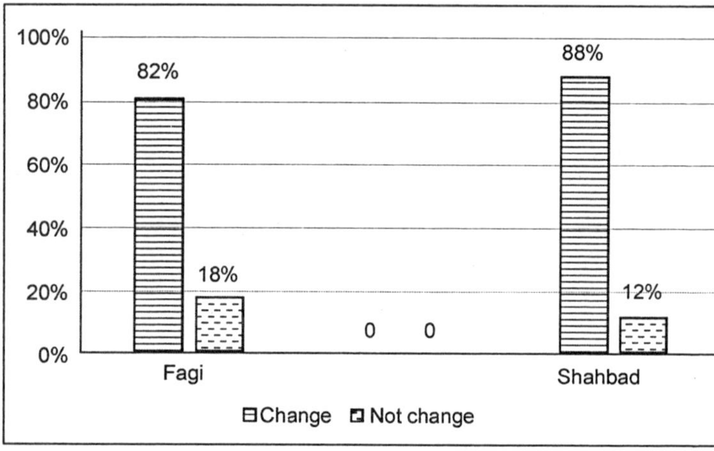

Fig. 14.2: Impact of Agricultural Activities on Farmer's Occupation
Source: Field survey 2014.

To fulfil the income gap from agriculture the households are engaged in alternative profession like business, migrate to industrial area for employment and wage labour. According to collected data from two region 82 per cent respondent from Fagi and 88 per cent from Shahbad change their occupation due to low production from agricultural activity. These people are migrating to Sanganer, Jaipur, Gujarat, Kota and Madhya Pradesh for crop cutting, construction work and labour work for daily wages.

Adoption of Seed for Production Enhancement

Most of the farmers have lost their indigenous varieties of seed and now they have to dependent on the market for the seeds, which resistant to dry spells, high temperatures and other detrimental weather influences. While planting traditional crop varieties, farmers used to get some yields under conditions where the new varieties fail completely. Five decades ago, most of the farmers were using indigenous seed. Now, around half of the farmers are completely dependent on hybrid seeds.

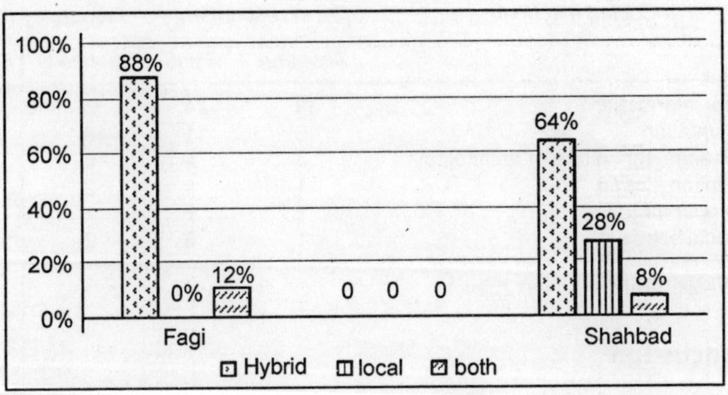

Fig. 14.3: Adoption of Seed
Source: Field survey, 2014.

According to the study 88 per cent respondents from Fagi and 64 per cent from Shahbad were adopting Hybrid seeds for more production, which is having resistance capacities and takes less time in comparison to local seeds. Even some of them knew that by using fertilizer there is reduction of soil strength. In Shahbad most of respondent belongs to Sahriya and Bhil community, so, they have believed more on traditional way of cultivation and another reason was unable to buy hybrid seeds due to poverty.

Adaptive Measures on Coping Mechanism

In two agro-climatic zone of Rajasthan has been affected, as result of study shows the figure of respondent that they are unable to cope with changing pattern of climate which affected their livelihood. Seventy eight per cent respondents from Fagi and 48 per cent respondents from Shahbad do not have any information how to cope with climate change and what should be the coping mechanism to deal with climate change. Respondents of both zones said plantation is one of the ways, which help to cope with changing pattern of climate. While conducting focus group discussion in Shahbad it is found that there is a demand from villagers for better irrigation system from government.

Table 14.2: People's Perception on Coping Mechanism

Coping mechanism	*No. of respondent*		*Frequency (%)*	
	Shahbad	*Fagi*	*Shahbad*	*Fagi*
No. information	39	24	78	48
Plantation	5	11	10	22
Change agriculture or technology	3	4	6	8
Minimize need	1	1	2	2
Proper irrigation	1	7	2	14
Local seeds	1	3	2	6

Sources: Field survey, 2014.

Conclusion

Climate change is a natural process, but human activities are accelerating the speed of change. Deforestation leads to increase in temperature and unseasonal rainfall, which is major consequences in agriculture and livestock asset. Due to the scarcity of water for irrigation, agricultural production and productivity is decreasing. Threat to agriculture and livestock also has been experienced on different geographical region. Because of less adaptation and mitigation capacity Rajasthan have been affected more in comparison to other states from climate change. Rajasthan is the most vulnerable state on the basis of water resources, reason behind less numbers of rivers are flowing. Even Thar Desert also situated in this state, so annual temperature rise higher in comparison to other states.

The production and productivity of the food grain as well as cash crops has been decreasing every year. Due to low productivity threat to food security is rising as a big issue. Cultivation of crops is being difficult because of scarcity of water for irrigation and excess rainfall on crops harvesting time. Area for livestock rearing, getting grass and fodder is reduced because of drought. Due to less availability of fodder livestock pattern has been decreased, resulting in reduction of milk and milk products. On the other hand decreasing the domestic animals like commercial poultry, goat and seep farming due to unseasonal rain, excess winter and new borne diseases. Natural hazard and uncertainty of whether threatening on agricultural production which is leading towards less production and threat on food security. Cash crops such as Soybean, wheat, coriander, mustard are also threatened from extreme drought, unseasonal rainfall and incest. Overall economic status of people of the study area seemed to be unsatisfactory. Unsustainable genetic hybrid seeds and traditional patrons of agriculture is threatening the life of people in rural areas and opportunities for livelihood have been narrowing down. Traditional sources of income are being inconvenient for survival. Poor, marginalised farmers are affected more from climate change.

Recommendations

Agriculture is a science which teaches us what crops are to be planted on each kind of soil and what operations are to be carried out. For this the land have to be over-exploited. When applied to agriculture, a sustainable system of production should achieved for economic viability of farmers and others engaged in agriculturally related enterprises. There is requirement of preservation and enhancement of environmental quality which contribute to local community development. This means, a system of agriculture that involves sustainable management of natural resources and progressive enhancement of soil quality, biodiversity and productivity is ever required. Several farming systems can help to produce more from the available land, water and labour resources without either ecological or social harm. The sustainable agriculture is integrated with sustainable rural development through technological and knowledge empowerment of rural communities.

Training and capacity building enables the rural resource-poor farming, fishing and landless farmer's families to manage successfully the various farming enterprises. Technological development, knowledge and empowerment of the rural communities fall within the domain of village knowledge centre. There should be plan for realisation of sustainable agriculture practices by considering a mix of modern scientific methods with traditional wisdom, participation of farmers, scientists, planners, policy-makers etc., as well as market and trade linkages that are not only free but also fair. In addition, the developing countries mostly India should contain their population growth without further delay. Sustainable agriculture holds out hope for humankind it can succeed only if all the developed and developing nations stand together for common good. Sustainable agriculture and development is for our common future. Shifting cropping patterns to adopt heat and less water consuming varieties of seeds and fertilizers should be practiced by farmers for the sustainable development of agriculture. The cropping patterns to local varieties of pulses, green gram, millets and mustard, which need less water and less time to harvest may also be promoted. Plantation, Rain water harvesting, Multi-crops' cultivation and worm fertilizer are the ways, which help to cope with changing pattern of climate which leads agricultural sustainability.

References

Cindy, J. (2007). Agricultural Sustainability: Review. *Economic Botany, 61*(4): 397.

Conway, G.R. and Barbier, E. (1990). After The Green Revolution Sustainable Agriculture for Development, *Earth Scan*, London.

Dennis, E.S., Ellis, J., Green, A., Llewellyn, D., Morell, M., Tabe, L., and Peacock, W.J. (2008). Genetic contributions to agricultural sustainability. Philosophical Transactions of the Royal Society of London B: *Biological Sciences, 363*(1491): 591-609.

Faeth, P. (1993). *Agricultural Policy and Sustainability: Case Studies from India, Chile, and the U.S.*, World Resources Institute, Washington, DC.

GoI (2008). *Climate Change*, Ministry of Environment and Forests. New Delhi: Government of India. Retrieved from http://envfor.nic.in/cc/what.html.

IPCC (2007). *Climate Change 2007: The Physical Science Basis.* Contribution of Working Group I to the Fourth Assessment Report of the Intergovernmental Panel on Climate Change—Solomon, S.; Qin, D.; Manning, M.; Chen, Z.; Marquis, M.; Averyt.

Jackson, K. (1990). *Making Sustainable Agriculture Work. Sustainable Table.* San Francisco: North Point Press, pp. 132-41.

Kesavan, P.C., and Swaminathan, M.S. (2008). Strategies and models for agricultural sustainability in developing Asian countries. Philosophical Transactions of the Royal Society B: *Biological Sciences, 363*(1492), 877-891.

Lal, R., and Bruce, J.P. (1999). The potential of world cropland soils to sequester C and mitigate the greenhouse effect. *Environmental Science and Policy*, 2(2): 177-185.

Leigh, R.A. and Johnston, A.E. (1994). *Long-Term Experiments in Agricultural and Ecological Sciences*, CAB International, Wallingford, UK.

Matthews, S., and Brand, K. (2004). *Africa invaded: the growing danger of invasive alien species.*

Rajasthan State Action Plan on Climate Change (RAPCC) Report. (2014). Retrieved February 2014 from http://timesofindia.indiatimes.com/city/jaipur/Climate-change-adversely-affecting-agriculture/articleshow/14218321.cms

Rasmussen, P.E., Goulding, K.W., Brown, J.R., Grace, P.R., Janzen, H.H., and Körschens, M. (1998). Long-term agro-ecosystem experiments: Assessing agricultural sustainability and global change. *Science*, *282*(5390), 893-896.

Rupakumar, K., Kumar, K., Prasanna, V., Kamala, K., Deshpande, N.R., Patwardhan, S.K., and Pant, G.B. (2003). *Future Climate Scenario. In Climate Change and Indian Vulnerability Assessment and Adaptation.* Hyderabad: Universities Press (India) Pvt. Ltd.

Ruttan, V.N. (1991). *Sustainable Growth in Agricultural Production: Poetry, Policy, and Science.* CREDIT Research Report 91(13), University of Nottingham, Nottingham, UK.

Sathaye, J., Shukla, P.R., and Ravindranath, N.H. (2006). Climate change, sustainable development and India: Global and national concerns. *Current Science-Bangalore*, *90*(3): 314.

Sontakke, N.A., Singh, N., and Singh, H.N. (2008). Instrumental period rainfall series of the Indian region (AD 1813—2005): revised reconstruction, update and analysis. *The Holocene*, *18*(7): 1055-1066.

Swaminathan, M.S. (1983). Genetic conservation: microbes to man. Presidential address to the 15th Int. Cong, of Genetics. In *Genetics: New Frontiers*, Vol. 1. New Delhi, India: Oxford and IBH Publishing Co.

Times of India, June 18 (2012). Climate change adversely affecting agriculture. Retrieved from: http://timesofindia.indiatimes.com/city/jaipur/Climate-change-adversely-affecting-agriculture/articleshow/14218321.cms

UNFCCC. (2007). *Climate Change: Impacts, Vulnerabilities and Adaptation Countries.*

15 Characterization of Isolates of *Ralstonia Solanacearum* (E.F. Smith) Yabuuchi *et al.*, Causing Bacterial (Hooghly) Wilt of Jute (*Corchorus* spp.) in West Bengal

A.N. Tripathi and *Rajib Kumar De*

Introduction

Bacterial wilt is one of the most important diseases of jute (*Corchorus olitorius* and *C. casularis*). Ghosh (1961) coined the term "Hocghly wilt" (Mandal, 1986; Mandal and Ghosh, 2002) which is caused by plant pathogenic bacteria *R. solanacearum* (Hang *et al.*, 2000; Tripathi *et al.*, 2014a and 2014b). *R. solanacearum* (E.F. Smith) Yabuuchi *et al.* (synonyms *Pseudomonas solanacearum* and *Burkholderia solanacearum*) is one of the most widespread and economically important bacterial plant pathogens in the tropical and subtropical region of the world (Hayward, 1991; Champoiseau *et al.*, 2009). It has an extended host range that includes more than 450 plant species in 54 botanical families (Kelman, 1953; Allen *et al.*, 2005; Wicker *et al.*, 2007 and Chakraborty, 2011). The disease is most prevalent in the areas where jute is followed by potato or other solanaceaous crops. During 1950 typical wilt disease in jute (*C. olitorius*) was observed in Tarkeshwar area in Hooghly district of West Bengal. The benchmark survey estimated 30-34 per cent loss of jute crop each year between 1950 and 1954. During late eighties and early nineties, 5–37 per cent disease was recorded in Kamarkundu area of Hooghly district and 2–20 per cent in some area of Nadia and North 24 Parganas districts (Mandal and Mishra, 2001). Epiphytotic record of it in 1950–1970 declined due to break down the cropping sequence of jute after potato and implementation of jute-paddy/potato-paddy crop rotation. *Olitorius* jute CV more prone to bacterial wilt than *capsularis* jute. Wilting of jute results in cent per cent losses and loss directly proportional to disease incidence (Fig. 15.1). In India, the economically important hosts include potato, tomato, brinjal, chillies, groundnut, fennel, cumin, *ajwain*, cotton, jute, ginger and broad bean. Bacterial wilt in jute was observed in Burdhman, Hooghly, Jalpaigudi, Murshidabad, North 24 Parganas, Nadia, and Pundibari districts of West Bengal (Mondal *et al.*, 2011; Tripathi *et al.*, 2014a and 2014b).

Fig. 15.1: Diagnostic symptom of bacterial wilt in jute (Cv JRO 524)
Source: Author's Survey.

Bacterial wilt pathogen *R. solanacearum* is a gram negative; rod shaped, mesophilic, non-fluorescent pigment producing phytobacteria, which exhibits great degree of both phenotypic and genotypic diversity/plasticity and is comprised five strains/races and six biovars (Buddenhagen *et al.*, 1962; He *et al.*, 1983; Hortia and Tsuchiya, 2000; Denny and Hayward, 2001; Gadevar *et al.*, 2003, Xue *et al.*, 2011). Race 1 biovar 3 is the most ubiquitous and widely distributed biovar in South-East Asia. In order to devise successful breeding and integrated management programme a detailed study of the pathogen diversity is a must (Sanchez Perez *et al.*, 2008).

Better understanding of variability in the pathogen would lead to more detailed and precise studies on the genetics of wilt resistance, geographical distribution and development of targeted diagnostics targeted diagnostics for effective and economically viable management strategies. Information on existence of variability in *R. solanacearum* and detection techniques is not available for proper and economically viable management strategies.

In the present study we tried to characterize cultural, physiological and biovar diversity in isolates of *R. solanacearum* causing bacterial wilt in jute.

Methodology

Collection, Isolation, Establishment of Pure Cultures and Maintenance of Bacterial Isolates

The samples of bacterial wilt infected jute plants were collected from Murshidabad, and North 24 Parganas, district of West Bengal. Each sample was composed of three plants showing typical symptoms of bacterial wilt. Samples were placed in plastic bags and brought to the laboratory for isolation of the bacterial pathogen. The specimens were washed thoroughly in running tap water and the presence of bacterium in the wilted plants was confirmed by performing the ooze test. Two to three surface sterilized bits were placed on a sterilized clean slide containing 2-3 drops of sterilized distilled water in the centre and crushed with the help of sterilized scalpel/blade and dissecting needle. A loopful of bacterial cell suspension sufficient for three Petriplates was streaked on Kelman's 2, 3, 5 triphenyl tetrazolium chloride agar (TZCl) medium (10.0 g of peptone, 1.0 g of casamino acid, 5.0 g glucose, 20.0 g agar per litre and added 5 ml of 1 per cent sterile stock solution of 2, 3, 5-triphenyltetrazolium chloride to the sterilized molten medium) under aseptic conditions. Inoculated Pertriplates were incubated at 24 ± 1°C and after 36-72 h of incubation the Petriplates were examined for bacterial growth. The virulent colonies showing profuse extracellular polysaccharide (EPS) production and having pinkish centres were selected. A typical virulent colony was picked up and suspended in 10 ml sterilized distilled water in a glass vial and a loopful of this suspension was again streaked on TZCl plates for establishing pure culture of each isolate separately.

Cultural/Morphological and Physiological/Biochemical Variations

For morphological, cultural and biochemical or physiological studies, various solid, semi-solid and liquid media were used. For conducting such type of studies the protocols outlined in the laboratory manuals edited by Cappuccino and Sherman (1992); Schaad (2001) and Harley and Prescott (1999) were followed.

Each treatment was replicated thrice along with a suitable control. The colony characteristics like colony size, pigmentation, EPS production, form, margin, elevation and abundance of growth were recorded after 48 hrs of incubation at 24 ± 1°C on TZCl medium.

Physiological/Biochemical Tests

The various physiological/biochemical tests were performed for all test isolates of *R. solanacearum*. In order to determine the ability of *R. solanacearum* isolates to produce hydrolytic extracellular enzymes, Carbohydrate fermentation, Citrate utilization and Indole production.

Differentiation of Isolates into Biovars

Hayward's (1964) scheme was followed for the differentiation of *R. solanacearum* isolates into biovars as per their ability to oxidize three disaccharides (lactose, maltose and cellobiose) and three hexose alcohols (mannitol, sorbitol and dulcitol). To the molten basal medium (1.0 g of NH_4 H_2 PO_4, 0.2 g of KCl, 0.2 g of $MgSO_4.7H_2O$, 1.0 g of peptone, 1.5 g agar, 0.3 g bromothymol blue per litre; *p*H 7.0), 0.5 ml of sterilized carbohydrate solution (1%) was added to each tube and allowed to cool.

The basal media containing test carbohydrates were inoculated separately with cell suspension of each of 5 *R. solanacearum* isolates. Each treatment was replicated thrice along with a control in which no carbohydrate solution was added. The test tubes were incubated at 24 ± 1°C up to 6 days and the experiment was repeated twice to confirm the results. The utilization of sugar and sugar alcohols was observed by the growth of the respective isolate and change in turbidity/colour of the basal medium as compared to control treatment.

Results

Isolation, Identification and Characterization of Morphological/ Cultural Variations

Pure cultures of pathogen were established on TZCl medium. The bacterial cells of all the test isolates were gram negative and rod shaped. Colonies of all the isolates on TZCl medium formed irregularly round, fluidal, creamy white colonies with either light pink or deep pink centres. Such virulent colonies could easily be distinguished from the avirulent ones on the TZCl medium which were round, butyrous and uniformly deep red without any EPS production (Figs. 15.2 and 15.3).

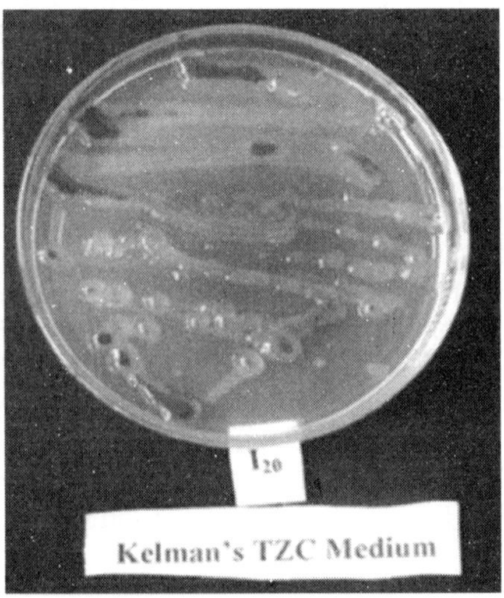

Fig. 15.2: Virulent colonies of *R. solanacearum* on TZCl

Source: Author's Study.

In order to characterize the 5 isolates of *R. solanacearum*, various morphological, cultural and biochemical studies were revealed some important observations are presented in Table 15.1. There was no differentiation of isolates on the basis of

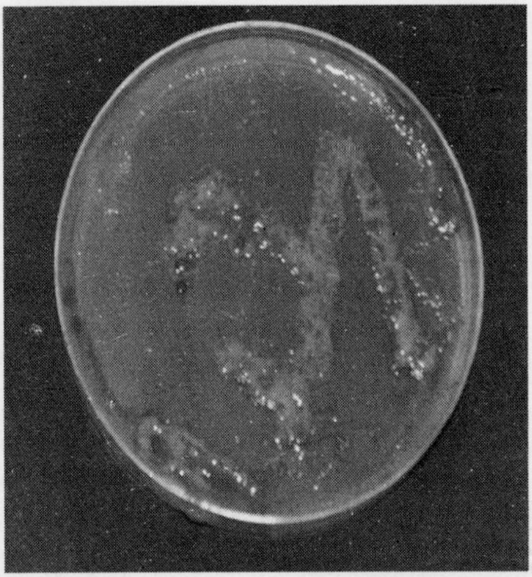

Fig. 15.3: Growth of *R. solanacearum* isolate Rsj-1 on TZCl medium

Source: Author's Study.

pigmentation, EPS production, margin and elevation of the colonies and gram reaction.

Physiological/Biochemical Variation

All the 5 test isolates gave positive results for the hydrolysis/ utilization of tryptons, lipid and urea after 48 h of incubation at 24 ± 1°C on the three media tryptone soya agar (TSA), tributyrin agar base (TAB) and urea broth base (UBB). All the five test isolates could utilize citrate as a carbon source on simmons citrate agar (SCA) medium after 48 h of incubation at 24 ± 1°C which was detected by the growth of the isolates in the medium and change of colour of the medium from green to blue (Fig. 15.4).

Indole production by *R. solanacearum* isolates was detected on sulphide indole motility (SIM) and tryptone soya broth (TSB) media after 24 hrs of incubation at 24 ± 1°C and was detected by the hydrolysis of tryptophan and change of Kovac's reagent colour from black to cherry red ring compared to black colour of the medium in control treatment (Fig. 15.5). All the 5 test isolates were found to give positive reaction for H_2S production which was detected by the change of colour of TSI medium from red (control) to back (Fig. 15.6).

Table 15.1: Morphological/Cultural/physiological/biochemical characterization of *Ralstonia solanacearum* isolates on various medium after 48 h of incubation at 24 ± 1°C

Parameters		*Isolates*					
Morphological/cultural	*Characteristics*	*Rsj-1*	*Rsj-2*	*Rsj-3*	*Rsj-4*	*Rsj-5*	*Remarks*
	Colony size	L	L	L	L	L	*
	Pigmentation	+	+	+	+	+	*
	EPS production	+	+	+	+	+	*
	Form irregular	+	+	+	+	+	*
	Gram staining	-	-	-	-	-	*
	Sulphide Indole Motility Agar	+	+	+	+	+	*
Physiological	Tryptone Soya Broth	+	+	+	+	+	*
	Triple Sugar Iron Agar	+	+	+	+	+	*
	Gas Production	+	+	+	+	+	*
	H_2S Production	+	+	+	+	+	*
	Simmon Citrate Agar	+	+	+	+	+	*
	Tryptone Soya Agar	+	+	+	+	+	*
	Tributyrin Agar Base	+	+	+	+	+	*
	Urea Broth Base	+	+	+	+	+	*
	Lactose	+	+	+	+	+	*
Biochemical test/categorization of isolates into biovars	Maltose	+	+	+	+	+	*
	Cellobiose	+	+	+	+	+	*
	Mannitol	+	+	+	+	+	*
	Sorbitol	+	+	+	+	+	*
	Dulcitol	+	+	+	+	+	*

Note: Rsj = *Ralstonia solanacearum* jute; L = Large colonies; + = Hydrolized/utilized/complete positive indicator for respective tests, * = No variability observed

Source: Author's Study.

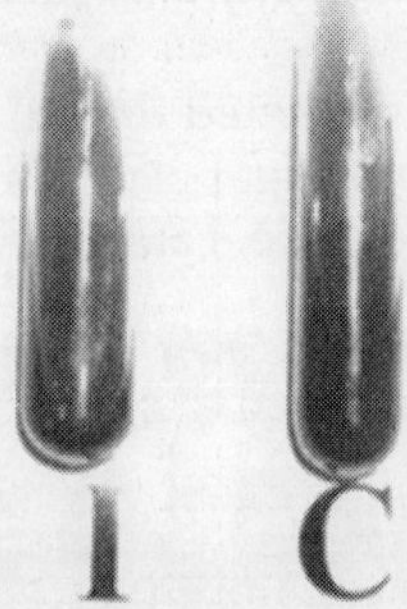

Fig. 15.4: I = Citrate positive and C = Citrate negative
Source: Author's Study.

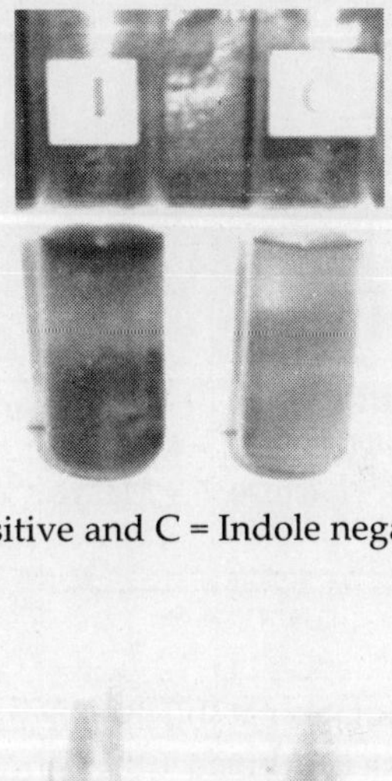

Fig. 15.5: I = Indole positive and C = Indole negative
Source: Author's Study.

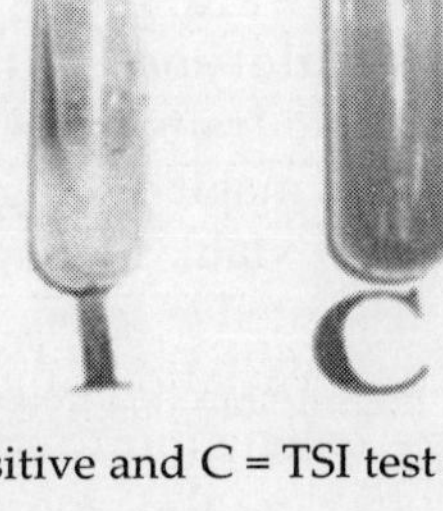

Fig. 15.6: I = TSI test positive and C = TSI test negative
Source: Author's Study.

Categorization of *R. Solanacearum* Isolates into Biovars

Biovar characterization indicated that all the 5 test isolates could oxidize the six sugars and sugar alcohols as compared to control treatment and were, therefore, categorized as biovar 3 of race 1 (Fig. 15.7).

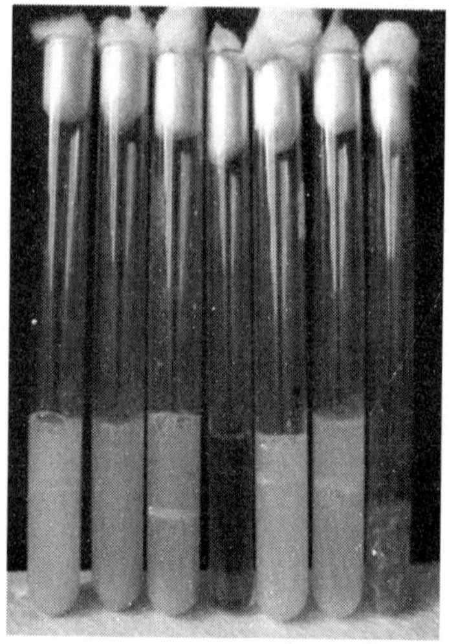

Fig. 15.7: Oxidation/utilization of sugars and sugar alcohols by *R. solanacearum* (Rs. 28) 1 = Mannitol, 2 = Sorbitol, 3 = Dulcitol, C = Control, 4 = Lactose, 5 = Maltose, 6 = Cellobiose

Source: Author's Study.

Discussion

In the present study, isolates established from jute were identified as *R. solanacearum* on the basis of phenotypic characters by producing typical white coloured fluidal colonies with pink centre and irregular in shape (Hayward, 1964). Tested isolates were exhibited as an array of biotypes with varying cultural, physiological and pathogenic traits. However, information on existence of variability in this major pathogen is not available for devising proper economically viable management strategies.

In the present study all 5 tested *R. solanacearum* isolates showed morphological and cultural variation among the isolates with respect to their colony size, colony form and abundance of colony growth. Similar observations were also reported by Banymandhub-

Munbodh (1997) who studied the variation among 140 isolates of *R. solanacearum*.

None of the 5 tests isolates could be differentiated on the basis of utilization of tryptone, lipid and urea on three different media. Similarily, the tested isolates of *R. solanacearum* could not be differentiated on the basis of utilization of citrate as carbon source. The results of the present study corroborate the findings of Hayward (1964), French and Sequeira (1970), Tripathi and Sood (2005) and Tripathi and Sood (2009).

The phenotypic variation in the form of carbohydrate fermentation and H_2S production among the tested *R. solanacearum* isolates were clearly detected. These two biochemical tests are important for characterization and differentiation of the isolates and have been used by many workers (Swanepoel and Young, 1988). Various workers have tested the above mentioned biochemical/physiological tests for characterization of *R. solanacearum* isolates for the purpose of identification of the species (Leifson, 1933; Hayward, 1964) and also for the differentiation of the isolates (Kelman, 1954).

Contrarily, all the 5 isolates of *R. solanacearum* isolates used in the present study were categorized as biovar 3 of race 1. These results are in conformity with the findings of several workers (Kalha and Sood, 1994; Eden-Green, 1994; Mehan and McDonald, 1995; Gupta *et al.*, 1998; Denny and Hayward, 2001; James *et al.*, 2003; Singh *et al.*, 2010) who have reported the occurrence of race 1 biovar 3 on various solanaceous hosts in South-East Asia including India. With the present and previous studies (Rathaiah *et al.*, 1993; Hang *et al.*, 2000; Bhattacharya *et al.*, 2003; Tripathi *et al.*, 2014a and 2014b), it could be firmly established that race 1 biovar 3 of *R. solanacearum* is prevalent in different jute and solanaceous crops growing areas of West Bengal.

The pathogen is very difficult to manage because of its wide host range, exceptional ability to survive in the roots of non-host plants and in the soil, susceptibility of the commercial cultivars, and non-feasibility of chemical control.

Information on the cultural, morphological, physiological/biochemical, pathological and molecular variation in the pathogen is important in establishing rational management strategies including the development of resistant varieties and appropriate cultural management practices.

Acknowledgements

The senior author is thankful to Director and Head, Division of Crop Protection, ICAR- Central Research Institute for Jute and Allied Fibres (CRIJAF), Barrackpore for providing required assistance for conducting of the experiment.

References

Allen C., Prior, P., and Hayward, A.C. (2005). Bacterial wilt disease and the *Ralstonia solanacearum* species complex. (528). USA: APS Press.

Banymandhub-Munbodh, K. (1997). Studies on bacterial wilt caused by *Ralstonia solanacearum* on *Anthurium andreanum. ACIAR Bacterial Wilt Newsletter*, 15, 11.

Bhattacharya, P., Samajpatti, N. and Bhattacharya, P. (2003). Characteristics of *Ralstonia* (*Pseudomonas*) *solanacearum* from Gangetic West Bengal. *Journal of Mycopathological Research.* 41: 15-19.

Buddenhagen, I.W., Sequeira, L., and Kelman, A. (1962). Designation of races in *Pseudomonas solanacearum. Phytopathology*, 52: 726.

Cappuccino, J.G., and Sherman, N. (1992). *Microbiology: A Laboratory Manual*, 3rd edition. (462). California: The Benjamin/Cummings Publishing Company.

Chakrabarti, S.K. (2011). *Ralstonia solanacearum*—an enigmatic bacterial plant pathogen. *Indian Phytopathology*, 64 (4), 313-321.

Champoiseau, P.G., Jones, J.B., and Allen, C. (2009). *Ralstonia solanacearum* race 3 biovar 2 causes tropical losses and temperate anxieties. Online Plant Health Progress.

Denny, T.P. and Hayward, A.C. (2001). *Ralstonia.* In Schaad, N.W., Jones, J.B. and Chun, W. (Ed.), *Laboratory Guide for Identification of Plant Pathogenic Bacteria*, pp. 154-174. USA, APS Press.

Eden- Green, S.J. (1994). Diversity of *Pseudomonas solanacearum* and related bacteria in South-East Asia: New directions for moko disease. In A.C. Hayward and G.L. Hartman (ed.), *Bacterial Wilt: The Disease and its Causative Agent, Pseudomonas solanacearum*, pp. 25-34. Wallington Wallingford: CAB International.

French, E.R. and Sequeira, L. (1970). Strains of *Pseudomonas solanacearum* from Central and South America: A Comparative study. *Phytopathology*, 60: 507-512.

Gadewar, A.V., Chakrabarti, S.K., and Khurana, S.M. P. (2003). Diversity in *R. solanacearum*, the incident of plant wilt in Asia. *Journal of Mycology and Plant Bacteriology*, 33 (1): 160-161.

Gupta, S.K., Dohroo, N.P. and Shyam, K.R. (1998). Occurrence of bacterial wilt of tomato in Himachal Pradesh. *Plant Disease Research*, 13: 174.

Hang, J.C., Hseu, H.S., and Sen, B.K. (2000). Bacterial wilt of jute caused by *Ralstonia solanacearum. Plant Pathology Bulletin,* (9): 35-38.

Harley, P.K., and Prescott, L.M. (1999). *Laboratory Exercises in Microbiology,* 4th edition. (979). Texas: WCB/McGraw-Hill Publishers.

Hayward, A.C. (1964). Characteristics of *Pseudomonas solanacearum. Journal of Applied Bacteriology,* (27): 265-277.

Hayward, A.C. (1991). Biology and epidemiology of bacterial wilt caused by *Pseudomonas solanacearum. Annual Review of Phytopathology,* 29: 65-87.

He, L.Y., Sequeira, L. and Kelman, A. (1983). Characteristics of strains of *Pseudomonas solanacearum* from China. *Plant Disease,* 67: 1357-1361.

Horita, M. and Tsuchiya, K. (2000). Genetic diversity of Japanese strains of *Ralstonia solanacearum. Phytopathology,* 91(4): 399.

James, D., Girija, D., Shaly, K., Mathew, K., Nazeem, P.A., Baboo, T.D. and Varma, A.S. (2003). Detection of *Ralstonia solanacearum* race 3 causing bacterial wilt of solanaceous vegetables in Kerala, using random amplified polymorphic DNA (RAPD) analysis. *Journal of Tropical Agricultural,* 41: 33-37.

Kalha, C.S., and Sood, A.K. (1994). Occurrence of race 1 biovar III of *Pseudomonas solanacearum* on tomato in Himachal Pradesh. *ACIAR Bacterial Wilt Newsletter,* 10, 10.

Kelman, A. (1953). The bacterial wilt caused by *Pseudomonas solanacearum.* North Carolina Agricultural Experiment Station, U.S.A. *Technical Bulletin,* 99: 154.

Kelman, A. (1954). The relationship of pathogenicity in *Pseudomonas solanacearum* to colony appearance in a tetrazolium medium. *Phytopathology,* 44: 693-695.

Leifson, E. (1933). The fermentation of medium malonate as a means of differentiating Aerobacter and Escherichia. *Journal of Bacteriology,* 26: 329.

Mandal, R.K. (1986). Wilt disease of jute and its management (in Bangali) *Sabuj sona,* March issue.

Mandal, R.K. and Ghosh, T. (2002). Hooghly wilt of jute in retrospect (1949-2000). *J. Mycopathol. Res.,* 40 (1): 67-69.

Mandal, R.K. and Mishra, C.D. (2001). Role of different organism in inducing Hooghly wilt symptom in jute. *Environmental Ecology,* 19 (4), 969-972.

Mehan, V.K. and McDonald, D. (1995). Techniques for diagnosis of *Pseudomonas solanacearum* and for resistance screening against groundnut bacterial wilt. *ICRISAT,* Hyderabad, 68.

Mondal, B., Bhattacharya, I. and Khatua, D.C. (2011). Crop and weed host of *Ralstonia solanacearum* in West Bengal. *Journal of Crop and Weed,* 7(2): 195-199.

Rathaiah, Y., Robin, G., Phookan, A.K. and Rahman, F. (1993). Bacterial wilt in jute in Assam. *Journal of the Agricultuiral Science,* 6: 85.

Schaad, N.W., Jones, J.B., and Chun, W. (2001). Laboratory guide for identification of plant pathogenic bacteria. 3rd edition. (4-10). U S A, APS Press.

Singh, D., Sinha, S., Yadav, D.K., Sharma, J.P., Shrivastava, D.K., Lal, H.C., Mondal, K.K. and Jaiswal, R.K. (2010). Characterization of biovar/races of *Ralstonia solanacearum*, the incitant of bacterial wilt in solanaceous crops. *Indian Phytopathology*, 63(3): 261-265.

Swanepoel, A.E. and Young, B.W. (1988). Characteristics of South African strains of *Pseudomonas solanacearum*. *Plant Disease*, 72(5): 403-405.

Tripathi, A.N. and Sood, A.K. (2005). Variability studies on *Ralstonia solanacearum* causing bacterial wilt in Himachal Pradesh. *Indian Phytopathology*, 58(3): 350.

Tripathi, A.N. and Sood, A.K. (2009). Cultural and physiological variability in *Ralstonia solanacearum* causing bacterial wilt in Himachal Pradesh. 5th International Conference on Plant Pathology in the Globalized Era, November 10–13, 2009, New Delhi, 134.

Tripathi, A.N., Meena, P.N., De, R.K., Kar, C.S., and Satpathy, S. (2014). Prevalence of bacterial wilt/Hooghly wilt on jute caused by *Ralstonia solanacearum* (E.F. Smith) Yabuuchi *et al., JafNews*, 12(2): 29-30.

Tripathi, A.N., Sarkar, S.K., Kar, C.S. and Satpathy, S. (2014). Characterization of *Ralstonia solanacearum* (Yabuuchi *et al.*) causing bacterial wilt of jute (*Corchorus olitorius* and *C. capsularis*). Book of abstracts, International Conference on "India Biodiversity Meet 2014", 21-23rd November, 2014, Agricultural and Ecological Research Unit Indian Statistical Institute, Kolkata, West Bengal. 68.

Wicker, E., Grassart, I., Coranson-Beaudu, R., Mian, D., Guilbaud, C. and Fegan, M. (2007). Ralstonia solanacearum strains from Martinique (French West Indies) Exhibiting a new pathogenic potential. *Applied and Environmental Microbiology*, 71: 6790-6801.

Xue, Q.Y., Yin, Y.N., Yang, W., Heuer, H., Prior, P., Guo, J.H. and Smalla, K. (2011). Genetic diversity of *Ralstonia solanacearum* isolates from China assessed by PCR-based fingerprints to unravel host plant and site dependent distribution patterns. *FEMS Microbiology Ecology*, 75: 507-519.

16

Cities and Economic Growth

Mitigating Urban Transportation Issues in Kohima: A Theoretical Framework

Tumbenthung Humtsoe

Introduction

It is now a familiar established fact that cities are the *engines of economic growth*. Cities are subjected to agglomeration economies, which make them store-houses of skill and capital, hubs of knowledge and innovation, sources of informal and formal employment, hopes of millions of rural-urban migrants, and generators of public financial resources for socio-economic development including rural development. To quote Jane Jacobs, "... Among all the various types of economies, cities are unique in their abilities to shape and reshape the economies of other settlements, including those far removed from them geographically" (Jacobs, 1984).

The world has witnessed Industrial Revolution (18th and 19th centuries), and like many other countries India has also witnessed Green Revolution (1960s), and according to Mohanty (2014), "the twenty first century will witness urban revolution sweeping through the developing countries." A strong positive correlation coefficient of 0.85 is observed between GDP per capita and level of urbanization in cross-section of developing countries. Urban-based economic activities account for up to 55 per cent of GDP in low-income countries, 73 per cent in middle-income countries, and 85 per cent in high-income countries (Mohanty, 2014). According to Mckinsey Global Institute analysis, cities accounted for 58 per cent of India's GDP in 2008, and are projected to account nearly

70 per cent by 2030. The statistics speaks of the economic significance of cities, and the economic reality is such that it is increasingly more apt to talk about wealth of cities rather than Wealth of Nations.

Urbanization is historically associated with economic and social transformations, and the "2014 Revision of World Urbanization Prospects" captures this fact, "The process of urbanization...has brought greater geographic mobility, lower fertility, longer life expectancy and population aging. Cities are important drivers of development and poverty reduction in both rural and urban areas... urban living is often associated with higher rate of literacy and education, better health, greater access to social services, and enhanced opportunities for cultural and political participation."

The unfounded thinking dictated by Harris-Todaro over-migration argument (...the main defect being of the neglect of agglomeration economies in their otherwise popular model), especially in developing countries is now substituted by a new thinking led by urban economists regarding the current trend of urbanization in DCs as a welcome development, while emphasizing the need to mitigate the accompanying urban issues. The economic significance of cities is unparalleled. However, in order not to negate the benefits of cities agglomeration one has to look at the urban challenges and issues so as to mitigate those problems. It is often the case that there is a divergence between private costs/benefits and social costs/benefits, and this gap has to be bridged in order to reap greater external economies. Recognizing this fact and the possibility that causes the same problem and the required policy intervention could be region-culture-specific, the present chapter will attempt to analyse traffic congestion in Kohima, the capital city of Nagaland. The analysis can be extended to other cities with similar characteristics facing traffic congestion problem. This is especially the case of most North Eastern states.

In the first section, recognizing the fact that, in India the importance of cities as *engines of economic growth* has not received much attention in the academic discourse and government(s) policies (until recently in the form of Smart Cities), the aforesaid importance is spelt out. Having briefed in the next section the significance of urban transportation, the background and the theoretical frame is staged in the succeeding sections. In the following sections, traffic congestion and the policy responses are assessed. The last section deals with traffic air pollution in the city. Policy responses towards abating air pollution in the context of Kohima city are scrutinized. Some topics related to congestion pricing are not covered in this review due to space constraints.

Significance of Transport

It needs no mention that there is a strong positive correlation between urban road or transport infrastructures on the one hand and city denizens' well-being and economic growth on the other. Besides, the interaction of transport economies and scale economies largely contribute to the creation of a city. Urban transport contributes to market development including development of new market. As Smith argued, this will lead to specialization and eventually knowledge spillovers. It is a fact that the most accessible lands are generally put to the highest and best use, and hence tends to be more developed. Accessible land gets what is known as *accessible premium,* which inaccessible land do not enjoy. Besides, road infrastructure leads to *agglomeration economies,* which increase land value. And, such lands enjoy agglomeration rent. In short, transportation makes or bars a city.

Transport not only creates or facilitates economic activities, but transport *per se* is an economic activity, directly employing large number of people as shippers, freighters, drivers, managers etc. Indirectly also, transport creates employment in the forms of travelling agents, transit operators, repair mechanics etc. Transport contributes six to twelve per cent directly to GDP in Developed countries. In India, it contributes around 6.5 per cent to GDP (CSO). Transport as we all know is the key component of public capital investment. And public investment in the short run boost aggregate demand and in the long run boost productivity. Empirical evidence abounds as to the positive correlation between public and private sectors investments. According to CSO data, the boom in private corporate investment during the high growth phase during 2004-05 to 2007-08 was accompanied by an increase in public investment by 1.5 per cent. And a decline in public investment by more than 1 per cent during 2007-08 and 2012-13 was accompanied by a general decline in private corporate investment by more than 8 per cent.

Also, in India, the long run multiplier of capital outlay on GDP is 2.4 (Reserve Bank of India, Annual Report 2012). Rodrik and Subramanian (2005) found that, after allowing for a lag of five years between infrastructure spending and economic growth, the former can explain around 1.5 to 2.9 per cent of overall growth. Besides, urban transport system is the key critical response to the challenge of changing the nature of urban development to a more ecological, sustainable model (Kenworthy, 2006).

Given the pathetic and inadequate Public Transport System (PTS) in Nagaland coupled with people's aspirations, the State is witnessing a rapid mushrooming of private cars on the roads of the cities. Kohima boasts of more cars per person than any other city of India. What is abysmal of this trend is that *Second-hand cars* that are worth discarding—at least on pollution considerations are increasingly filling the city's roads. It is a common sight to behold cars zooming pass in an unpaved road, leaving behind dust suspension, and thus polluting the air. Besides the chronic traffic congestion, this has serious adverse environmental and public health implications both in the short and long runs. With no railways or metros, the problem is more pronounced, as road transport is likely to remain the most important mode of transport in the city. The fact that Kohima which has PTS—thanks to JNURM, but is inadequate and lacks city planning and inadequate road infrastructure, begets the question as to whether this fact at least partially explains the congestion and consequently air pollution in the city. Like many cities, the cases of ailments related to air pollution will be increasing in at least Kohima. Against such background, an economic analysis of the issues will be made within the following theoretical framework.

Theoretical Framework: Speed Function Extended

The theoretical framework under which I will analyse the congestion is through Speed function analysis. Theoretically, speed (S) is taken as a function of the number of vehicles per lane hour (T). Algebraically,

$$S = S(T)$$

$dS/dT \leq 0$, i.e. as T increase, S may or may not fall. If speed falls, it means the *marginal* or additional one car causes congestion. Otherwise, there is no congestion. Thus, when $dS/dT = 0$, there is no congestion.

And, when dS/dT < 0, there is congestion. Diagramatically it is illlustrated below (Fig. 16.1):

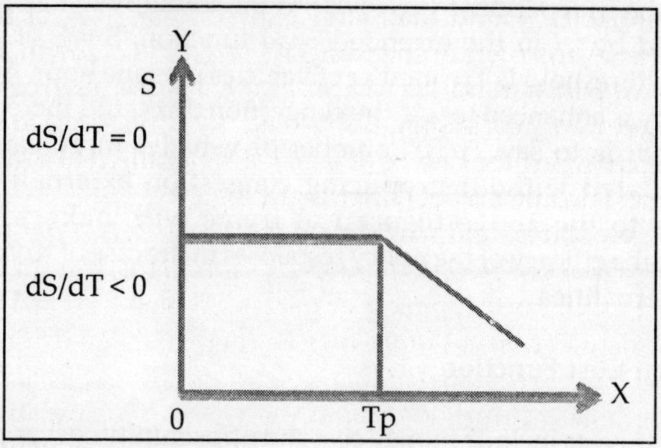

Fig. 16.1: Speed Function.
Source: Author's Study.

In the above diagram, Tp is the *traffic threshold* after which speed decreases. In other words, congestion sets in beyond Tp. Now, I will expand the speed function to include road capacity, S = S(T, C). Here, road capacity (C) is defined as number of lanes in one roadway so that as capacity increases Tp increases. That is to say, when capacity is enhanced more vehicles can ply at the same time without causing congestion externalities. This case is graphically explained below (Fig. 16.2):

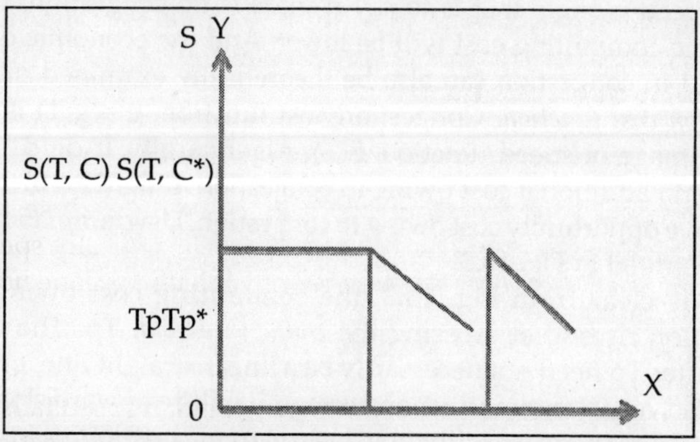

Fig. 16.2: Extended Speed Function
Source: Author's Study.

In Fig.16.2 speed function is extended to include road capacity as one of the independent variables. At the initial road capacity represented by 'c' in the extended road function, S = S (T, C), congestion threshold is Tp number of vehicles per lane hour. After the capacity is enhanced to 'c*,' the congestion threshold increases to Tp*. That is to say TpTp* number of vehicles more can be accommodated without producing congestion externalities. Reference to the above theoretical frame will make while evaluating the efficacy of the policy responses in the case of Kohima Traffic externalities.

Congestion Cost Function

Commuting costs include money cost and opportunity cost or time cost. The former refers to the money spent on per unit distance travel cost, e.g. ticket cost paid by a commuter. The later can be thought of as the potential amount of wage lost by a labourer owing to the time lost stuck in congestion. Thus,

Commuting cost (g) = Money cost + w.d/S (Opportunity cost)

where, w = wage rate; d = distance; S = speed

It is quite clear from the above equation that there is an indirect relationship between economic commuting cost and speed. Thus, if the speed is high, that is to say if there is no congestion, then economic commuting cost will be lower. And the economic costs involved in congestion can also be theoretically examined under *congestion cost function*. Congestion cost function, g = g(T) is the mirror image of speed function, S(T). Algebraically, If $dg/dT = 0$, there is no additional cost owing to congestion. If $dg/dT > 0$, there is positive opportunity cost owing to congestion. Diagrammatically, it is illustrated in Fig. 16.3.

As is clear from Fig. 16.3, the commuting cost owing to congestion rises after crossing the *traffic threshold,* Tp. The g(T) curve after Tp need not necessarily be a linear straight line, or the shape can vary over time. But, on average, it will be upward sloping as congestion increases with time. In an extreme possibility, in case of 'hyper-congestion' the curve may bend even backwards on itself (*see* Lindsey and Verhoef, 2000).

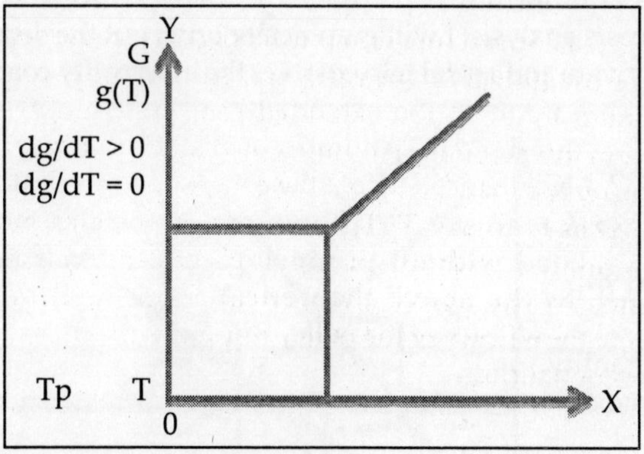

Fig. 16.3: Congestion Cost Function

Source: Author's Study.

Policy Responses

Having outlined the theoretical frame, I will now assess the possible policy responses in the context of Kohima traffic congestion. However, before going into the different policies, it will be helpful to bring out the divergence between private and social trip cost.

Social and Private Trip Cost

The private trip cost is the cost per driver, and hence is the same as average cost. It is the sum of the money cost (say, Rs. 10 per km.) and trip time times the opportunity cost. For instance, if the commuter/driver is a worker, his private trip cost will also include trip time times wage per hour besides money cost. Social cost on the other hand is the sum of private cost and external cost. It is associated with the last or marginal vehicle, and so it is also called marginal cost.

An individual will commute by private car as long as his/her willingness to pay for the trip (marginal benefit) exceeds the private trip cost. From micro-economics, we learn that each point on the demand curve represents willingness to pay. Thus, the inter-section between the demand curve and private trip cost curve will give the equilibrium traffic volume and equilibrium trip cost. Analogously, the inter-section between the demand curve and marginal or social trip cost will give the optimum social traffic volume and the associated equilibrium trip cost. Now, using average cost and marginal costs analysis, I will graphically bring out the divergence between private and social trip cost, i.e. the externality cost.

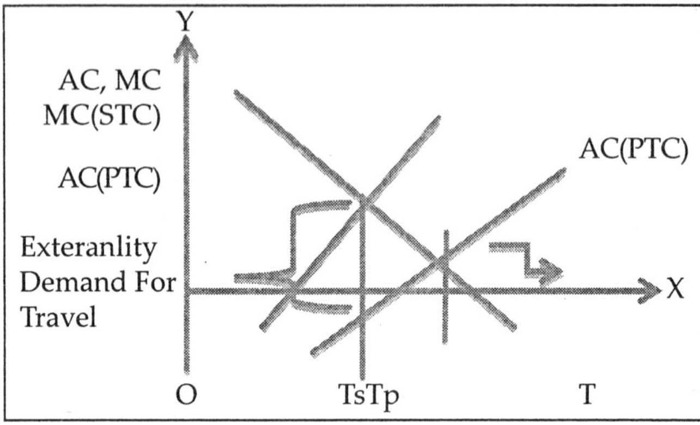

Fig. 16.4: Divergence between STC and PTC
Source: Author's Study.

In Fig. 16.4, the X-axis measures total number of vehicles per lane hour (T), and the Y-axis measures AC and MC. From the private point of view, Tp number of T is optimum. However, from the society point of view, Ts is the optimum, and Ts < Tp. The divergence is because while the private driver does not consider the externality, the society has to consider in its reckoning the externality that has been generated with additional T. The portion in the diagram marked externality is the externality cost, and it has to be internalized or removed by bringing down T to Ts level. Reference to this will be made while discussing policy responses.

In the context of Kohima, this divergence is observed in the fact that despite chronic traffic congestion, the trend of owning private cars is on increase. The fact can be explained partially by the fact that the PTS is inadequate, even for student commuters. Thus, personal cars become more like basic necessity, and this fact is attested by the purchasing behaviour of the people in buying second-hand, even third-hand or cars in very poor conditions.

Going by income indicators like per capita income, Kohima is very unlikely to be the city with highest car per person in the State. Having said so, the question arises why increasingly more people are buying/can afford personal cars? This can be partially explained by supply-demand analysis. The demand for personal car is high owing to people's aspirations and poor PTS. The supply of cars in Nagaland constitutes brand new, second-hand, third-hand or over-used, but very cheap cars, from within the State and outside. Thus, over the years the supply of cars increases more than the rising demand. The simple graphical presentation would make this line of argument more strong.

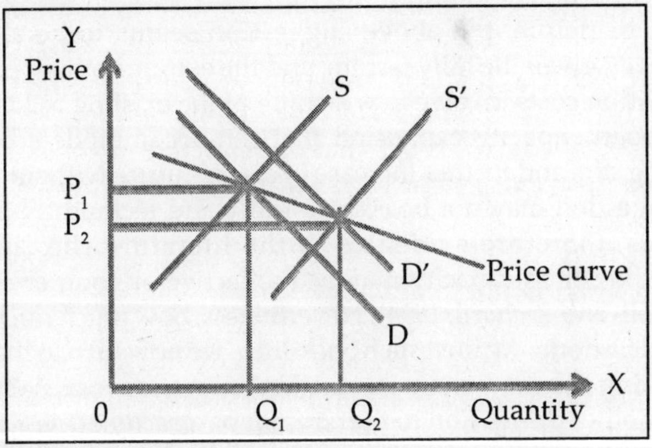

Fig. 16.5: Supply-Demand Analysis

Source: Author's Study.

As we see from the figure above when the shift in supply curve is more than the shift in demand curve, there is decrease in price, but the increase in quantity is more pronounced. This being the case, in the face of downward sloping price curve, and as their income increases the people in Kohima can purchase cars. This trend cannot be observed in cities where there are pollution regulations; like banning cars from use after ten years or so. Each individual calculate at his/her personnel level considering only his needs, ignoring the fact that his decision will add to congestion and environmental pollution. This is optimum from the individual point of view, however, the society as a whole bear the burden of congestion.

Different Policy Options

Capacity Expansion: Kohima boast as the city with the highest car per person in India. Hence, the two lanes main road of the city is profoundly inadequate and has to be widened. This is more so as the city is an elongated city. Besides, in-city roads branching out from the main road are inadequate and hence have to be lengthened and the existing roads widened. Besides, new roads have to be paved so that traffic in the existing roads will be eased. As we have seen in the theoretical analysis, all these capacity expansion will increase the *congestion threshold*. That is to say the expanded capacity will able to handle the existing high traffic load (large number of T), and in the process the current severe traffic congestion will be eased.

In principle, the above suggestion seems to be all right. However, given the hilly terrain, and the extremely high potential demolition costs involve in widening of the existing roads, large-scale road capacity expansion that can accommodate both the existing cars and further increase in cars in future without leading to congestion may not be economically and technically feasible. Besides, there are evidences in the literature showing how expanding road capacity may be ineffective or counter effective (Kenneth and Richard, 1994). Nevertheless, how much can be done should be done. Against such backdrop, we now turn to the policy of making the car owners internalize congestion externalities.

Another dimension to the concept of *capacity expansion* in the form of mass transit (Kenneth and Richard, 1994) can be emphasized here, especially in the context of situations comparable to that of Kohima."Public transit systems typically feature significant economies with respect to ridership that often outweigh any congestion externalities"(Kenneth and Richard, 1994). Capacity can be enhanced by means of introducing quality public transport services like buses, metros etc. Metro is technically not feasible in Kohima, but introducing quality buses attractive even to those using private vehicles can go a long way in serving the purpose. If a switch towards buses can be affected, the number of vehicles per lane hour will be reduced, thereby easing congestion. In other words, that will amount to enhancing capacity and the threshold level will be increased.

Congestion Pricing

Congestion pricing is one effective way to internalize congestion externalities. Pigou (1920) and Knight (1924) were the first to advocate it. However, William Vickrey, was arguably the most influential in making the case on both theoretical and practical grounds (Lindsay, Robin and Erik, 2000). One can give several rationales for introducing congestion tolls, however, a context in which one argues is crucial. Without providing good or adequate public transportation system, it does not seem proper or justifiable to levy congestion toll. Those who buy cars out of necessity, in the face of lack of PTS and inadequate road infrastructure, will find their tight budget reduced, especially those relatively poorer people, and hence will be not be Pareto optimal. Evidence shows that congestion pricing by inducing travellers to re-route to less congested roads, also had a tendency to increase travel distances—with potentially adverse environmental effects (May and Milne, 2000). Besides, such a tax would need to be accompanied by effective emission monitoring, which is difficult to implement in India (Fazal, 2006). Having said so, given the poor public transportation system, congestion pricing is not the right move in Kohima as of now. Besides, the city municipality may not possess the administrative and technical requirements to levy congestion toll.

As a policy response to the noticeably increasing number of private cars on the roads of the city, as suggested by Montek and Mathur (2014), "provision of bus services of a quality that would be acceptable to those currently using private transport and also provision of pedestrian and bicycle friendly infrastructure" will be a better policy here. A privately owned and managed bus system can be encouraged subjected to price regulation or through subsidized price in order to safeguard *Commoner's interests*, while assuring fares structure and ambience that ensures reasonable profits. This coupled with provision of roads infrastructure can reduce operational inefficiencies and inadequacies of PTS.

Differential Timing

From the theoretical analysis it is implied that *ceteris paribus*, if the number of vehicles per lane hour (T) is reduced, the *congestion threshold* will be reached late. This is equivalent to increasing *congestion threshold*. Now, it can be understood that if traffic or 'T' can be reduced to certain level, congestion during peak hours can be eased. Towards this end, many countries like Singapore, UK etc. levy higher congestion toll during peak hours. However, for the reason stated above, such toll is no appropriate to be levied in Kohima. The feasible option is to alter schools and office timings to differential timings (e.g., making some schools and offices start later/earlier while keeping the timings of the rest unaltered) so as to ease congestion during peak traffic hours and to increase traffic during off-peak hours. It is observed that congestion tends to be more severe during wee hours (between 7:30 am to 9:30 am) when students go to schools and colleges; and government employees go to offices, and during late noon (2:30 pm to 4:30 pm) when people start returning home. Thus, this policy intervention will ease traffic during the peak hours, thus saving commuting costs.

Private Cars and Air Pollution

Besides congestion externality, there is this severe environmental externalities—air pollution. This problem merits immediate attention because as noted above Kohima boast of the highest number of cars per person, and more and more second-hand cars are hitting the city roads. The cars emit volatile organic compounds (VOC), carbon monoxide (CO), nitrogen oxide (NO), sulphur dioxide (SO_2), smog, and particulate matter. It needs no mention of the adverse impact of air pollution on climate change, especially global warming as well as respiratory health issues.

Physical geographers call these emissions that also form part of the constituents of the atmosphere as *variable constituents,* i.e. they vary with place and time. Oxygen and nitrogen are the permanent constituents, i.e. their percentages in the atmosphere remain more or less constant with time and place. Ignoring the natural causes, we see here that the emissions in a particular region are the result of human actions in that region. Likewise, the adverse impacts of those emissions are also largely confined to that particular place, excepting the contribution to overall climate change through CO_2. Likewise, the health hazards and environmental degradation arising from such emissions have to be mitigated locally.

Internalizing Pollution Externality

One way to internalize air pollution is to internalize by imposing pollution tax equal to the marginal external cost of pollution. Such tax, according to O'Sullivan, "would cause drivers to incorporate the full costs of driving into their decisions, leading to the socially efficient level of pollution." He further argued that such tax would encourage people to buy cleaner cars and drive fewer miles. The tax can be implemented by installing a monitoring device in each car to measure its emissions and then charge the owner accordingly (O'Sullivan, 2009). However, such direct approach seems to be unviable in the context of Kohima. This is because of the record of low enforcement record in the state due to resource constraints of the government.

Another way to internalize is by imposing **one-time pollution tax** on each new car. Sullivan suggests that the tax can vary by car model and would equal the estimated lifetime emissions times the external cost per unit of emissions (O'Sullivan). This seems to a better option. But in the context where transaction of second-hand cars happens in informal market or setting outside the radar of relevant authorities, this alternative may not work.

One means towards the social optimum end is through **gasoline tax.** The tax would increase the cost per mile driven, and hence would generate incentives for the drivers to drive less, and decrease air pollution. However, the job is not that simple, as this alternative also suffers from certain problems. In this case, as pointed out by Sullivan, "…every driver would pay the same tax per gallon, regardless of how much pollution is generated per gallon of gasoline." Thus, such tax would "decrease pollution by decreasing miles driven but would not encourage people to drive cleaner cars." Besides, as pointed out earlier in Kohima context, the majority of the cars are not clean in environmental sense, and hence the solution should be more towards encouraging people to use cleaner cars, or to discourage people to abandon/use lesser poor quality cars.

However, as demand for gasoline is relatively inelastic in the short-run, notwithstanding the increase in the price of gasoline, people will not shift to *cleaner* cars in weeks or few months. Given the inadequate public transport and their aspirations reflected in their preferences for private cars, they would exhibit an inertia using the 'unclean cars'. Reporting on the relative efficiencies of different charges like km-charges, fuel charges, parking charges and public transport pricing for different cities and countries, using the multi-modal TRENEN-model De Borger and Proost (2000) concluded that the potential of fuel pricing and public transport pricing is rather limited. However, in the long run, provided there is a provision of better and adequate means of public transport and an increase in the income of the residents, the residents will either shift to public transport, or to fuel-efficient or cleaner cars in environmental sense.

Conclusion

The situation on the ground as presented above merits immediate policy intervention. However, it should be noted that the policies should be assessed in the context of the applicability to the city in question. Expansion of roadcapacity coupled with provision of adequate and quality public transport system is the need of the hour. Only after meeting these two, the authority can think of other market failure corrective measures of Pigovian nature or non-Pigovian alternatives. Failure to do that will lead to loss of welfare of the citizens.

References

Ahluwalia, M., and Mohanty (2014). *Urbanization in India: Challenges, Opportunities and the Way Forward*, Sage India Publications.

Jacobs, Jane (1985). *Cities and the Wealth of Nations*, Vintage: Vintage Books Publication.

Kenworthy, J. (2006). "The eco-city: Ten key transport and planning dimensions for sustainable city development", *Environment and Urbanization* (2006). *18(1)*: 67–85.

Lindsay, C.R., and Verhoef, T.E. (2000). Tinbergen Institute Discussion Paper, *Traffic Congestion and Congestion Pricing*.

Mohanty, P.K. (2014). *Cities and Public Policy: An Urban Agenda for India*, Sage India Publication.

Population Division of the Department of Economic and Social Affairs of the UN, "Revision of world Urbanization Prospects" Report (2014).

Reserve Bank of India, *Annual Report 2012*.

Rodrik, D., and Subramanian, A. (2004). From Hindu Growth to productivity surge: The mystery of the Indian growth transition, *IMF Working Paper*.

Shahab, F. (2006). Addressing congestion and transport-related air pollution in Saharanpur, India, *Environment and Urbanization* (2006). *18(1)*: 141–154.

Small, K., and Arnott, R. (1994). "The economics of traffic congestion", *American Scientist, 82(5)*: (September-October 1994), 446-455.

Sullivan, A. (2009). *Urban Economics*, McGraw-Hill Publication.

Index